Black Eye

Black Eye

*Escaping a Marriage,
Writing a Life*

Judith Strasser

THE UNIVERSITY OF WISCONSIN PRESS / TERRACE BOOKS

The University of Wisconsin Press
1930 Monroe Street
Madison, Wisconsin 53711

www.wisc.edu/wisconsinpress/

3 Henrietta Street
London WC2E 8LU, England

1   3   5   4   2

Printed in the United States of America

Library of Congress Cataloging-in-Publication Data
Strasser, Judith, 1944–
Black eye: escaping a marriage, writing a life / Judith Strasser.
        p.   cm.
ISBN 0-299-19930-4 (cloth: alk. paper)
   1. Strasser, Judith, 1944—Marriage.
       2. Kingsley, Stu—Marriage.
   3. Married people—United States—Biography.
   4. Problem families—United States.   I. Title.
          CT275.S87855A3   2004
      306.89´3´092—dc22   2003021175

Terrace Books, a division of the University of Wisconsin Press,
takes its name from the Memorial Union Terrace, located at
the University of Wisconsin–Madison. Since its inception in 1907,
the Wisconsin Union has provided a venue for students, faculty, staff,
and alumni to debate art, music, politics, and the issues of the day.
It is a place where theater, music, drama, dance, outdoor activities, and
major speakers are made available to the campus and the community.
To learn more about the Union, visit www.union.wisc.edu.

for my sons

and in memoriam
Maxine Strasser, my mother
and
"Helen," my mother-in-law

Table of Contents

Introduction

I learned that the University of Wisconsin Press would publish my memoir, *Black Eye*, on December 5, 2002, sixteen years to the day after my husband gave me the black eye for which I named the book. It was an astonishing coincidence.

It also made it hard to ignore how long I'd been working on the memoir: sixteen years, or seventeen, if you include the year I wrote the journal that serves as a chronological spine for the narrative. Of course, most of that time, I wasn't actually writing. I was getting up the courage to write. Or taking my kids to school. Or transcribing the handwritten journal. Or making supper. Or trying to find a publisher. Or going to work. Mostly, I was living my life as a single parent, a public radio producer, a poet working on a memoir. At the same time, I was getting older. And changing, as we do when we age. In many ways, I am no longer the woman whose husband slugged her in 1986. The story of my life sounds different now than it did when I wrote my journal.

In *Black Eye*, I've tried to convey the patchy manner in which I came to understand two braided strands of that story: how my marriage ended and how I came to be a poet. The events of a single year—1986—triggered both the divorce and the writing, and at the time I chronicled those events obsessively, mostly by speaking into a handheld tape recorder. I spoke into the recorder two or three times a day. Every day or two, I transcribed the tapes into a notebook, copied them down by hand. The whole thing came to more than six hundred pages when I finally typed it out.

After he'd read a draft of my manuscript, a writer who's published two memoirs told me that journals are "private" writing. "As a reader," he said, "they don't interest me." He advised me to delete all the journal entries from my manuscript.

I refused. It took me more than forty years to find the courage to use my voice. The entries are testament, proof of what really happened: how my marriage ended; how I began to write. *Black Eye* includes sections of the journal, severely pruned; they provide a chronological narrative of 1986, a pivotal year in my life.

But I didn't understand, when I was writing the journal, what was happening to me. The understanding came more than a decade later, as I tried to find a way to tell my story. I began work on the first draft of *Black Eye* in late 1996 at Norcroft, a writing retreat for women on the North Shore of Lake Superior. I continued writing after I returned home and completed the draft late in 1997 at the Ucross Foundation in Wyoming, another writing retreat. The chronological narrative of that year of writing weaves in and out of the journal excerpts from 1986. The 1996–97 narrator knows a great deal more than the woman who wrote the journal. She is a published poet; she has spent ten years raising her sons by herself; she is a different woman, with a different voice.

As I worked on these intertwined narratives of two years in my life, I realized that I could not ignore what filmmakers call the "back story." My new interest in writing and the end of my marriage were both triggered by events that occurred in 1986, but 1986 wasn't the beginning of the story. I could trace the beginnings back to the 1970s, the early years of my marriage; to the Vietnam War years of the late 1960s, when I met my husband; to the 1950s, when I was a child whose mother developed a crippling, and ultimately fatal, disease. I couldn't explain either the events that occurred in 1986 or the insights I was having in 1997 without referring to incidents that had happened decades before. Unlike the 1986 and 1997 narratives, these incidents refused to fall into line chronologically. Rather, they popped out of memory and into my consciousness in response to whatever I happened to be writing. They enriched my understanding and they demanded space on the page.

Black Eye is not a straightforward narrative. But I trust that you'll find your way—as I did—through the braided chronologies, the fragments of memory, the anecdotes and metaphors, to a greater understanding of the way all our lives are shaped. We are each unique, a product of our own individual psychology and family history. But we are molded, too, by context: by the social, economic, and political environment that surrounds us. I was born in 1944. Like many baby boomers, I came of age in the 1960s. My story is not only my own.

Black Eye

Unpleasant Truths

My husband punched me in the eye.

What is wrong with that sentence? It follows all the rules. Subject, verb, direct object. A simple sentence. I could go to the board and, chalk dust flying, diagram it just as Miss Montgomery taught me to in seventh grade.

The sentence is true. My husband is no longer a husband, much less mine, but he did punch me—and it was in the eye, the right eye because he's a lefty—in December 1986.

Why, then, does this sound better to me: He gave me a black eye?

I have been mulling this question over. My poet's ear prefers "he" to the more awkward "my husband." My aggrieved soul wants to keep "him" at bay. But this does not have to do with me alone, or even with me and him. That form—X gave Y a black eye—is the one we more often hear.

I am at a writing colony for three weeks. I have nothing else to do; I intend to figure this out. I look up synonyms in the thesaurus I find in my writing shed. *Hit, strike, smite; poke, jab, smack;* and then the "nonformal terms". *belt, bush, paste, bonk, slug.* They all work pretty well in the simple subject-predicate form. He hit her in the eye, struck her, smote her, poked, jabbed, and smacked her, slugged her, pasted one on the kisser. But he didn't punch me in the mouth. He gave me a black eye. I suspect that we pull our punches, when it comes to blackened eyes.

It is mid-October 1996, not quite ten years since he punched me, and I am at Norcroft, a writing retreat on the North Shore of Lake

3

Superior. I have come to find the story; to shape the narrative; to write, if I can, about the last year of my marriage, the year of the black eye.

I look out the big windows of my writing shed, set deep in the woods, at balsam firs and silver-trunked paper birches that shimmer with a wealth of gold leaves. The sky is perfectly blue. The sun reflects on the water, a gigantic rippling patch, white-hot, almost molten, on a deceptively calm slate blue sea. The air is warm and dry, but the breeze carries sharp undertones of winter, the clean, crisp feel of warning, or of possibility. We are far north in Minnesota, almost to Canada. It snowed here two weeks ago. Any day now, winter could come.

When does a marriage turn cold? I remember October 1985, a day very much like today: blue skies, hot sun, cool breeze. I was looking for a building in an unfamiliar part of Madison. I have to trust memory on this; I wasn't keeping a journal. I remember old wood-frame houses perched on the side of a hill. Tall front stoops of cracking concrete led up to rickety porches. Flocks of students rented the houses. They aimed speakers out the second-floor windows, cranked up their stereos; they sunbathed on flat porch roofs, basking in fugitive warmth while they read lit or poli sci.

I had just turned forty-one. My sons were at Wingra, a private school five miles from our big house on Lake Mendota. David, an active sixth-grader starting to take on a chunky pre-growth-spurt heft, might have been shooting rubber bands off a ruler at his teacher. Eli, an elfin child with big brown eyes and long lashes, was no doubt carefully printing his name to make his second-grade assignment as perfect as possible. Their father—my husband—was out of town, at a regatta, racing his flat-bottomed scow. Stu, who parted his thinning hair low and combed it over his bald spot, didn't have to take the day off from work; he'd lost his job as a researcher in early 1982. Let's be precise: he was fired. After that, he called himself a consultant, a "scientific jack-of-all trades." He'd had only one client in nearly three years, an attorney, a friend of a friend. He had plenty of time to sail.

I didn't take the day off either. I worked part-time, writing grant proposals for public radio and television. I took the job after Stu was fired, so we would have health insurance. In 1981, I'd come down with Hodgkin's disease, a form of lymphatic cancer. The doctors removed my spleen. I spent the next year in treatment: three rounds of chemotherapy, each followed by a month of radiation. Enough radiation to kill me, if they'd zapped me all at once.

Stu's boss fired him as soon as I finished treatment, in January 1982. Maybe the company didn't want to pay higher premiums to keep insuring me. Maybe Stu wasn't productive enough to suit the company. Maybe they wanted to fire him earlier, but his boss was a humane sort who thought they should wait until I seemed to be out of the woods. I never knew; I still don't know. By 1985 it hardly mattered. We fed our family with money Stu inherited.

⊛

I open an old file folder I have brought to my Norcroft writing shed. It's stuffed with letters I never mailed, notes from Stu, handwritten pages of journals I began long ago and abandoned: a scrappy written record of my seventeen years of marriage. In the folder, I find a list I made in 1980, before Stu was fired, before I got cancer, when David was in kindergarten and Eli was not yet two.

Reasons to Leave:	I would be free to come and go as I please; to decide what sorts of entertainment I want; to choose and see my friends without fear of them being chased away.
	I don't like living in a house full of cigarette smoke, with an alcoholic.
	I do not want to feel a constant need to apologize for my existence.
Reasons to Stay:	Children probably better off with two parents present.
	I would be lonely if I left.
	Life is financially easier.

Five years after I wrote that list, on that sunny day in October 1985, Stu was still drinking heavily. At the edge of downtown Madison, I found the address I was looking for: an old house with a sign on the porch. PICADA, Prevention and Intervention Center for Alcohol and Drug Abuse. I hoped the people inside could answer some questions for me. Does the definition of "social drinking" include four or five double shots of Jack Daniel's on the rocks? Could someone be an alcoholic if he only drank after six o'clock? Do alcoholics pass out on the couch after dinner every night?

I wanted those questions answered. But I didn't want to go inside. I looked up and down the street. I saw only porch-roof students. Still, someone I knew might see me. And inside, they might have answers I didn't want to hear.

I took a deep breath, opened the door. The room was small, full of chairs, an old couch, a battered reception desk.

The receptionist asked, "Can I help?"

I flushed, confused and embarrassed. "I'm looking for information about alcoholism." It sounds stupid now; it sounded stupid then. It was all I could think of to say.

"The library's in there." The woman pointed me toward the next room, floor-to-ceiling books. I browsed for a few minutes, nervous and uncertain. Was this a lending library? Could I borrow these books? Or did I have to read them there? I found a shelf full of pamphlets: "Facts about Alcohol and Alcoholism," "Alcoholic in the Family?" "Crossing the Thin Line between Social Drinking and Alcoholism," "Alcohol: Simple Facts about Combinations with Other Drugs." They seemed to be for sale. I grabbed an assortment, gave the receptionist twenty dollars, rushed out into the calm October air.

At home, I flopped on the couch to read in privacy. By the time I got halfway through the pamphlets, I was pretty sure Stu had a serious problem. I finished reading. The kids came home from school. Sara, our housemate, came home from work. I couldn't wait to talk to her. Her father was an alcoholic. I knew she'd understand.

The kids were up in their playroom, creating thrilling adventures for Lego "little guys." I stood with Sara on our deck, looking out at shadows lengthening over the lake. "I went to PICADA," I said. Telling her made me nervous. "I did a lot of reading." It occurred to me that Catholics might feel like this at confession. I took a deep breath. "I think Stu's an alcoholic."

"So what's new?" Sara turned away from the lake and looked me in the eye. "You told me that at least a year ago."

⬡

Here at Norcroft, a skinny birch tree outside my window is shedding a lot of bark. The papery skin hangs like rags all up and down the trunk. I have no idea why birches flake off old skin, although I've loved birch bark since I was a little girl, playing with sweet-smelling birch-bark wigwams and tiny souvenir canoes. I grew up in Pittsburgh, too far south for paper birches. Later I lived on the West Coast. The first time I saw birch bark peeling off trees I had come with Stu to Door County, the thumb of Wisconsin that sticks up into Lake Michigan. It was October 1972; we had just gotten married. We were traveling in our van, heading east to spend time with our very different families. My father, the son of Jewish immigrants, lived a solidly middle-class life in Pittsburgh, with a new wife (my mother had died in 1968) and my two youngest sisters. Stu's family could trace its roots back to the Mayflower. I'd spent a couple of evenings with his parents, Helen and Richard, when they visited Stu in California, but I'd never been to their elegant house in Madison, full of family heirlooms and the art Helen collected. Stu thought it would be easier for me to really get to know these rather formal people at their Door County cottage, where we could all relax. We crossed the country on U.S. 2, followed fall colors through Michigan's Upper Peninsula, hooked down through Wisconsin to Green Bay, and followed the limestone shoreline north to the birch and cedar woodland Helen and Richard owned. We arrived at their lakefront cottage late on a Saturday.

Helen embraced me and kissed Stu's cheek. Richard and Stu shook hands and carried our duffel bags up to a room tucked under the eaves. Helen followed with a stack of ironed sheets.

I helped her make the narrow beds. We plumped the feather tickings and smoothed comforters over the sheets. "Ready for a nightcap?" Richard called up the stairs. I accepted a tiny etched-crystal cordial glass of Kahlua coffee liqueur. Helen asked for a tall drink, gin with Bitter Lemon. For Stu and himself, Richard poured Jack Daniel's on the rocks. Birch logs in the woodstove crackled and shifted. We talked late into the night, telling Stu's parents about our travels, our months of living in the van.

Sunday, we slept in. The phone woke us about ten. Madison friends were up for the weekend. Helen invited them to brunch, to see Stu and meet his bride. They arrived at half past eleven. Richard offered drinks: Bloody Marys, screwdrivers, sherry. Which would I like, he asked. In my family the liquor cabinet contained a souvenir bottle of champagne from my parents' wedding in 1943, a single joke bottle of Olde Frothingslosh, The Pale Stale Ale with the Foam on the Bottom, and one partly full fifth of rye. My father took out the rye when my mother's Uncle Al, who lived in New York and wholesaled ladies' underwear, came to Pittsburgh on his annual selling trip. "Want a drink, Al?" my father would say. And he would pour rye into a shot glass for Al and take a shot himself. Uncle Al always had seconds. My sister Shelly and I thought he might be a drunk.

I had nothing against alcohol. I'd consumed my fair share in college and afterward, mostly cheap California wine. I'd had seconds of Kahlua only the night before. But I couldn't imagine drinking first thing in the day. "Nothing for me, thanks," I told Richard. He frowned. Helen suggested, "A glass of sherry?" I declined. She thought for a minute, then brightened and turned to Richard. "Why don't you make her one of your sweet vermouth drinks for nondrinkers?" He started pouring Martini & Rossi before I could protest.

Stu's parents' Door County routines made me uncomfortable. We spent hours in the car, driving the back roads, admiring the changing leaves. We took walks prescribed by tradition: park at the old church camp and climb up the bluff to look across to Michigan. We bought fresh whitefish from the fisherman's wife Helen always patronized, limpa rye from a Swedish bakery. Jellies and relishes

8

came from Koepsel's farm market stand. Before dinner each night, Richard made killer old-fashioneds. Helen boned smoked whitefish and served it with Triscuits. No other cracker would do.

I shrugged off my discomfort. I didn't know why I felt so uneasy. What could be wrong with this cottage, with its rocky beachfront, its built-in bookshelves, its antique rolltop desk? It wasn't a wilderness retreat, but it was simple, tasteful, not at all ostentatious. As for the routines—doesn't every family have its own traditions? I'd just have to get used to the Kingsleys'. I was married—well married, obviously. And my in-laws could not have welcomed me more.

I found a piece of smooth birch bark on the cedar-strewn path to the cottage. It was just about postcard size. I addressed it with a ballpoint pen and mailed it to an old friend in birchless California: proof, I wrote to Gwen, that I'd entered a whole new world.

✦

In the folder I brought to Norcroft, I find a few pages I wrote in January 1985. Stu was in the Bahamas; he'd left town before Thanksgiving to sail on his brother's boat. *Dream: I call Stu in Marsh Harbour. After some heavy conversation, I hear nothing on the phone but faint sounds of breathing. He has passed out, drunk. Later we have an angry argument. He is drunk again, abusive. When I go into his room to retrieve my shoes so I can take Eli to gymnastics, Stu is fucking someone else.*

By the time I had that dream, we'd been married thirteen years, and Stu and I had our own traditions and routines. He sailed every weekend on Lake Mendota; I made soups and casseroles to feed the hungry crew. He did laundry; I shopped, cooked, cleaned up the kitchen, but never fast enough. He wanted the kitchen run "like a chemistry lab." He bought packs of gummed labels. I was to label the jars of brown rice and whole wheat flour; I was to mark leftovers with name and date before I stored them in the fridge. I did as he directed. And I stockpiled anger too.

Most of our arguments started in the kitchen. Stu criticized me: I didn't label the leftover chicken; I piled dishes too high on the drain board; I left the crusted frying pan soaking in the sink. I screamed:

"If you want things done a certain way, why don't you do them your-self?" I dredged up old resentments. I complained that he didn't make school lunches; that he refused to drive the car pool; that he'd never take family vacations; that he ignored me and the kids. I erupted in fury, accused him of sleeping with other women; of tak-ing them to fancy restaurants; of giving them expensive gifts. "Don't tell me how to lead my life," he warned. I dissolved in hysterics, cried, shrieked like a banshee. He called me a "crazy woman," poured another drink. He retreated to his study. I followed him up-stairs. I tried to explain my anger, tried to apologize. "I'm sorry I screamed," I said. He didn't want to talk. "Get the hell out of my study," he roared. The silent treatment lasted for days.

I don't imagine the birch tree outside my writing shed, its bark in tatters, feels any pain. But I did. Sometimes I hated my life, really hated Stu. His reaction to my hatred, which must be visible, I wrote in a journal I started December 7, 1985, has been retreat and noncommu-nication. That just infuriates me even more.

✿

A few days after I visited PICADA in October 1985, I found a classi-fied ad in *Current,* the trade paper for the public telecommunica-tions industry. A new public radio station in Valdez, Alaska, needed a manager. It sounded good to me. I was bored with my job; it was time for a change. I'd always wanted to see Alaska. I'd produced some programs for public radio. I had grant-writing skills and start-up experience with nonprofit organizations: for three years, I'd worked half-time as the volunteer executive director of the new Madison Children's Museum. I sent in my resume.

One day late in October, the Alaska people called to interview me. The satellite connection was weird. My voice echoed in my ear. The Alaskan voices came at me from a great distance, after a several-second delay. They wanted someone to start the job, and start lobby-ing the Alaska legislature, right away. I said they'd be better off with someone who knew Alaska politics. They weren't convinced, or maybe they didn't have any politically savvy applicants. A few days later, one of my references told me she'd been called. They liked me, she said. Did I really want the job? I talked with Stu. Sure, he said. Take it. It's a terrific opportunity. But I'm not going with you. And the kids are staying here.

⊛

Do I stay or do I leave? Ten years later, the question still plagues me, even here at Norcroft, here in my writing shed, a few hundred feet away from the lodge where we eat and sleep. Every morning, about nine-thirty, I pour coffee into a thermos and walk down the gravel driveway to this small building, about nine by twelve feet, with a sloping roof, painted red on the outside. But it's hard for me to stay in the shed, staring at the computer screen or gazing out at the birches and evergreens through the big windows above my desk. Writing makes me so anxious, I keep trying to escape. I go back to the lodge again and again, for coffee, for candy, for anything that's not 1985. I *have* to get away. This morning, I was walking back to my writing shed eating handfuls of peanut M&M's, thinking about this need to get away, when suddenly, I slipped back into adolescence, into a scene from more than thirty years ago:

Passover, 1962, my senior year in high school. My grandmother is visiting from New York. She's in a spring cleaning frenzy. She's re-cruited me to help with the cupboards. We take out all the company dishes, the ones with the apple pattern. Nana wipes down the dusty shelves while I wash the bowls and plates. My mother sits in the living room, in a green upholstered armchair, leafing through magazines. For years, she's had multiple sclerosis, the progressive form that sends you downhill fast. She walks with a cane. She doesn't think clearly. She's much too weak to work with us.

I have just won a scholarship to Reed College in Portland, Oregon. I can't wait to leave home, to escape. But who will make sure supper's ready, who will iron the laundry, who will sew on the buttons, who will care for my sisters if I'm two thousand miles away?

"Don't worry," Nana says. "We'll manage. Get out and save yourself."

❀

Get out and save yourself. The message stayed with me, deep in memory. It surfaced in November 1985, as I wrestled with the big question: Should I move to Valdez? I had a vivid, unsettling dream: *My sister Shelly and I are in a large laboratory or a test kitchen, a big open space. We are having a serious conversation, a conversation that requires privacy. I have something very important to tell her, but every time I open my mouth, some friend or relative wanders past. I am enormously frustrated.* I woke from the dream in the middle of the night with the clear knowledge of what I was trying to say: I applied for the job to escape Stu's alcohol, his disease.

I had a real conversation with Shelly a few days later—after researching the price of milk in Valdez, which was pretty high. I told her it was an old story: sick mother, sick husband, the urge to save myself. But this time I couldn't run away. I couldn't leave the kids, who were only seven and ten. Escape wasn't possible. But Stu has to agree to counseling, I wrote in my journal, or I really will go.

I called Alaska and withdrew from consideration. I called a marriage counselor; he was booked until after Christmas. I called my college friend Rachel, a psychiatrist in San Diego. I told her my waking dream. "I can't leave," I said. "But sometimes I hate Stu so much, I feel it in my gut. My insides seize up at the mere thought of him."

"Find a therapist," she said. "Not an analyst. Someone who does brief therapy."

I called around and found Paul Bergeson. Saw B for an hour last Monday, I wrote on December 7, and have felt enormously better since; in fact I have been smiling, looking different to myself in the mirror. I feel I am really going to accomplish something, whatever the end results may be.

❀

That December 7 entry was the first in an obsessive journal I kept for more than a year. I *had* to describe what was happening to me; it was a compulsion. Recording the events of my life—my daily routine, my fights with Stu, my therapy sessions, my dreams—seemed almost as important as living them. But it wasn't easy to find either a time to write or a place. Less than a week into the journal, on December 13, I described my misery: Last night, Stu decided to go to a basketball game instead of the Wingra holiday festival where both David and Eli performed. I felt quite lonely at the event, like a single parent. I told him I thought his decision was reprehensible.

I am writing at a coffee shop. I don't know how to get the privacy to write in a journal at home.

⊛

I started keeping a diary in 1957. I was in seventh grade. Someone gave me an official Girl Scout diary, bound in green leathcrette, embossed with a gold trefoil, secured with a strap that fitted into a brass-plated lock. Later, I lost the tiny key and used scissors to cut the strap.

Under the illusion that my diary was private, a place to record my secret thoughts, I groused about my sisters, confided my crush on my classmate Lenny, complained that my parents mistreated me. One day my father took me for a walk. We were going to Forbes and Murray, to pick up bagels and the Sunday *New York Times*. Under the canopy of leaves that bowered Beechwood Boulevard, he told me I was old enough to know that my mother was very sick. She had MS, multiple sclerosis. The doctors thought it was better that she didn't find this out. I was to keep it a secret; I was not to tell anyone.

I didn't tell, and the secret grew until it took up all the room in my head. I couldn't think about anything else. I had to let it out. I confided it to my diary. Later, my father, apoplectic, yelled at me. "Why did you do that?" It was the worst thing I could have done. "Don't you know your mother reads your diary?"

I didn't know, until he told me.

But she did. She read my diary. That's how she learned she had MS.

⊛

13

My mother might discover my secrets by reading my diary, but still, I kept writing things down. What's a secret, anyway, but a socially sanctioned device for hiding unpleasant truth? I believed in the power of truth. I kept diaries and journals, sporadically, through high school and college and into graduate school. Some months I wrote obsessively, day after day. Some years I didn't write anything at all. I never thought much about whether anyone read what I wrote.

✦

Monday, December 16, 1985

Yesterday, Stu initiated a skating expedition onto the middle of the lake. There was wonderful ice, smooth and clear, not far from our shore. We had so much fun that Stu invited some friends over to skate this afternoon, a couple with a son who's David's age.

But when I went to pick up the kids at school, David's teacher told me that he has not done his assignments for the past two weeks. She wanted me to leave him at school to make up the work. I felt trapped. It's very rare for Stu to take the initiative in our social life, and I wanted to encourage it.

I was livid, too, because my idea of making a kid know that work is of prime importance is to make him do it, first thing upon arriving home each day. But I am usually at work when David gets home from school, and Stu doesn't agree with me about this. He thinks we should let David learn the hard way that he has to get his work done, by having his teachers point out when he is in a deep hole. So today he was in a deep hole, and I was the one who was caught. I wanted to make him stay at school, but really felt I couldn't. David told his teacher, in front of me, that "Stu doesn't care whether I get my work done," with elaborations.

I came home terribly upset and realized it was because once again Stu has all the authority. My views count for nothing, and David knows it. If Stu cracks the whip, David will toe the line (at least for a while); but where do I come in? I wanted to discuss this when we got home, but Stu wouldn't let me say anything. "Can I do the talking?" he snarled. He allowed that I could be present while he talked with David, if I kept my mouth shut. When I said I wanted a three-way conversation, he said, "Do I have to get a separate office? Or a separate house?"

⊛

I've brought all my old journals to Norcroft. The one that covers June 30, 1968, to August 7, 1969, fills 150 lined and numbered pages of a small "Record" book I bought in Berea, Kentucky, at a stationery store. Some time that year, my sister Shelly calligraphed a big "Hi" inside the pebbly black cover and added "P.S. I am not snooping. I am a big grown-up now and I am just saying hi."

She was twenty or twenty-one when she did that, and she's three years younger than I am, so I was a big grown-up too. In fact, by June of 1968, I had graduated from college, moved to Haight-Ashbury, and worked for a year and a half as a training course writer for Ma Bell, Pacific Telephone and Telegraph. San Francisco was filling up with flower children wearing tie-dyed T-shirts and beads. The six o'clock news was filling up with body counts and clips of napalm in Vietnam. I wore little knit suits by day, attended antiwar organizing meetings at night, and on the weekends, got stoned and hung out in Golden Gate Park, listening to Jefferson Airplane and the Grateful Dead. Several times, my roommates and I hosted big contingents of friends descending on San Francisco for major antiwar demonstrations. I tried not to think about Pittsburgh, about my mother's crippling illness. I succeeded, most of the time.

In the spring of 1968 I quit the phone company. I planned to start graduate school in the fall, but for the summer, I joined a Peace Caravan sponsored by the American Friends Service Committee. We traveled by van through Ohio, Kentucky, and Indiana, showing films about peace, talking to Rotary Clubs and church groups, bringing the truth about the war in Vietnam. In Berea, Kentucky, I finally filled the last lined page of a lab notebook bound in gray cardboard in which, for more than four years, I'd been keeping a sometime journal. It was a relief to give up the notebook, its pages smudged with soot that leaked from an envelope I'd stapled into the book on October 24, 1965, the beginning of my senior year in college.

I'd labeled the envelope: These are the ashes of some very scary things I wrote today. Right now, I remember what they are, but I am trying to forget them. I tried to kill them by writing them out and then burning the paper. My thoughts are most coherent on paper.

And then, on the facing page, just before graduation seven months later, the next entry: That succeeded. I don't remember it at all.

And I don't. But I can guess what it was. I'm pretty sure I wrote, on that paper I burned in October 1965, that I wished my mother dead. By then, she was severely crippled by MS, incontinent, crazy, depressed. She sat in the living room, turning the pages of *Woman's Day* without ever looking at them. Sometimes she shrieked at my father, who tried to ignore her, or at my sisters, or at me, if I happened to be home. Almost anything we did could provoke an irrational screaming fit. But mostly she withdrew into herself. Shelly got meals on the table. Daddy escaped into work. My two youngest sisters, grade-schoolers, more or less took care of themselves. I'm pretty sure I wrote that the whole family—my father, my sisters, even my mother—would be much better off if she died.

In Berea, nearly three years later, I bought the "Record" book with the pebbly black cover to replace the smudged lab notebook. After the Peace Caravan, before I went back to California to start graduate school, I spent some time in Pittsburgh. My father had finally been forced to acknowledge that there was something irreversibly wrong with my mother, something he could no longer ignore by hiding behind the *New York Times.* He had put her in the Jewish Home for the Aged. When I went to see her she lay, emaciated, in an iron bed, her body frozen into a fetal curl. She couldn't talk. I think she recognized me, because her expression changed. She grimaced. I think she was trying to smile.

My mother died in mid-September 1968. She was forty-eight. I have just turned fifty-two. I can't be sure how much I'm making up about the time I saw her in the nursing home. According to my journal, I was in Pittsburgh for about ten days after the Peace Caravan. I barely mentioned my mother. On Monday, August 12, I wrote Practiced flute—first time in weeks; saw Mother—first time since Thursday. A few days later, I left for graduate school. Before classes began, I returned to Pittsburgh for the funeral. There are no entries in the journal between September 3 and October 23. Nothing about my mother's death. I suppose I didn't want to think about it. I didn't write anything down.

Stu shows up in the journal the following spring, brief mentions in pages that are full of reports on other men: fellow graduate students, political activists, a married medical student, a couple of rock musicians. It's hard to tell, reading those pages, whether I spent more time in bed or protesting the war in Vietnam. Stu first noticed me— he told me later—speaking at an antiwar rally. We actually met at a mutual friend's house, drafting a manifesto. It demanded that Stanford University take control of its think tank, SRI (Stanford Research Institute), and stop all classified research, including research on chemical and biological warfare and counterinsurgency. We spent at least a half hour arguing about where the commas should go.

Questions of Politics

Friday, December 20, 1985

Can't remember ever being so depressed about Christmas. Fought with Stu this morning about whether we would go together to look for a new TV for his mother; best I can figure out about why I was so angry is a feeling that he has once again dumped all responsibility for this alien holiday on me. I'm sure this is made more annoying by his having left me holding the bag—as B so aptly summed it up—last year, when he spent the holidays sailing in the Caribbean with his brother, and I was left with his mother and children. But I was in a rage this morning, for reasons that I'm sure were not really apparent to Stu.

Left the house with the kids and seven coffee cakes I made for teacher presents; spent an hour at work, including two screaming phone calls with Stu; then went to Hilldale Mall to try to find presents for Stu and his mother. I could barely keep from crying at a scene in the Misses' dress department. "Do you think Mother will like this?" an older man asked his grown daughter, running his hand down the skirt of a red jersey knit.

She nodded. "She'll love it because you picked it out."

I wanted simply to not buy anything for Stu and Helen, just to avoid Christmas. To leave. Finally got Helen a cashmere sweater and a duffel bag for her many travels. Stu will also get her a fancy new TV. I know part of what makes me angry is the shabby treatment of my own family. For example, for Chanukah I sent my stepmother a $20 pin and my father a $25 gold coffee filter and a $1.95 joke book about apples. They would not ever expect me to spend hundreds of dollars on them—but they would like to see us more often (and I, them). I'm glad I never changed my

maiden name. I hate having to live a Kingsley life when I will never be—
would never want to be—a Kingsley.

⊛

Wednesday evening, December 25, 1985

Almost through this crap. Depressing dinner at Helen's last Friday. Brick
red chili in the green hand-painted Chinese bowls. Everything was very
Christmas with a capital C. A Yule log crackled in the fireplace. The living
room was fragrant with wood smoke and piney evergreens. Helen had
picked up David and Eli after school to trim her tree. She'd decorated the
mantel with miniature revelers, town and country scenes, inch-high angels
gathered around a tiny creche. And I got the old "You don't mind this
Judy, do you, because it's really just a pagan festival, right?"

After a lot of argument, Stu finally set out to do some Christmas
shopping on Monday afternoon (Dec. 23). He made it as far as the corner, where someone skidded into the front of his car.

I spent much of Monday and Tuesday in a frenzy: wrapping presents,
grocery shopping, making a yeast coffee cake. The kids stayed overnight
at Helen's after Christmas Eve tenderloin. Stu and I went back with the
coffee cake this morning for breakfast and presents, from ten until two or
so. Stu gave me a turquoise-and-liquid-silver necklace from Katy's American Indian Arts. It is not as nice as the one I told him I saw there a few
weeks ago. He'd said, "Call them and tell them to put it away, and I'll go
get it." But I didn't. Why couldn't he put a little effort into getting me a
present, thinking of what I might like or at least making the phone call
himself? On Monday, before Stu started out to go shopping, he wanted
to know if I'd asked them to set the necklace aside, and got very annoyed
when I said, "No."

"So I'm at ground zero with you," he said. ("Yes," as Shelly said when I
told her about this on the phone. "And square one.")

If life here were not so pleasant. . . . Helen gave us big checks for
Christmas, so now we talk of replastering the living-room ceiling, and I
dream of an Eames chair, something very comfortable for reading. I have
no guts, no initiative.

❋

No initiative. This is an old, old story; I can trace it back to sixth grade. Miss Larson is standing in front of the room. She is fed up with our class. What have we done? I no longer remember. But there she is, in front of the blackboard, wringing her hands and naming faults around the room. Marcie chews gum like a cow. Billy cracks his knuckles. If he keeps that up, he will never be a famous surgeon. I am too good. I do exactly what I'm told, nothing more, nothing less. I lack initiative.

❋

I sat on the edge of the couch in B's office at my second therapy session. He switched on the floor lamp and leaned back in his armchair. His long legs jutted into the space between us. Four o'clock, mid-December, daylight fading fast. I stared out the window, into the darkening courtyard, reconstructing dreams, searching for answers to his questions in the failing light. At the end of the session, he summed up my dilemma:

"When you try to talk with Stu, he dismisses your descriptions of his behavior as 'grudges,' unbelievable or unreasonable. So then you feel contempt for him and you ignore him. He reacts by looking around for other women. That makes you mad. But you can't blow the whole thing up because you're afraid of losing another intimate relationship."

That—fear of loss—is the hardest to deal with. One minute I am certain that I am fucked to be staying and putting up with all the bullshit, the next minute certain that it would be fucked to leave. I imagine B as some sort of savior, and yet am irritated by his interpretation of a dream fragment. When he says, "It's all in the dream, the mind is truly amazing," I don't know if he means my mind or his.

❋

I met Stu six months after my mother died. In September 1969, exactly one year after her death, I moved into his three-bedroom, two-bathroom ranch house. My journal-writing habit soon faltered. You can see the end coming on the blue-lined pages of a bound gray notebook, the sort Stu used when he worked in a chemistry lab. I report the move—Don't quite know why—it just seemed to be the logical, obvious, and right thing to do—and in the same entry, comment that I'm keeping the journal in my grad school office. Will I write in it?

I didn't, for more than six months. The next entry is April 5, 1970; by then, I'd brought the notebook home. I wanted to record the activities of the antiwar movement at Stanford. It seemed to me that the movement had historic significance; and of course it did, although my journal entries are too garbled, cryptic, and sporadic to contribute much to posterity. On April 5 I wrote a short paragraph about what I did that day: Read several chapters of Woody Guthrie's autobiography, made spaghetti, and saw Godard's *Sympathy for the Devil.* Then I wrote a paragraph about how Stu spent the day: Saw the Bullets beat the Knicks, fried bacon, did the laundry, ate a lime sherbet sugar cone, read the first half of *Factories in the Field,* and saw a movie too. In the margin next to the second paragraph, I noted: Dictation.

On April 6 I wrote a longer entry about my day. It's followed by a long paragraph in Stu's handwriting about his day. He added, in the margin, Nondictation.

Two weeks later, after I wrote a page about my activities, Stu initialed his approval: Good Report, SK.

In May we visited my college friend Rachel in Los Angeles, and I described our drive home through the Central Valley. Stu added a paragraph about irrigation, corporate agriculture, and ominous signs of future developments.

A month later, at bedtime, I sat in my turtleneck and underpants on the edge of Stu's double bed. Stu, also half-dressed, sat cross-legged behind me. I opened my journal, wrote Wednesday 24 June, skipped a line, and added Stu is looking over my shoulder. He asked me for the pen and wrote No—it is more like your writing hand. And then, Question: Why, if you skip a line between date and first line, do you indent the date? I took the pen back: Why do worms crawl?

He proposed An alternative and drew an arrow to the margin next to the first line, where he dated the entry Wed 6-24-70.

This back-and-forth game annoyed me. But I put the date in the margin after that.

The journal ends on August 7. We'd had several arguments—usually at bedtime—about the value of diaries. I didn't really know why I wanted to keep one. I just knew I did. "It helps me understand myself," I told Stu, but I knew he had no patience with that kind of self-indulgence. "These are important times," I added. "It's important to take notes."

One night, Stu delivered the coup de grace: "What do you think will happen if the pigs get their hands on your journal?" We both knew the answer. Someone would get busted. The journal was full of descriptions of our political activities, legal and quasi-legal, and the names of our radical friends.

⊛

Friday, December 27, 1985

Before dinner, I was looking at the Outings issue of the Sierra Club magazine, daydreaming about expeditions that would be fun to make with Stu and/or the kids. I mentioned some to Stu, and we talked briefly about summer vacation. "I don't really care where we go," I said, "but it's important to me to spend my vacation being active. Canoeing or backpacking, something like that."

Stu, very angry, accused me of insisting on "the terms." Well, yes, as a matter of fact: I have very limited vacation and an insatiable desire to be physically challenged, skiing, or whatever. Surely related to being alive and well. And I won't compromise away my desire to backpack with David and Eli every summer, so long as they're willing. Last summer we went to Isle Royale in Lake Superior. I made every effort to time the trip so it would not conflict with Stu's sailboat racing schedule, but still he refused to come with us. After we got back, he allowed as how perhaps he'd take a vacation with us next summer. But I should not have been fooled about his terms.

Terms. As in:

If one of us has a study of his own, it will be Stu.
If we go to a movie, it will be one Stu wants to see.

Oh, why do I go on with this? A year ago, I was sure we would separate in 1985. We have come pretty damn close, but here I am, a chicken-ass masochist. In agony.

✺

At noon today I took a break from writing: grabbed some trail mix and drove up a gravel road near Norcroft to the Superior Hiking Trail. It's two or three miles around the Oberg Mountain loop, a good length for an hour-long walk. Rain and wind the past two days have muted a lot of the color. When I walked the road just after I got here I noticed a pretty yellow tree hung with clusters of red berries. The word *pinnate* floated by; somehow I knew it applied to the leaves, strung along pink stems. Suddenly, somehow, I knew the tree's name: this was a mountain ash.

Not "somehow." I should give Stu credit for this; in fact, for most of the botany I know. He taught himself botany the year we traveled the country in our van: memorized words like *pinnate* and *oblate*, describing the shapes of leaves; tore flowers apart to examine the stamens with his pocket microscope; insisted we call the wildflowers by their Latin genus and species names. After all, he pointed out, "How many dozen *compositae* go by the name of daisy?" I learned more than I intended.

Today, all the ashes had lost their leaves. The berry clusters hung on bare limbs like Christmas ornaments. I passed a Forest Service sign: Approaching Scenic Overlook, carved into wood, the letters painted yellow. And in red: *Caution* Keep Children in Hand. It made me think of my children: Eli in New York, David in Connecticut.

And then I arrived at the overlook. The day was overcast, low clouds, flat light. A cliff dropped off, hundreds of feet, from the lichened rock under my feet. In front of me, nothing. A child could easily fall into the leafless stands of birch, the spiky bare branches below. I focused on the near distance, noted the dark evergreens, the few remaining patches of greeny-yellow in winter's approaching gray. When I raised my eyes, I was surprised to see the vast wrinkled skin of the lake.

❧

Sunday morning, December 29, 1985

Finally a day—yesterday—that was altogether fine. The kids and I went skiing with Bill and Linda Lange at Indian Lake, about twenty miles out of town. I'd forgotten all the birches there. Really beautiful: blue sky, snow on the branches. I fell many times—perhaps not quite so many as Eli, but certainly more than David. By the end of the trip, Eli could probably ski as well as I, and I think he really enjoyed it. Stu was appalled and perhaps annoyed that we were going. "It's too cold," he said as we left the house.

But it was not too cold: probably about five to ten degrees, but mostly sheltered from any wind. Anyway, I didn't let his attitude affect me. I just went. We five (the Langes, the kids, and I) now call ourselves The Grasshoppers, because a few days ago when Stu said he was "too busy" to go skiing with us, he taunted us: "Just a bunch of grasshoppers, nothing but play, play, play."

❧

My father could never have been accused of "grasshoppering." He worked as a physicist for the U.S. Bureau of Mines. This day job ended at half past four; he was home by five o'clock. Supper had to be cooked and the table set so we could eat the minute he came in the door. He didn't have much time: he had night jobs, too, teaching college math, and radio and television repair.

We did not say grace. My father turned on the hi-fi and we listened to the news while he dished out food from the pots, canned butter beans and frozen mixed vegetables. He'd cut up the chicken my mother had put in the oven half-frozen. "Maxine," he'd say in an annoyed voice, "can't you remember to take the chicken out of the freezer first thing in the morning?" He hated bloody joints.

24

She never remembered, I suppose because she was sick. By the time I was in junior high, she mostly sat in the green armchair in the living room, leafing through the *Ladies' Home Journal* or *McCall's*. The house was pretty much a mess. My littlest sister, Bobbi, cried in her crib upstairs. The green armchair, the living room, maybe the whole house, smelled sickly sweet from Mother's piss.

"WHIST?" Daddy asked when the news was done and he'd loaded up our plates. Shelly and I would tell him "what happened in school today." "Another movie!" He'd raise his eyebrows when we'd had a filmstrip day. "What's this world coming to? Don't they teach you girls anything?" He especially liked to hear how well we'd done on tests.

One day, when she was in fourth grade, Shelly said her class was taking a trip to Norway, a pretend trip, but just like the one Miss Larson had taken the summer before. They would cross the Atlantic west to east on the posh *Oslofjord* and come back on the *Stavangerfjord*, a student ship with no cabin toilets, or so Miss Larson had said.

"Then where do you pee?" my father asked, and we made it a family joke. Either the bathroom ship sailed alongside or you held it until you got home. All it took was the name: *Stavangerfjord*, and we laughed until it hurt. We said it night after night. *Stavangerfjord*. The word stretched out on our tongues. *Stavangerfjord*. It made Daddy forget the bloody chicken. It made Mother laugh with her mouth full. She grabbed for a paper napkin when the coffee came out her nose.

⊛

Monday morning, December 30, 1985

A friend brought over Jill Krementz's picture book, *How It Feels When a Parent Dies*, and left it on the living-room table. Eli immediately glommed on and started reading. When I asked, "Is that a good book?" he assured me that he was only reading the comments "by kids my own age."

(You can tell from the drips and smears on this page that I have taken to writing in the bathroom, before and after showers.)

Eli was in nursery school when I was diagnosed with cancer in November 1981. David was in first grade. I'd had more than enough secrecy about my own mother's illness; I thought my kids, however young they were, deserved to know what was going on. After school one day, I suggested a walk in the neighborhood. We headed for the breakwater near the Tenney Park locks. The trees were already bare; all the piers had been pulled for winter; not a single boat cruised the flat surface of the lake. I told David and Eli that I had Hodgkin's disease. I described the bad cells that keep growing and dividing. I said I would take medicine to kill the bad cells, but it would make me feel really sick. I told them that the doctors would also zap the bad cells with something like X-rays. "All the treatments," I said, "might make my hair fall out. And I won't get better right away. I'll be sick for a long time, but I won't have to stay in bed." I looked across the lake toward the State Capitol, the dome golden in the setting sun. "Sometimes I'll have to go away," I said. "I'll go to see a doctor in California, Dr. Henry Kaplan, who invented the cure for my disease." When Stu and I were at Stanford Hospital, I told the kids, Pops and Grandma—my father and stepmother—would come from Pittsburgh to stay with them.

It was almost suppertime. I'd left the chicken roasting in the oven. I had to go home and put on the rice. "You probably have some questions," I said. "I'll answer the best I can."

Eli asked, "If your hair falls out, will it grow back in again?"

David said, "Can I tell you what happened in school today?"

Tuesday morning, December 31, 1985

Sara (our housemate) took David and Eli to see the Harlem Globetrotters last night; Stu and I went to see *Out of Africa*. I was not overly impressed with the film, but Stu was blown away. He was stunned by the movie's explication of the differences between men and women (he wants freedom, she wants to settle down) and came home in some sort of rhapsodic transport. I asked him to help me finish getting food ready for the New Year's Eve party we are having tonight, and we worked in the kitchen from eleven-thirty until two in the morning, preparing dishes for an elaborate Indonesian *rijstafel* using recipes I clipped years ago from an old *Sunset* magazine.

Stu drank steadily all that time and ended up slurring words and being really nasty. "You always find something else to do besides cleaning up," he snarled at me while I was still in the midst of cutting vegetables. And "Be sure you don't leave the house too early tomorrow morning, before I see if you really did put a check on my desk to cover property taxes." For the most part, I just ignored it.

I was too busy all day to open my mail. Finally, at 2 A.M., I read a letter from an old college friend who lives in Seattle saying that Chuck Gold mark's family had been found badly beaten by an intruder on Christmas Eve; his wife dead, his two sons and he in critical condition.

Unnerving, and somehow, a terrible symbol of transience and lack of control.

Chuck Goldmark was a Young Democrat, blond haired and blue eyed, sharp featured, the roommate of my college boyfriend, Tom. About the time Tom and I got together, Chuck started going with Sandy, a friendly girl from southern California who had an infectious laugh.

One day in the fall of 1963, my sophomore year, Sandy and I walked up the hill from campus to the five-and-ten. We bought fake gold wedding bands, and then we took the bus downtown. I can still see the Planned Parenthood clinic—the pregnant women in the waiting room, the white walls, the nurse in a starched white hat who came out with a clipboard and asked for "Mrs. Smith." The clinic visit, in fact, remains more vivid than the night in Tom's Chevy Impala when I lost my virginity. That happened sometime freshman year. After that, Tom and I had sex without birth control. I knew I was pretty lucky. I didn't want to get pregnant. I didn't want a baby, and I had no idea what I would do if I had to have an abortion. I heard rumors about girls going to Tijuana. That sounded dangerous. Anyway, I didn't have much money, and Tijuana was a long way from Portland, Oregon.

I left Planned Parenthood with several months' supply of Ortho-Novum, flat cardboard-and-foil discs, each with twenty-one pills spaced evenly in a circle. I also got a plastic dispenser. You put the disc in the dispenser, and every day (if you remembered) you pushed down on the plastic blister covering a pill. The Pill popped out through the foil.

I didn't get pregnant. Chuck and Sandy broke up after a year or two. Tom broke up with me after I graduated. In the odd and incestuous way life sometimes loops around, Tom and Sandy got married.

✿

Wednesday noon, January 1, 1986

Had a very nice New Year's Eve party last night: five couples, lots of board games, and an Indonesian feast. I was a little concerned at first because Stu spent most of the time in the kitchen, making sure things got cleaned up immediately. He was either sulking or being self-righteous; I couldn't be sure, but it made me uncomfortable, especially when he told me, "We'd be great in a restaurant together. You're a good cook and I run a smooth kitchen. We'd make a great pair, so long as you remembered who was boss."

After the guests left (about 1:45 A.M.), we cleaned up and talked until about 4:30. Stu was fantasizing about where environmental cleanup research work might lead him. "How would you feel if I was gone six months of the year on consulting jobs?" Again, he identified heavily with Robert Redford's character in *Out of Africa*.

"I gave up my freedom to marry you, the same way Robert Redford did when he agreed to marry Meryl Streep," he said. "That should be enough to satisfy you." (I don't think the Redford character did decide to settle down and get married, but that's another story.)

Stu also said: "I've spent the past three years staying at home instead of pursuing career alternatives so that you would be free to develop your career."

And: "I'm afraid you'll divorce me if I get very involved in consulting. You won't like it if I set up an office away from home and spend a lot of my time out of town."

I told Stu, "You need to be honest with yourself about why you've done so little for the past three years." I said I thought it was because he was depressed, not because he'd made some decision to encourage my career. And I added, "I'm not so concerned about what you do when you're not here—or with how much you are or aren't around—as with the quality of our life when you are here." Stu didn't understand what this meant. "I wish we'd play together," I said.

"Then you have to use a carrot and not a stick," he insisted and implied that I have to do what he wants to do, not what I want to do (for example, camping with the kids or skiing every few days with them and Bill and Linda).

I told Stu that, at my last session, B posed a question he wanted Stu to answer: "Judy has the idea that if she exerts control or takes action, you will drag your feet or not go along. I'm not sure whether she's right or not. What things does Judy do when she wants to take control that allow you to join her, and what sorts of things does she do that make you drag your feet or not go along?"

Stu said, "He should go see *Out of Africa.*" When I asked him to elaborate, he said, "Just tell him carrot and stick."

Six years after I went on the Pill, the summer of 1969, I started to think about children. I'd been dating Stu for a couple of months. I was almost twenty-five. That seemed pretty old. Back then, a lot of girls got their bachelors' degrees and, the same June, married their college boyfriends. They had their first babies at twenty-two or twenty-three.

That summer Shelly and her boyfriend Patrick moved from the West Coast to New York to go to graduate school. I went along for the road trip. We stopped to visit friends and check out a lot of sights in the Southwest that Stu told us we shouldn't miss. At the hot, dusty rim of the Black Canyon of the Gunnison, I heard two sweaty little boys hatching a plot. They had just run up the trail far ahead of their parents. "When they come back," one said, "let's complain about leaving so soon. Let's say how *interesting* it is."

I began to think of how much fun it would be to discover Indian cliff houses and gigantic chasms with a child, I wrote in my journal, and then to think about Stu saying that he'd decided that the greatest challenge man can have is that of raising a child. And, not for the first time, but for an early enough time to be notable, I began to think that perhaps I would like to have a child, fairly soon.

We spent a night in Manhattan, Kansas, with my college friends Sandy and Tom. Tom was back from Vietnam, where he'd served a year as a medic. He and Sandy lived in a small apartment near the army base. When we arrived, Sandy was folding diapers. A toddler was helping. Sandy was pregnant, if my memory serves me right.

No matter how cute I'd found the kids at the Black Canyon of the Gunnison, I didn't envy her. There but for the grace of God, I thought.

Life with Stu, I knew, would be entirely different. For one thing, I would never be an army wife. Stu was thirty, too old for the draft. More important, he was an antiwar activist. When I considered what we had in common, politics was high on the list. I moved in with him as soon as I got back to California. We lived together for three years, going to meetings and demonstrations, doing "power structure" research and making speeches, fighting to end the war in Vietnam. In 1972, as the war was winding down, we got married. David was born three years later, and Eli, three years after that.

❀

In high school, if anyone had asked me what kind of boyfriend I wanted, I would have said "someone very smart." But politics was just as important. I couldn't imagine falling in love with a Republican. The summer after ninth grade, I volunteered as a "Kennedy girl." I wore a white plastic boater with red, white, and blue streamers and waved a campaign sign high when JFK stumped for votes in Pittsburgh. I listened to the convention on the radio, kept a running tally of the delegates' votes. I cheered when Kennedy was elected and cried when he said, "Ask not what your country can do for you; ask what you can do for your country."

What I could do for my country, I thought, was to hold it to its guarantees of life, liberty, and the pursuit of happiness; to help make it truly a place of freedom and justice for all. After Kennedy's election, I joined work camps and seminars for high school students, sponsored by the American Friends Service Committee. We spent our weekends painting houses in the slums and discussing the Civil Rights Movement and the Soviet threat. We sang folk songs and marched up and down the sidewalk outside the Jewish Y and the public television station when they wouldn't host Pete Seeger because he'd been a Communist. We marched on Washington because nuclear war scared us and we wanted to Ban the Bomb. We wore sandals and woolen ponchos. Our classmates called us "beatniks" and "radicals."

Before I left for Reed College in 1962, my father warned me about Communists. "They get into peace organizations," he said, "good organizations, organizations you would want to join, and then they take them over because they're the hardest workers." During orientation week at Reed, I met red diaper babies, members of the Student Peace Union, including the son of Dorothy Healey, secretary of the American Communist Party. When SPU organized a protest in downtown Portland, I joined the picket line. (As I recall, it was a response to local investigations of "un-American activities.") But I was already spending too much time reading Homer and Plato to be able to out-work any possible Communists who might want to take over the organization. Besides, I soon fell in love with Tom. I met his roommate, Chuck, and began to hang out with their friends. They seemed less dangerous, and a lot less work. They were Young Democrats.

I was no democrat as a child. In the summer of 1953, Queen Elizabeth had just been crowned. I was nine; Shelly, six. We lay on our stomachs on the living-room rug, turning the pages of *Life* magazine, absorbed in the fairy tale lives of England's royalty. We were avid monarchists. We played Princess Margaret (Shelly) and Princess Elizabeth (me). More than anything else, we wanted a life-size playhouse like the one at Buckingham Palace. We spent hours on our swing-set ladder, watching for the prince in shining armor (my grade-school boyfriend Howie) who would ride up on a great white steed, clip-clopping down the alley, past the garbage cans, transforming our lives as he entered our backyard through the rusted gate.

By the mid-sixties, I had no use for such childish fantasies. I was in college. The war in Vietnam was heating up. I campaigned for Lyndon Johnson in 1964. Johnson, at least, said he wouldn't use the Bomb. Barry Goldwater, the dread conservative, said, "Extremism in defense of liberty is no vice." On October 31, just before the election, the Reed College Young Democrats blanketed southwest Portland with elegantly calligraphed leaflets paraphrasing Robert Burns: *From ghosties and ghoulies and long-legged beasties and things that go bump in the night, Good Lord preserve us! Goldwater for Halloween.*

It took me years to realize that Barry Goldwater wasn't the problem; that the good Democrats, Kennedy and Johnson, had embroiled us in war. It wasn't a simple case of political loyalty. My boyfriend was a Young Democrat. Then he dropped out of school and enlisted, to avoid being drafted. I was in love with a soldier. I sensed danger in knowing too much about Southeast Asia. I focused instead on school, on my senior thesis about the history of some other time and place. After I graduated from college, after Tom broke up with me, I started to pay attention to politics again. I discovered that I hated what our boys were doing in Vietnam. I wore my phone-company-little-knit-suits to antiwar organizing meetings in San Francisco. Once again, I marched and waved picket signs. I joined the Peace Caravan. Freed to think clearly, I reclaimed the radical self I'd abandoned when I fell in love with Tom.

And then I married into the upper class.

⊛

I've brought Eli's old bike to Norcroft; I ride along the shoulder of Highway 61, thinking about place names. Schroeder. Tofte. Lutsen. Were these towns named after people? Who were they? How much land did they own?

I started thinking about place names after I married Stu. His family was "old Madison." They'd come to Wisconsin when it was part of the old Northwest Territory. They helped establish the city's institutions; they invested in Wisconsin's oldest firms. They bought land when it was cheap and plentiful. As Madison grew, they sold some of their properties and invested the proceeds. They donated some of their land for civic projects. Family names appeared on building facades, on business letterheads, on parks, on plaques in front of schools.

Stu's parents drove Fords; they lived in a relatively modest house near the university, not a mansion on the lake. They owned a beachfront cottage; they collected art; and they traveled frequently, to exotic places like Morocco and Afghanistan. But they scorned the nouveau riche, Johnny-come-lately businessmen who drove new Cadillacs and flashed their money around. The Kingsleys didn't need to prove anything to anyone. They carried the unmistakable mark of old money: names rooted in the history of the city's development.

⊛

In the spring of 1970 I stood on the Atherton train platform, the station in the wealthy San Francisco suburb closest to Stu's house in Redwood City. We'd been living together for nearly half a year. I was studying communications research at Stanford, but mostly I was an antiwar activist. Stu spent his time organizing scientists and engineers against the war.

The two of us fed on a volatile stew of patriotic rage and shame. Our rich and powerful country, the country we loved, was destroying a tiny nation, bombing and napalming children, doing this in our name. We didn't know how to stop it. But we would try whatever we could. This meant endless organizing meetings. It meant nonviolent demonstrations. It meant taking over campus buildings and shutting down research centers. "By any means possible," we vowed.

I was headed up to the city for a meeting of antiwar media activists. As I waited for the train, I watched a well-dressed man dial a pay telephone. I walked toward him, heard him get a number from Information: a multinational corporation, a defense contractor with interests in Vietnam. He placed his call. I felt a sudden surge of adrenalin. He was one of Them. I had him cornered. "By any means possible." I couldn't help myself. My fury overflowed. I started screaming. I asked how he lived with himself. I called him a fucking pig. I shrieked, "Do you tell your kids that you kill babies in Vietnam?"

Stu and I were united in our rage against the war. Indeed, his anger was greater, fueled, I think, by embarrassment at being a son of the upper class. When we met, he had no job. I wondered how he got money to buy food, to pay the mortgage on his three-bedroom, two-bath ranch. He didn't tell me, and I didn't ask; I gratefully accepted his support, once I moved in, as a supplement to my $2,200 fellowship. Stu was so secretive about his past that, for a short time, I was afraid that the rumor I'd heard circulating in the Stanford movement was true: maybe he *was* an undercover agent.

Eventually I realized that we were living on Stu's small inheritance. Of course, this made him even more attractive. Nana, my mother's mother, had told me over and over: "It's just as easy to fall in love with someone rich as someone poor." Even as a child, I understood her mantra of upward mobility to be in the category of "do as I say and not as I did."

❧

Tuesday morning, January 7, 1986

Stu and I got into another vacation argument in the kitchen yesterday. It started when I asked what makes him willing to do something that I suggest. "For example, why did you agree to ski up north next month with the Langes, the kids, and me?"

"You just made it as a suggestion. It wasn't like last summer, when you announced that you were going to Isle Royale and I could come along if I wanted to."

"First I suggested that we all go to Isle Royale," I pointed out. "I only announced that I was going after you said you weren't interested. It's really important to me to backpack every summer."

This set him off. "Now you're trying to change the plans for next summer," he complained. "You're insisting on backpacking. I thought we agreed to take a car trip and do some day hiking."

Before I could reply, he headed down to the basement to do some laundry. When he came up, he got ice cubes out of the freezer and poured himself a drink. I said, "I'll probably have enough vacation this summer to backpack with the kids and do a car trip with you."

He didn't answer, just picked up his glass and walked through the kitchen past me.

I said "Hey!"

"I don't have time to discuss next summer," he said. "I'm trying to get ready to go to California tomorrow."

He did take time to blame me for the fact that when he hung his silk turtleneck to dry on the wooden rack, it got discolored: red, so he decided it was from my red wool ski socks. He started yelling about what a "mess" it is downstairs, how I don't do laundry right. "When I get back from California we'll change jobs," he said. "You can take over the grocery shopping and I'll do the laundry again."

During our first seven years together, Stu had no regular jobs around the house. I was responsible for the grocery shopping, the laundry, the cooking, cleaning the bathrooms—the traditional housewife's tasks. This division of labor seemed unfair, and I resented it, but the work didn't overwhelm me until we moved to Madison. In the fall of 1976, six months after the move, we lived around the corner from

Stu's mother in a huge, formal, three-story house: five bedrooms, living room, dining room, sunporch, family room in the basement. We had no household help. It was a question of politics. People should take responsibility for the space they occupy.

David was eighteen months old. Every week or ten days, he stayed overnight with Helen. That was the thing I liked best about living in Madison: I got to sleep in once in a while. Stu never woke up with the baby. When David cried, Stu pulled a pillow over his head. I thought fathers and mothers should both do child care. That, too, was a matter of politics.

Stu and I discussed these questions—who should clean the toilet, who should feed the baby, who should make the meals. The discussions escalated quickly into full-blown arguments. I screamed and cried. Stu retreated to his study. We did agree on two things: one, we shouldn't oppress other people; two, our house was much too big for just the three of us. We invited someone to live with us, rent free. Our housemate cooked one dinner a week and vacuumed the first floor. I cooked six dinners a week and cared for the rest of the house.

Stu spent most of his time at work. I wrote some freelance articles for a progressive newspaper; I volunteered on the news staff at WORT, the community radio station. I was learning how to write grants. I was learning how to do radio. I was cleaning house; I was planning menus; I was making meals; I was washing clothes; I was paying bills; I was changing diapers. A housemate wasn't enough to take the pressure off. I was exhausted most of the time.

One day, I had an epiphany. The problem, I realized, was political principle, our dogged determination not to oppress anyone else. But if it was a question of our politics or our marriage, the politics would have to yield. I told Stu I wanted to talk. I didn't scream; I was very rational. "I've decided that there's no use asking you to help around the house," I said. "We have all these arguments and nothing ever changes. You just get mad at me for nagging. So I've decided not to expect you to do anything anymore. Instead, we'll use your money to hire a cleaning lady."

I expected an argument about politics, about oppressing other people. But Stu saw nothing wrong with the arrangement I proposed. To him, it seemed perfectly logical. After all, Helen had live-in help while he was growing up. The hang-up about having a cleaning lady was entirely mine. Nana was right: marrying a rich man was a good idea.

Stu even volunteered to take on the laundry as his job.

⊛

Tuesday evening, January 7, 1986

Aha! Stu has gone to California, and I am able to write this openly, in the lake room, listening to Glenn Gould play Bach on the new record Helen gave me for Christmas.

I took him to the airport about half past nine this morning, after working an hour at home on the facilities grant for work. Went from the airport to work and stayed there until about two; then had a hurried lunch before seeing B. During the session, I felt close to tears talking about Stu.

At the end of the hour, B summed up the situation:

Like many men, he said, Stu is only really comfortable if he has the power in a relationship. In our early years together, when both of us acknowledged his superiority, the relationship was stable. Now, as I am asserting myself, Stu reacts with "fight or flight." This surprised me, because I always thought Stu liked me to be strong. B said, "He probably was attracted to your strength at first, when he was clearly in charge."

B helped me see that I began to make the transition from accepting Stu's authority to rejecting it years ago, when David was an infant. I felt trapped and desperate. I found part-time child care so I could have time for myself, and hired someone to help with the cleaning chores that Stu refused to do. But the transition has become much clearer—and perhaps even completed—in the past three years, as I recovered from Hodgkin's disease and from the chemo and radiation. I have become more assertive, more certain of what I do and don't want to do. In fact, maybe I'm stronger than I was before I got sick. At any rate, Stu reacts irrationally to what B agrees has been my reasonable response to my situation.

The problem now, as I see it, is that I have two alternatives. I can stick around, if Stu will change. But what most provokes his flight or fight reaction is my "using the stick," as he puts it, to make him change his behavior. (B made a wonderful allusion to the shape of carrot and stick: both long, similarly shaped . . .) Or I can leave. But what other prospects for intimacy do I have, forty-one years old, with two children and a questionable health history?

Intimate Strangers

Last night, I worked in my writing shed later than I'd intended. It grew dark, and I didn't have a flashlight to show me the path back to the Norcroft lodge. The sky was cloudy; there were no stars, the moon had already set. I stepped outside my shed, turned off the lights, and waited for my eyes to adjust to the dark. But it remained pitch black, with only an occasional flash of headlights off to my left, where the highway was, and to the right, in the distance, the lighted windows of the lodge. My shed is thirty or forty yards off the driveway, down a narrow path through the woods. I stepped onto the path and moved very cautiously, shuffling my feet a few inches at a time, guided only by the feel of the leaf-covered gravel underfoot. More than once, when I thought the path must have met the driveway, I veered to the right and was gently nudged back on track by a hillock of grass, a slight dip underfoot, once by the long stem of something brushing my cheek.

⊕

Thursday, January 9, 1986, late night

Went to Helen's for a quick dinner before the University of Wisconsin basketball game. As we were walking to the Field House, she slipped on the ice and gave her head a good crack, so we went back to her house. I stayed there for a while to be sure she was OK, began to leave, and then started telling her about seeing B and sat back down again. We had a

39

good talk, and I gathered some history for B, who says next session we will talk about Stu's family. Some of Helen's points:

Her husband, Richard, was never a "bully," but he let you know how he wanted
   things to be. He permitted no squabbling or "nit-picky" arguments.
Richard never interfered in Helen's "province." He respected what she did
   (volunteer work, homemaking) and her right to make her own decisions
   and have her own opinions. In the early '50s, they settled this issue when
   he supported Joseph McCarthy and she did not.
Richard was quite unlike his own father, whom Helen described as "an autocrat
   and a bully of the old school."

Most interesting: Helen has no memory of the only anecdote that Stu has ever told me about his father. According to Stu, when he was in grade school, Richard punished him for lying. As Stu tells it, he had permission to go to a movie with a friend and the friend's older sister. But Richard saw Stu and friend—and no sister—at a bus stop. Stu says that for the next year, he had to get Richard's permission whenever he wanted to go to a movie. Even on Saturdays, Helen would not allow him to go to a movie until he had called Richard at the office, interrupting whatever he was doing, to ask permission.

Helen said she wished Stu would also get some help from a therapist.

❦

The first time I met Stu's parents, they had come to California to visit. Stu and I had been living together for a couple of years. Stu's younger brother, Hal, also lived with us, more or less camping out in the bedroom Stu used as a study.

Richard and Helen stayed in a motel, but one night they came for dinner to our house in Redwood City. I made chicken paprikash, one of my specialties. I suppose I was trying to assert my identity. My father's parents were both born in Hungary. But they were poor, observant Orthodox Jews. If they could have afforded a chicken, they would never have cooked it in sour cream.

Another evening, Stu's parents took us out for dinner at L'Auberge, a fancy French restaurant. We all had cocktails with appetizers; some of us had two. The maitre d' served wine with our entrees. The conversation grew loud. I fingered the starched edge of the linen tablecloth while Richard, Hal, and Stu argued about Vietnam. Richard supported Nixon; he believed in bombing the enemy. Hal said that the country might never recover from the napalm, the defoliation of the jungle. Stu condemned the war as genocide committed in the interests of a ruling class of privileged white Americans.

The maitre d' refilled our glasses and asked if we'd like dessert. The man's tuxedo, his manner—haughty, but somehow servile—made me intensely uncomfortable. He was treating us as though we were of the ruling class. Well, I thought, the Kingsleys might be. But I was only their guest. Under the tablecloth, I unzipped my macrame evening bag. The waiter rolled up the pastry cart. The Kingsley men held their fire, stopped their argument. The waiter described the amaretto cheesecake, the tarte au poivre, the chocolate decadence. All eyes were on the desserts. Quickly, I slipped a silver-plated teaspoon off the table and slid it into my purse.

※

Friday, January 10, 1986, 4:30 A.M. (and freezing!)

Just awakened from an intense, pleasurable dream: I am at a party, a New Year's Eve party, to which I have driven Helen and B. The party is at a very warm, rough-hewn wood house—a cottage really— and by the end of the dream I think it is B's house. There is a piano in the cottage and a lot of good classical music. I am having a good time, and then B begins to tell me that he finds me attractive. When I joke and protest that one's therapist ought not to say such things, he gets quite serious, and says that a therapist's job is to show the possibility of changing one's situation, and he would like to change mine. I give in completely. I ask him to tell me something about himself; I have been very curious, I say, but reluctant to ask questions. He doesn't say much, but I know somehow that he is single and really available and that he means what he says about me and us. As all the other guests leave, I find myself in his arms and the dream becomes quite romantic and erotic. Helen wanders through the living room and sees us, and I am afraid there will be problems. I tense—but she gives us her approval and even joins the hug. David suddenly materializes. He is talking with B, and then he accepts and returns a hug from B. I am suffused in growing warmth, hope, possibilities, happiness, and then I wake up.

⊛

Possibilities. How do we know what is possible? I turned twenty-one in 1965. I expected to be a wife; a mother; to have an education, but not a career. A few years later, the second wave of feminism washed over college campuses. By then I was in graduate school, living with a man six years older than I, a man who'd come of age in the fifties.

Picture this: I am in a dingy church basement somewhere in Palo Alto in 1970, one of a dozen women sprawled on brightly colored pillows spread across the linoleum. We are going around the circle, telling our life stories. One of the women has just walked out on her husband, leaving two small children behind. "I couldn't take it anymore," she says. She's loud and sarcastic. "All that washing and cooking and cleaning! Taking care of other people! Now it's time for *me*."

I am appalled. I am all for women's rights: equal pay for equal work, sharing jobs around the house, admission to law school and med school. But I don't understand this sobbing sister, this woman who's abandoned her kids.

How much of a feminist was I in 1970? I hated ironing, but I always ironed my boyfriends' shirts. Fortunately, Stu sent his to the laundry. Still, there was the cooking conundrum. When I moved in with Stu, he and his housemates seemed very well fed. They all knew how to cook. But I took over the kitchen. I made all the dinners—chicken in wine sauce, clam spaghetti, Swedish meatballs—elaborate meals that were very well received. Was I showing my love through food? Proving my wifely credentials? Was I just happy to have an appreciative audience after years of cooking for myself?

Or was I simply stupid?

It's not that Stu never cooked. He turned out big weekend breakfasts of sausage or bacon and highly seasoned eggs. He specialized in refried beans made from scratch. But by the fall of 1975, when we'd been together for six years, I was tired of doing most of the cooking, the housework, and—lately—the child care. David was six months old. I understood how a wife and mother could yearn to do something for herself. When the National Organization for Women called a strike for Wednesday, October 29, I was ready to walk out. For the morning, at least.

Stu took David to the food co-op to do our share of work, cutting cheese and sorting produce. I stayed home to write.

I don't know whether to be amused or outraged at the irony, I typed. Stu has already been complimented for his liberated stance by a local reporter who came to interview me yesterday, and by our next door neighbor. Yet on this unusual "liberating" day I got up at six to feed and dress David, squeeze in a shower, and make breakfast before Stu got out of bed. At noon, I will meet Stu on campus and resume "primary responsibility" for David. I packed the diaper bag with the essentials Stu needs for three hours this morning. I snorted with disgust when I read that the Department of Motor Vehicles has designated this Women's Week and placed women in positions of management for the week, but I think I'm a "token" too.

A few weeks after David was born, Stu and I bundled him into his car seat and drove to an ice cream parlor near our house in Davis, California. Over coffee and sundaes, we talked about the future. Should Stu accept a new job in Madison? He asked me what I thought.

I didn't want to move. We were just getting established in Davis, where we'd settled after a year of traveling in our van. We'd bought a house on an acre of land a few miles outside town. The house was nothing special, but the lot was one-of-a-kind. We had wonderful neighbors, a field of corn across the road, and behind us, pasture, part of the University of California–Davis farm. When we moved in, I was six months pregnant. In the evenings, Stu and I sat on hay bales overlooking the irrigation stream at the back end of our lot and watched the sun set and the moon rise and the burrowing owls that nested in the opposite bank. Stu built a big compost pile and put in a beautiful garden, including artichokes we dropped, like corn, right into boiling water.

In a booth at the ice cream shop, Stu stubbed out a cigarette and described the two-year postdoc he'd been offered at the University of Wisconsin. The work excited him. "And it would be good for Mother," he said, "if we were in Madison." Helen was recently widowed; Richard had died in 1974.

I agreed that Helen would love to have her only grandchild nearby. But I was nervous about living so close to Stu's family and its ties to "old Madison." Besides, I'd just found a pediatrician in Davis; I knew some baby-sitters; we had begun to make some friends. Nan Houck, a woman I'd met on the Peace Caravan, lived with her husband and year-old son in Woodland, ten miles away. She ran the food co-op and I was editing the newsletter. Mostly, though, I just didn't want to be the kind of wife who followed her husband wherever he went.

The baby began to fuss, and I turned away from the table so I would have room to nurse. My shirt—an old maternity smock—made a tent over David. He tugged at my nipple. My milk let down. I looked out the plate-glass window, avoiding Stu's eyes. "I'd rather stay here," I said.

Stu had asked me what I thought. But we were talking about his career, and I knew it was his decision. My wishes in this matter had no more importance than David's. We moved in May 1976. David turned one the day we crossed the Continental Divide.

❦

Wednesday, January 15, 1986

Stu—back from California—just asked what I was writing. "My journal," I said.

"Do you think you have to put a lock on it?" he asked.

"Do you?"

"No, but I worry about Eli."

I have had to come into the bathroom and sit on the can to finish writing this entry. Stu is very talkative, interrupting. So far we are going along smoothly, though my irritation has been triggered twice, first by the smell of cigarettes when I came home from my piano lesson and later by Stu repeatedly filling his glass with liquor.

☞

Friday, January 17, 1986

Stu has been home two days. I feel distant, detached, and beginning to itch for contact. It occurred to me to walk into the study and ask him why he's avoiding me—but that would be provocative. So I will stay distant and will seethe inside. This is interesting, because I'm not sure what Stu has done (or not) to annoy me. Nothing big. More little picky things like telling Helen and me, this evening, where and when to cross a busy street; telling David this morning that if David didn't tidy his Legos, Stu would step on them, "or maybe step on you"; reducing Eli to tears at dinner when Helen and Stu were talking about different words that mean the same thing and Eli piped up (interrupting), "That's like all the words for rear end." I understand why Stu got upset: Eli interrupted, and Stu didn't consider his comment appropriate dinner conversation, especially with Helen present. But Eli had discussed synonyms and body parts in school this week, and he wanted to join the discussion.

With both incidents involving David and Eli, I rushed to the kids' defense. This morning I jokingly asked Stu, "How would you like someone to tell you, 'I'll step on you'?" That gave him pause. He said he was only joking. This evening I explained that Eli had been discussing synonyms at school, using "rear end" as an example, and Helen joined in Eli's defense. But this "women and children vs. The Boss" sucks.

☞

Saturday, January 18, 1986

Almost predictably, Stu came into the bedroom last night to see if I wanted chocolate, dope, and a fuck after I had crawled into bed with a novel. Leaving him alone does please him, turn him on. I was not averse to rolling around, but could not feel warm toward him because of the ways he'd annoyed me yesterday.

Spent a lot of time this afternoon on a walk, thinking about writing fiction, and will try to set aside at least a half day each week for this, again. (I tried this for a while in the fall, and actually drafted a short story, but dropped it out of lousy-ness and fear.) For the next nine months, I am on leave from grant writing so I can write and produce audio programs for a college-level sociology distance learning course, *Marriage and the Family.* Maybe I could just not work after the course is done in September: I could get continuation health insurance from the state and write for a year or eighteen months. This really is in conflict with my other urge: to seek a high-paying, exciting job. But today I felt more the urge to expand artistically . . . .

❀

When my fourth-grade classmate Barry Golden died, my mother took me across the street to pay a condolence call. A grand piano filled the living room. I sat on a straight-backed chair while the grown-ups talked. My mother asked how Barry's sisters were "taking this." Mrs. Golden said the older one, a high-school girl, spent hours each day "working it out on the piano." I couldn't believe that anyone would really *want* to practice piano.

Barry and I used to ride the bus home from Colfax School with Howie Katz. Howie lived around the corner, on Beechwood Boulevard. I knew him better than Barry; in third grade, Howie and I declared our love, and he kissed me on the hand. Every year he was going to give me another kiss, first on my wrist and then up my arm and neck until, by the time we were old enough to get married, he reached my lips. He came over to play, or I went to his house, almost every afternoon. Sometimes Barry joined us. We played on the swing set, made up games of cowboys and Indians, placed strips of gunpowder caps at the weighted end of a rocket-shaped metal toy. When you threw the rocket straight down, the cap hit the sidewalk with a bang.

Barry died just before Christmas vacation. I had a hard time understanding why a kid my age would die, but I finally figured it out. Barry was Jewish, like me, like Howie, like most of the kids in our neighborhood. (It was easy to tell the non-Jews: they wore dark blue uniforms and got off the bus at the stop near Saint Philomena's.) God, I decided, needed more angels to help Him get ready for Christmas. To be sure, I'd never heard about angels at Rodef Shalom Sunday School. And I wasn't so sure I believed in God. But if He existed, I didn't think that just before Christmas, He'd kill a Saint Philomena's kid.

⊛

Tuesday, January 21, 1986, 4:50 P.M.

Just back from seeing B. A wonderful experience! I read him the dream about the party at his cottage, and then we talked about it. The most difficult part for me was learning the symbolism of the cozy, warm house: the house of my early childhood, spiritually, although not physically. "Coziness" evokes the image of the big green upholstered chair in which I curled up to read; the classical music reminded me of Daddy and his love for Beethoven. The whole dream, as we interpreted it, was a merging of my desire for early childhood comfort and erotic pleasure. B kept asking, "Why are you embarrassed to talk about this?"

"I don't think you'd like to be put in this position in my dreams," I said, and then realized that it could only be flattering to be incorporated into someone's fantasy, providing love and warmth.

Perhaps I am embarrassed to be such a needy person or to reveal myself as so needy?

⊛

Tuesday, later

Stu was out this evening, curling. Have had almost no conversation with him since he came home. I feel in a different world. How would I (why would I?) even begin to tell him about the dream, the conversation with

B, my desire to let the spiritual and artistic side prevail, the connection of that with my childhood of warmth, intellectualism, books, and music? Now the question seems to be: how the fuck did I get into this cold drafty barn of a life? And: can I get myself out of it without losing too much? Can I become the intellectual—or the artist—and still live on the lake with a compulsive, neurotic autocrat, an alcoholic who watches football on TV?

My father used to say that if I was going to be a writer, I should be a good observer. "Writers," he told me, "can only write what they know." It was good advice, but it produced a writer's block of epic proportions. Over the years, I turned out plenty of grant proposals, training manuals, even magazine articles. But nothing I called "creative." When I wrote what I knew—even in my diary or journals—it just made people mad.

In the fall of 1985 I decided to see if I could write fiction. Barry's death seemed a safe enough subject. For one thing, he'd been dead more than thirty years. For another, if I wrote about the little girl who imagined an anti-Semitic God, I was the only one who would come off looking bad. I changed people's names and invented some scenes, but overall, I stuck pretty close to the truth. Part of the action took place on the bus, going home from school. I moved Saint Philomena's down the street and surrounded it with a tall iron fence and a wooded cemetery, but otherwise, the bus in the story followed the precise route I'd taken back and forth to Colfax School every day for three years. When I went to Pittsburgh in the spring of 1986, I drove the route to check it out. In that stable neighborhood, nothing had changed. The same solid brick houses lined the same streets; the high school and synagogue held their ground. Still, the bus route looked nothing at all like I remembered it. When I thought I was writing objective fact, my memory created fiction.

Thursday, January 23, 1986
Sitting outside Eli's gymnastics class (5:30 P.M.)

Last night I got thoroughly caught up in Lillian Rubin's book *Intimate Strangers*. She explains so much that frustrates me about my relationship with Stu, from his resentment of my closeness with David and Eli when they were babies to his making fun of my long phone calls with woman friends, to his moody silences, to his lust. Getting such insight into male-female differences, and into Stu's behavior, at the same time as getting insight into my own fears of intimacy and my own behavior—and thinking about the institutions of marriage and the family while working on the tapes for the audio course—is almost too much. I was on campus this afternoon, and I felt like running all the way to the clinic to share all my excitement with B.

People are beginning to tell me how good I look. And I feel great—exuberant, high with discovery, and in love with me, which is pretty unusual.

※

Thursday, 8:30 P.M.

Stu and I were supposed to go to a basketball game this evening. I got supper ready before I took Eli to gymnastics so we could eat and be ready to leave by seven o'clock. I left Stu a note, asking him to add corn to the stew at 4:45, turn the heat off at 5:15, and make rice at 6:00. When I got home at 6:15, he took pains to point out to me how clean the kitchen was, with the clear implication that I don't clean up after myself.

I blew up. "You accuse me of being 'incompetent' every time you go into the kitchen," I screamed. "I'm tired of it." I'm not sure he understood me at all. He seemed to think I was trashing myself, calling myself incompetent! I need to figure out some other way to say this.

The baby-sitter didn't show up. At 7:15, I suggested that Stu go alone to the game. He ignored me, and I thought that maybe since he was feeling sick, he didn't really care about going. But at 7:25 he was looking and acting pissed.

"Stop being mad at me," I said.

"I'm not mad at you," he yelled. "I'm pissed at Jeremy."

"You're certainly taking out your anger at him on me," I said, and I reminded him that he could have gone to the game by himself.

David heard this conversation. He asked if we'd ever let Jeremy—his favorite sitter—come again. Stu said "No" very angrily, and I said "Yes" softly, at the same time. David was very upset.

Stu turned on me then. "I'll keep yelling at you as long as I feel like it," he shouted.

I said I'd leave if he kept it up.

"Fantastic," Stu said.

A little later he said, "Of course, I didn't really mean that."

I told him, "I think you did."

Before Eli's bedtime, David, very upset, came to hear me read *Twenty Thousand Leagues under the Sea*. I asked why he was upset.

"You won't let Jeremy baby-sit any more."

"I didn't say that," I tried to reassure him. "Stu did. But I don't think you have to worry. Stu hasn't called a baby-sitter in the past ten and one-half years, and I don't think he's about to start."

But who knows what David really was upset about? He said it was not because Stu and I were yelling at each other. "That's too usual to get upset about."

Thursday, midnight

In the kitchen about nine o'clock I apologized to Stu for blowing up and asked that he not trigger my anger by taking back with one hand what he gives with the other. I explained that every time he cooperates with me in the kitchen, he seems to show his anger at having to participate. "I wasn't doing that," he said. "I wasn't trying to tell you that you left the kitchen a mess today. It was fine today. I was upset about how you left it yesterday."

"I've fed a family for fifteen years without turning the kitchen into a pigsty," I said, "and I think you might respect that."

"If you're going to be rancorous, shit your way out of here," he hissed in his hateful, steely style.

I was so mad I went upstairs and packed to leave. David was in bed, listening—I'm sure—to the argument in the kitchen.

I went past Stu's study, packed duffel bag on my arm, to show that I was leaving. Stu pleaded with me to explain why I have blown up at him twice in the eighteen hours since he told me he was feeling sick. (Last night, after having a toothache for four days, Stu finally told me he was hurting.) I suggested—à la Lillian Rubin—that maybe Stu, terrified of having revealed his vulnerability, unconsciously provoked me to blow up. Then he had good reason to retreat, to lick his wounds and call me a crazy woman.

Of course, he hasn't read Rubin, and this made no sense to him. The bottom line is that in five hours I've gone from euphoria and a sense of possibilities and understanding to pure hatred of Stu and despair that my work will lead us anywhere positive. How can one person struggle alone constructively to improve a relationship? I just want out. I don't want to deal with the shit he dishes out any more.

⊛

My father used the *New York Times* as a shield against the world. Not the world of national politics and international affairs. He was absorbed in that world and happy to discuss it with us. What he wanted to fend off was the unreal world at home. The world in which my two-year-old sister hugged herself and rocked rhythmically, back and forth. The world in which Shelly said *Stavanger-fjord,* night after night, so that everyone would laugh. In which I sought out awards to win, conspiring with my father—I realized, much later—to prove I was well adjusted, that we were a normal family.

Just before Valentine's Day the year I was in sixth grade, we moved to a three-story house. It was a few weeks after Bobbi's birth; a few months after my mother was diagnosed with MS. I don't remember the move itself. But I remember walking along Beechwood

Boulevard through a snowstorm, headed from our new house over to Forbes and Murray to buy valentines for Shelly to take to school.

A few weeks later, my parents went shopping for furniture for the new living room. They came home with a Papa chair, a big, dark green comfortable armchair; a Mama chair, a smaller, modern curved-back design, upholstered in bright red; and a green plaid two-piece couch. The Papa chair was everyone's favorite. After school, I liked to curl up in it with a library book. My mother sat in it when she read her ladies' magazines. And in the evenings, when he wasn't teaching night school, my father sat in the big green chair, reading the *New York Times*.

He was a loyal, responsible husband. He did not leave my mother after she got sick, like a lot of men would. He did not complain about his problems. He sat in the Papa chair long after it started to smell like piss, the *Times* open in front of him, screening out the truth.

Losses

Friday night, January 24, 1986

Bizarre, horrible day. A letter from Shelly brought a *Guardian* clipping about the Goldmark murders. Apparently, an anti-Semitic, right-wing nut decided that they were Jewish Communists and their lives threatened our Christian democracy. On Christmas Eve the murderer knocked on their door, pretending to deliver presents. He chloroformed Chuck and his wife, shot the kids first, and then the grown-ups. Chuck's wife died immediately; one son died within a few hours. Chuck and the other child lingered for several weeks.

When I first heard about Chuck's death, I was shocked and sad. But the clipping terrified me—as a Jew, as a leftist, as a parent. Chuck's boys were just a few years older than David and Eli. I was very upset and tried to talk about it with Stu. But the conversation consisted mostly of Stu grilling me about my friends at Reed.

In the evening, we rented *Tron* and *American Graffiti* and made pizzas with Bill and Linda Lange and David's friend Andy Thompson, who was staying overnight. The kids' pizza was done first, and Stu drank quite a bit —I'd say at least four or five big bourbons—before we got around to eating. At dinner, he and Bill started to tease Sara about feminism, as usual. Then Stu turned very ugly. "You're really just half a person," he told Sara, reducing her to tears. "It's because of you and your feminist friends that my dear, sweet, seventy-five-year-old mother has joined a group that reads only women's books." He was absolutely off his tree about the book group, accusing us of being anti–intellectual and ignoring half the human race. He was so abusive and rude that I couldn't stand it.

"Stop that! You're drunk," I yelled, and kept screaming, "Stop being cruel to Sara!" Bill had to grab my arm to calm me down.

Somehow we got it back together enough to play dominoes and watch *American Graffiti* after dinner. (Of course Sara disappeared.) After the Langes had gone home, I cleaned up the kitchen. Stu came in, poured himself a drink, and then began giving me lectures about my political responsibilities vis à vis the Goldmark case. I finally told him I didn't want to talk about it any more.

Stu said, "You owe me thirteen apologies for calling me drunk in public."

"I'm sorry I screamed like a banshee," I told him. "But I can only explain your cruelty to Sara and your inexcusable rudeness as drunken behavior."

I don't know whether he accepted that or not. He didn't argue about it very much. But he repeated, "Sara is just a fluff ball. She's half a person. She has only half a brain."

❧

Our housemate Sara was gay. I sit in my writing shed and think about the roots of homophobia. Norcroft is a feminist retreat, founded by a lesbian; a place that gives women permission to attend solely to themselves and their writing. A caretaker cleans the lodge and does the grocery shopping; we residents (some gay, some straight) have nothing to do but eat when we feel hungry, sleep when we feel tired, write whenever we wish. What would cause someone to vilify the woman who offers such a gift?

Maybe fear.

I think of the evening David played the ingenue in a vaudeville act at school. He was eleven, his voice not yet changed; he wore a long gingham dress and a wig of ringlets, strawberry blond. He was beautiful, and funny too. All of us laughed at his performance and praised him afterward, even Stu. But when I said I thought David, in drag, looked like my sister Shelly, Stu was angry and appalled.

"Don't tell him that," he snapped. "I'm sure they gave him that role because he could handle it. But this is a hard age for boys. They can easily be confused."

Wednesday morning, January 29, 1986

Fell into bed very tired last night. I slept restlessly, having many dreams, of which I only remember fragments. In one, I go into a government office and see an actor friend who tells me he has a new job and will be moving to Los Angeles. We go out to the street, and he watches me climb up a tall ladder to a thatched roof. I get something up there—something small, like a comb or a candy bar—and begin to bring it down, but I am suddenly paralyzed by fear. I realize that only one side of the ladder is resting against the edge of the roof.

I've been trying to think about B's suggestion that I am resisting having him help me. The idea didn't have any emotional meaning until this morning. Now I am very upset that I will lose him too—because we have a professional, not personal, relationship, one with a defined end. That makes it very hard for me to trust him, to put myself in his hands, however competent and appealing they are.

Loss runs in my family. My father lost his father, who abandoned the family when Daddy was four years old and his brother Ed was two. Daddy describes his father—my grandfather—as a no-account young Hungarian who passed bad checks. My great-grandfather was a lawyer, the Hapsburg equivalent of a district attorney. It was an extraordinary position for a Jew. He didn't plan on losing it because of a no-good kid. "Get out," he told his son and paid his passage to New York.

A couple of years after her husband left her, Daddy's mother, Julia, contracted tuberculosis; she died when he was eight. Daddy and Ed were taken in by relatives, Tante and Unk. Julia's mother also lived with them, a superstitious old woman who spoke Yiddish, Hungarian, and Rumanian—but no English—and pulled balls of strudel dough into gossamer layers across the kitchen tabletop.

She kept live carp in the bathtub on Thursday nights; on Friday, she killed the carp and ground it into gefilte fish for the Sabbath meal.

Tante and Unk had a child of their own, a slightly older boy, clearly their favorite. Tante always served Morris first, my father said. He and Ed got to eat whatever might be left.

⊛

Thursday, January 30, 1986

Stu is doing taxes and *letting me know*. He asked me to transfer $1,000 to our joint checking account, and I got a little testy about it since I'd transferred $1,100 two weeks ago. Theoretically, we contribute equally to household expenses, me from my work income and some savings and Stu from the money he's inherited. He's supposed to reimburse me for the health insurance premiums that are deducted from my paycheck, but these smaller transfers back to me always get conveniently overlooked.

This evening, Stu collapsed on the bed for his after-dinner nap—an hour and a half or more. Then he came downstairs, where I was reading Harry Stack Sullivan's book on psychiatric interviews.

"You seem to be very absorbed in that book," he commented, very sarcastically.

"Actually, the book's not so great. But I couldn't work at my desk because you were napping," I explained. (My desk is next to the bed.)

"It wouldn't have bothered me."

But his presence would have bothered *me*. I didn't point that out.

⊛

In the big house on Lake Mendota, our bedroom furniture included not only my desk, but my "studio"—custom-made cabinets that housed a reel-to-reel tape recorder and other radio production equipment. The cabinets matched our high, custom-made captain's bed: a queen-sized mattress in a frame that sat on four chests of drawers, two on my side, two on Stu's. The chests, the bed frame,

56

and the studio cabinets were all crafted of Baltic birch, sanded silky smooth, with a natural finish.

One afternoon during the summer of 1982, I lay in bed on top of the quilt Shelly had made for us as a wedding present. In the center of the quilt, on a big blue patch, she'd appliqued a *J* and an *S*.

("For Judy and Stu," she told me. "Or Judy Strasser, if you ever get divorced."

"Or Just Stu," her boyfriend Patrick pointed out.)

It was hot. The windows were open. A soft breeze blew in from the lake. I'd just finished my second round of chemotherapy. In the backyard, David and Eli were laughing, playing, making the noises kids make when they are seven and four and having fun. The sounds drifted in on the breeze.

The noise pierced me to the bone. I understood why the frail elderly might choose to live in retirement communities. I couldn't bear to hear my own children play.

※

Sunday evening, February 2, 1986

Stu and I spent last night at the Gobbler—my Christmas present to him. Quite a bizarre place, all shag rug and fancy fieldstone. Definitely designed for Love; or at least our room was, from its seven-foot-diameter water bed (enclosed by a curved shaggy wall) to its tiled bathtub, five feet in diameter and three feet deep. We came armed with Godiva chocolates and good liqueurs and did quite a bit of rolling around, with an awful dinner sandwiched between. All I ordered were three gigantic, mealy, slightly old shrimp and a salad drowned in salty oil and vinegar. I had made dinner out of the fried potato skins at the bar, which were very good. Stu had a steak, which he said was excellent. The whole thing was rather like a time out from life.

I had two unsettling dreams in the midst of all the *amour*. In the first, I was in a car pulling away from our house in the snow, when I saw flames. I hesitated and did not run back in. Everyone got out safely, but I worried about the furnishings, which were not destroyed by the fire but seemed likely to suffer water damage. In the next dream, I was on some sort of tour boat with a great many people with backpacks, all very friendly. Then I discovered that someone had taken all my money out of my wallet, and all my credit cards. I woke up panicked and depressed.

Why such awful dreams of loss in the midst of all this lovemaking? On the other hand, *all* I lost were material things—things that could be replaced. Why be upset by such loss?

❦

I am not much attached to possessions, perhaps because I have very little that could not be replaced. I have a few things that belonged to my mother: a tall, light green vase, terribly ugly, part of her Wedgwood collection; another vase, hammered out of a brass shell casing, that an uncle brought her from Verdun; a miniature tea set—a tray holding a couple of tiny cups and saucers, a tiny chipped pitcher, all glazed in shiny green—that her best girlhood friend, Francine, brought back from Mexico.

Nana promised to leave me her wedding ring, a heavy, wide gold band set with a few tiny diamonds. Poppy gave it to her to replace the ring that disappeared when I was two. She'd taken it off so I could play with it. They thought I swallowed it and watched my stools for days. It never showed up. I never got the replacement band. As she grew old, Nana was hospitalized several times for heart trouble. The ring disappeared on one of her trips to the hospital.

I don't have any material objects that belonged to Nana's parents or Poppy's or to any of my family on my father's side. None of these people ever owned much of value. And how important are tangible heirlooms in the bigger scheme of things? I do have a story my father tells about the aunt he lost during World War II, his mother's sister, I think. She had stayed in Hungary. He wrote to her in Hungarian for years after his mother died. Then her letters stopped. She died in a concentration camp.

❦

Tuesday afternoon, February 4, 1986

I told B about my dreams at the Gobbler, my nightmares of loss the night of having fun. He suggested that I simply am so closely guarded, so tightly protected, that I can't allow myself to have any fun.

In the story I've been writing, the little girl says, "It's wrong to think of fun. Barry can't have fun anymore. It's wrong to have fun—even to think of having fun."

B asked if I wrote fiction and I mentioned the story, but didn't go into much detail. Perhaps I will finish it and give it to him. Writing fiction, playing the piano, and seeing B are all connected in some way—they have to do with a creative other path, something quite different from the rational competent front I present to Stu and at work.

It has been raining all day. Lots of rain. Big drops. The ground is icy, the rain sometimes is frozen rain. The world is a big slush puddle. I went out this morning, wearing my yellow sailing slicker and my black rubber knee-high boots from the irrigation ditches in the Central Valley and my umbrella, I felt impervious to the rain. It couldn't get to me. I was like Christopher Robin playing in rain puddles. It was lots of fun. I smiled—smiled a lot—and people *looked* at me. I looked peculiar but I was smiling. I felt the same way sitting in the car after I saw B. It was raining, spattering on the roof—lots of noise—sleety drops on the window pane. But it couldn't get to me.

And then I went home. Stu asked, "So how was your session with Bergeson?"

"Good," I said. "It's an interesting game."

"That's what I've suspected about psychiatry for the past twenty-five years. But it doesn't seem to be doing you any harm, so I don't begrudge the money."

I must have had an odd expression. He added, "I wouldn't begrudge the money even if it were doing you harm."

❀

When I went off to college Daddy said, "Don't get hitched." I thought it was a joke—like when he said "DGD" (for "don't get drunk") whenever we left the house. But he added, "I'll support you until you get your bachelor's degree, unless you get married first. After that, you'll be your husband's responsibility."

He meant to emphasize the importance of a college education. But I understood that men—my father, my husband—would, indeed should, provide my support, my security.

I don't imagine many young women think this way now. Everyone knows it takes two paychecks to live a middle-class life. And even before the economy drove women into the workforce, the women's movement had begun to turn the culture around. By the time Shelly, three years behind me, graduated in 1969, any self-respecting college woman knew she should have a career. But when I grew up, men brought home the bacon. Women cooked it. Tom, my college boyfriend, thought he wanted to enter the Foreign Service. I thought I might write; it was something portable, something I could do wherever he might be posted. I knew writers didn't make much money. That didn't matter; making money wasn't my job.

⊕

Wednesday, February 5, 1986

The Children's Museum fundraising committee met here from 7:30 to 10:00 P.M.; then I spent a long time doing dishes and broke a nice bowl, a present from Helen, by accident. (It slipped out of my hands while I was putting it in the dish rack.) Stu, who was standing in the kitchen, mewing at the fucking cats in his oh-so-loving voice, turned on me and yelled, "You broke our nicest bowl! You should dry things as you wash them."

"You could dry the dishes as I wash them," I said.

A few minutes later he "apologized." "I misspoke," he said.

"How did you misspeak?"

"I should have said it *was* our nicest bowl."

Fuck him. It was a nice bowl, but it was just a bowl.

Later, we had a major blowup because Stu wanted me to acknowledge that I was once again piling things too high in the dish rack and to apologize for breaking the bowl. Again, I suggested that he could help by drying things as I washed them.

"Next time you see your shrink," Stu said, "ask him why you blame me when you make a mistake."

I told him that he cared more about bowls and cats than about people—or at least acts that way toward me and the kids.

"You'd better find someplace else to sleep," he said.

Suddenly it occurred to me that perhaps there is a connection between my feeling that I am "bad" because of something that happened when I was eleven or twelve and my sticking so long with someone who regularly trashes me.

❀

In the beginning, I loved Stu for his lack of interest in *things*, his disdain for materialism. When we met, he didn't own a suit, unless you counted the outgrown tuxedo left over from his Harvard days. The only time I saw him put on a sports jacket was the day we tried to get into a stockholders' meeting at FMC, a big defense manufacturer. He'd furnished his house with brick-and-board bookshelves, furniture from secondhand stores, an olive green, kidney-shaped coffee table someone had put out for the trash. We watched a portable color television he'd won in a benefit raffle for Eugene McCarthy's presidential campaign. He did have a Nikon with several lenses, but friends had bought it for him in Japan, at a time when the yen was weak. He drove a two-door, two-year-old Volvo. It was his biggest luxury.

Stu combined a frugal lifestyle, contempt for bourgeois baggage, and real generosity. None of his housemates paid rent—not me, not his brother Hal, not the political comrades who sometimes lived with us. Soon after we met, he outfitted me with a pair of binoculars, the most expensive gift I'd ever received. He contributed to worthy causes. In the sixties and early seventies, he withheld his income taxes, because he refused to support the war in Vietnam.

After we were married, after David was born, after we moved to Madison, we got up the courage to see a lawyer. It was time to act like grown-ups, time to make our wills. We talked about money, about Stu's inheritance, about the almost unspeakable possibility that one or both of us might die. Stu assured me, as he always had, that whatever was his was also mine. The wills reflected this; in case of death, we would each inherit from the other. "But what about now?" Stu asked. We had moved from California, a community property state, to Wisconsin. What did the law say here?

At the time, Wisconsin had no marital property law. "Whatever's in your name is yours," the lawyer said. "Whatever's in Judy's name is hers." I had a couple of thousand dollars in a savings account. Stu had what seemed to me a fortune in stocks and mutual funds.

Stu saw the inequity. He loved me. He turned to me and asked, "Do you want me to put half my assets in your name?"

I loved him. I trusted him. I knew the right answer was no.

⊛

Tuesday, February 11, 1986

This afternoon I told B, "I feel I don't deserve any better life than my mother had." (In a dream fragment a few nights ago, voices chorused, "You're alive! What more do you want?") "But I do want more," I said, "I want more beauty, more joyousness, more 'rightness' than I have now. And so long as I arrange a relationship in which Stu devalues me, discredits my worth, I satisfy my guilt."

We talked about the kitchen fights. I said, "I feel a bit ungracious because I demand so much, but I get so much more help than most wives apparently do."

"But the help you get comes with demands for perfection," B pointed out. Then he remarked, "You seem to have a need to discredit and devalue your own thoughts, wants, and desires—even when you think they're perfectly reasonable."

⊛

One day in February 1986 I got home from work to find that Stu had already left for the curling club. Eli had been home all day, sick with yet another bronchial infection. He was on the lake-room couch, watching *Sesame Street*, a program he'd long since outgrown.

He was flushed, hot to the touch, spacey. I took his temperature; it was 105 degrees. Stu had only been gone for ten or fifteen minutes; how could he have left Eli alone, obviously very sick? I gave Eli a Tylenol and called the doctor, all the time trying not to be angry with Stu. I had to take David to a school potluck, so I made a batch of brownies and waited for Sara to come home from work. She would take care of Eli until Stu got back.

I was terribly upset: Eli had had pneumonia several times, and I was afraid it was happening again. At the potluck, my friend Maggie asked, "Where's Eli?" (No one expected Stu to show up at the kids' school.)

"Eli's sick," I said. And then I blurted out, "Stu left him alone at home with a temp of 105."

Maggie looked horrified. Her expression gave me courage. "Do you think it's OK for me to be angry about that?" I asked.

"Yes, indeed!" She was adamant.

"I guess it's really a matter of safety, isn't it?" I asked, and she nodded. I'd been thinking I should give Stu the benefit of the doubt, because after all, the poor man *did* stay home with Eli all day while I was at work. I decided I should say something about it.

After the potluck, I found Stu in the kitchen, finishing his dinner. "You shouldn't have gone curling, leaving Eli by himself," I told him. He was obviously upset when he learned how high Eli's temperature was. He finished his Jack Daniel's and lit a cigarette.

"You weren't here," he said. "If you don't like the way I do things, you should stay home and do them right."

"Don't hand me that," I told him. "I went to work, and that was Right, and you left Eli alone with a temperature of 105, and that was Wrong."

He changed the subject. "Where were you between three and four-thirty?" he asked. "Your boss called to ask you a question, so I know you weren't at work."

"You know that I always see Bergeson between three and four on Tuesdays."

"Are you sleeping with him?" he asked.

Tuesday afternoon, February 18, 1986

A remarkable session with B just now. I wanted to talk about Mother. I said I didn't really know who she was. We never discussed her illness, or how she felt about it, or how it affected Daddy or any of us kids. In fact, I would say there was no emotional openness or emotional honesty in our house.

"How come you're so successful in the outside world?" B asked. He asked if I'd been "parentalized"—made to act like a grown-up, a mother to my little sisters. I said I didn't think so. In fact, I think I was encouraged to be involved in a great many extracurricular activities that kept me away from home after school. Nana, Daddy, and AA (Aunt Audrey, Mother's sister) all encouraged me to "get out and save myself," to "escape," even to go to college two thousand miles away, rather than stay in Pittsburgh and help out with Mother, who was failing very rapidly, and with my little sisters Ellen and Bobbi, who were still quite young. "So," B suggested, "you're successful in the outside world because, as a child, you were 'entitled' in this area."

But I am not successful at interpersonal relationships. I don't know how to get what I need (in fact, I don't even know how to identify my needs) because there was no entitlement at home to be emotionally honest. When I act "not entitled" with Stu (B called it acting "schlumpfy"), I am just continuing this childhood pattern.

And then B said, "Children who lose their mothers at an early age often react by acting like their mothers." He suggested that, when I act like Mother—having screaming rages, acting unentitled—I am trying to stay close to her. "If you give that up," he said, "there will be a price."

"Well," I said, "it's a good idea to give that up and pay the price, whatever it is, because after all, she's dead and I'm not."

B said it was hard for him to talk about my holding on to Mother without choking up. In fact, I think he felt more empathy for me than I felt for myself. When he described how children hold on to mothers who have left them in childhood, I said, "That's sick!" And I think it is—but I don't know how to stop it. What do I replace my "schlumpfy" and screaming behavior with?

I'll tell you what Mother wasn't entitled to. What she wasn't entitled to was love.

⊛

Tuesday night

Figure this out. I suggested to Stu that for the first time in two weeks he come to bed and we make love. He joined me. He stroked my thighs, kissed my nipples, ran his tongue back and forth across my clit. Suddenly he stopped. He sat up and looked across the bed at my desk. "You have $2,400 worth of undeposited checks over there," he said. "If you want, I'll make you a little card with all the account numbers, and you can just put the account numbers on the checks and I'll deposit them for you."

"No thanks," I said. "I'll deposit them."

I turned on my side, with my back toward him. He lay down beside me and started caressing my breasts. I didn't respond.

"You seem to be going to sleep," he said.

"No, it just turns me off to be criticized about not depositing checks, and to be criticized in bed."

"It would turn you off anywhere—in the car, anywhere."

"Yeah, that may be so, but especially in bed."

Stu got up and left. Was this supposed to make me feel guilty? It didn't. I mean, I didn't care that he left.

(As I am transcribing this, about eleven-thirty Wednesday morning, Stu decides it is time to come into the bedroom and lie down. I am absolutely fed up with not having a room of my own.)

⊛

These days, I have a whole house of my own. It's small, but it's all mine. I don't have to share it with anyone. Still, sometimes I'll walk past a big house, like the one I lived in with Stu, and it will hit me: I'll never live in a house like that anymore. My life is scaling down. Now that Eli has left for college, I rattle around at home. I'm an empty nester, a single woman living alone, and it feels as though I am sliding down the back slope of a housing mountain. I picture the places I've lived since I graduated from college: first, a one-room apartment on fashionable Russian Hill. That place made me feel like a real San Franciscan: every day I commuted to the phone company on the Hyde Street cable car. I bought, for ninety dollars at a silent auction, a white Naugahyde hide-a-bed. (My friend Cassie called it a Naugahead hide-a-bod.) I furnished my room with the hide-a-bod; a collapsing, architect-style desk lamp that balanced precariously on the back of the couch; and all my college books, in boxes because I couldn't afford to buy shelves. One day, flying back from a training course in Los Angeles, I met a guy on the plane. We got to talking, and he drove me home. I invited him up. "Oh," he said, looking around. "I guess you just moved in!"

"Nope," I grinned. "I've been here about six months."

He didn't even stay for a drink. I guess he wanted the homemaker type.

Soon after that, Cassie and her husband, Ted, moved into the third-floor flat of a Victorian house in the Haight. I fell in love with the curved-glass windows and the turkey red carpet that climbed the long straight stairs and brightened the central hall. They invited me to move in. That lasted until Ted was drafted. Then I moved a few blocks to a chilly one-bedroom apartment. If I squeezed into a corner of the kitchen and looked out the window at just the right angle, I could see the Golden Gate Bridge.

When I started grad school an old boyfriend helped me move the hide-a-bod up a swaying flight of concrete-and-metal steps to the second floor of a shabby, motel-like building in East Palo Alto. I lived there until the end of the school year, sitting on the Naugahyde couch in the living room, entertaining gentleman callers in the bedroom, on a mattress on the floor. Then, for a couple of months, I moved to a communal house that stood on land that had once been orchard. In June, all the apricots on two trees ripened at once and splatted in the front yard. The owner of the house had a psych degree. He used the living room for weekend encounter groups. On

Saturdays and Sundays, the big pillows strewn all over the bare wood floor would be occupied by sobbing men and women who hadn't had any sleep. Soon after I moved in, someone's dog ate the brand-new *Joy of Cooking* my friend Rachel's mother had given me. My favorite mugs began to disappear. Stu rescued me from that house, but not before he shocked an elderly Palo Alto doctor by presenting with a full-blown case of crabs. Stu insisted that the lice came from one of the encounter groupies. "Someone must have crashed on your bed."

᭟

Saturday, February 22, 1986

Stu and I have barely spoken since the bedroom scene Tuesday night. But I woke up this morning feeling ready to talk. We started with the Tuesday night "deposit your checks" episode. After considerable discussion, he confessed that he was turned off by my crotch smell. The conversation went on from there. We did fine so long as I was explaining my need to change my behavior. I said I had to stop acting like Mother, for example, and explained that I thought I harbored grudges because I never successfully vented anger. Then he asked me why I was so angry with him back in 1976 or 1977.

"I think it started just after David was born," I said. "Every time you pulled the pillow over your head to block out the sound of the baby, I got angrier. It's not just that you weren't helping out. I felt that you were ignoring me and David, and three years later, Eli. You were excluding us from your life. And when I said it bothered me when you put the pillow over your head, you explained that the kids made too much noise."

I suggested that Stu had problems too; for example, trouble with controlling behavior. Requiring that I always be the one to get up with the kids was only one example. "You want things to be done *your* way, if at all," I pointed out, and I suggested that he couldn't simply view me as a "sickie" who needs to deal with my own behavior. This changed the conversation completely. Stu got very defensive, very angry that I had intruded on his morning.

So we stopped talking, and I gave him a note. It said that I appreciated his willingness to talk, but that it seemed to me the conversation deteriorated because he perceived himself as my therapist, rather than as one of two people who both need to work on changing behaviors.

Stu returned the note in little pieces and continued to mope, complain, and act weary all morning and afternoon. It really had me down, thinking that things would never get better, that I'd fucked up. I was near tears almost all day. So I decided to take a walk in the late afternoon. La di da! On the walk I realized that I was letting him get to me, letting him make me believe that I had fucked up. He does that by moping, complaining, acting weary, and getting down on me. But he is *dragging his wing* when he does that: trying, consciously or not, to distract me from seeing that I am right and my comments have hit home, whether he likes it or not.

After the walk, the first time he started acting put-upon, I told him to stop dragging his wing. He got righteously angry and snarled, "Lay off of me."

I feel so much better, seeing what's going on!

❀

The places Stu and I lived ranged in size from a 1972 Dodge B200 van with hand-built furniture to the summit of my housing mountain, the big house on Lake Mendota. On the first floor alone, that white elephant contained the cozy "lake room" where we usually entertained guests; a cavernous hall of a living room; a formal dining room (which, when we bought the house, boasted floor-length gold damask drapes and red flocked wallpaper in a pattern of fleur-de-lis); an "entry room" off the lake, as big as an average bedroom; a powder room; and an eat-in kitchen, which was gorgeous once we had it gutted and remodeled. The second floor included, in addition to the master bedroom where I had my desk and studio, Stu's study, a three-season sleeping porch, a bathroom, and two rooms—a playroom and a bedroom—for David and Eli. Our housemates—Tony and Claire and their infant daughter Frances, and later Sara—lived on the third floor, two rooms and a bath. The house also had a full basement, partly finished, and big decks off the first and second floor.

I found the house advertised in the newspaper one Sunday in the summer of 1979. We'd been living two half-blocks away from Helen, in a big brick house with a steep, north-facing driveway that we shared with the neighbors next door. The driveway dog-legged at the bottom to reach our garage, which was just big enough for a Model T Ford. It was a perfect house to live in for a couple of years, close to the university, in an excellent neighborhood. We knew our investment was sound; the house wouldn't depreciate. But it was too formal for us and too big for its lot. There was no place to keep the van And when it snowed, not even Stu's Swedish Volvo could manage the driveway and garage.

Besides, I'd had a taste of living on the water. At the beginning of our third summer in Madison, Stu's brother Hal invited us to join him at his cottage on Lake Mendota. The building was wood, sixty or seventy years old. Carpenter ants were slowly carrying it away. It had running hot and cold water, but no toilet; I emptied Eli's diapers in an outhouse attached to the garage. Laying out bread for peanut butter sandwiches on the rotting kitchen counters turned my stomach. But there was a pier for swimming, a place for a motor boat, and a glorious screened porch. At Hal's cottage, everyone stayed happy, no matter how hot and humid the summer got.

Very soon, I knew I wanted to live on the lake full-time. Stu and Bill Lange owned a sailboat that they kept at a friend's lakefront house. They raced three times a week. That meant Stu was gone every Wednesday evening, Saturday afternoon, and Sunday morning from mid-May to Labor Day. It wasn't just the races. The pier had to be put in at the beginning of each season and taken out at the end. An hour or two before each race, the sailors gathered to rig the boat, make repairs, check the wind speed and direction. After each race there were several hours of beer drinking and recapitulation of tactics and strategy. I didn't like being a sailing widow. At least if we lived on the lake, some of the sailing activities would happen in our backyard.

On Labor Day weekend, I saw a classified ad for a house on Lake Mendota. We went to see it. We calculated our finances and recalculated them. We couldn't afford the house. Helen offered to help us out financially; this involved considerable self-sacrifice since it meant her grandsons would no longer live around the corner. We moved across town a few months later, in the middle of January. A friend with a four-wheel drive came to the old house and loaded our big chest freezer into the back of his truck. He barely made it out of the driveway, which was covered with snow and ice.

I lived in the house on Lake Mendota for nearly seven years, longer than I'd ever lived anyplace, even when I was growing up. I loved swimming laps from our pier to the neighbors' buoy. I loved watching storms come in, rain advancing over the water, wind whipping up whitecaps across the lake. I loved our remodeled kitchen, the oak cabinets, slate-green counters, cork floor, and clean white walls. I spent most of my time in the kitchen.

I miss living on the lake. Now that my children are grown and gone, I miss living with other people. But I don't miss living in that big old drafty house.

❀

Sunday, February 23, 1986, 7:00 A.M.

I dream that we are living with a lot of people. I am making school lunches for David and Eli, trying to get organized, dressed, out the door in the morning. Stu comes in and I say something about having a party to celebrate a Jewish holiday. He will not allow it, and I get very angry. I insist that we are going to celebrate anyway. He says he's going to leave and wants to take the children, but I hold them to me and won't let them go. There is much shock and confusion: I am still trying to make lunches; woman friends are finding out what happened and supporting me; I am comforting David and Eli and talking with David about what kind of computer I will need now. "What if I want to live with Stu?" David asks. I assure him that we will see Stu again and that can be arranged. We talk about how custody is decided and how the courts enforce it.

Then AA, my aunt Audrey, shows up. She and Nana have learned about the separation; through some foul-up they have overheard Stu talking on the phone.

"We didn't have any money before you married Stu," AA comments, ironically, "and we'll get along fine without any money now."

Later in the dream, Stu says he wants to come back. I insist that I will live my life as I want to. "If that means I am getting increasingly religious, you will have to be tolerant of that," I tell him.

It is a very upsetting dream, but somehow we are making it, through the shock.

In real life, Stu slept on the third floor in the small bedroom last night. In real life, he also pushed my desk chair into the desk so hard that the middle drawer crashed to the floor. I can't see how it happened, really. In real life, David's friend Andy stayed overnight, Stu rented *Hammett*, which I dozed through, and we are not on speaking terms since I told him to stop dragging his wing. In real life, divorce seems like a real possibility and maybe a relief.

⊛

My father, raised on Orthodox Judaism and a strong dose of his grandmother's superstitions, pretty much gave up religion as soon as he got the chance. Still, he drove us every week to Sunday school at Rodef Shalom, the big Reform temple in Pittsburgh. I learned to sound out Hebrew, if the vowels were printed underneath. I sang in the choir, sometimes at services. I learned to chant the "mah nish-tanah," the Four Questions asked by the youngest child at the Passover Seder. Quitting religious school—which I yearned to do—was never an option. My father—or maybe my mother—insisted that I go for ten years, until confirmation, when I would reap the rewards of faithful attendance: a certificate (signed by the rabbis), a party (thrown by my parents), and presents (from adult friends and relatives).

During tenth grade the confirmation class gathered after school, on Wednesdays, and sat straight-backed on the pews in the small chapel off the main sanctuary. The assistant rabbis instructed us on things every Jew should know. One Wednesday Rabbi Schwartz stood at the pulpit and described how one went about getting a job like his. The stained-glass windows, lit by the afternoon sun, glowed as he described his own path through college and rabbinical school. "A rabbinical career," he said, "combines service and scholarship."

It seemed a noble calling, the most honorable kind of life. For a moment, I felt singled out, touched by the hand of God. I raised my own hand. "Can girls be rabbis too?" I asked.

Rabbi Schwartz said no.

I didn't really want to be a rabbi, but I was annoyed. Who was Rabbi Schwartz to tell me what I couldn't do? That afternoon reinforced my growing estrangement from Judaism. It wasn't just the misogyny. I was disgusted by the grubby materialism, the lust for *things,* apparent in our mostly Jewish neighborhood. (I didn't realize that grubby materialism was a general feature of American society.) The Quakers and Unitarians I knew seemed much more liberal than the Jews. The Unitarians had even let Pete Seeger sing in their church when the directors of the Jewish Y kicked him out. I went to the second concert. We sang "Kumbayah," "Take This Hammer," "This Land Is Your Land" late into the night.

I didn't want to be a Unitarian or a Quaker. Still, I couldn't help noticing that they thought peace was important. My favorite prayer started, "Grant us peace, Thy most precious gift, . . . and let Israel be its messenger unto all the nations." But there didn't seem to be much peace in Israel, and I never saw our rabbis marching to ban the bomb.

When I was in college, my father started going to Rodef Shalom on Sunday mornings. He took my mother along. After an abbreviated service, the head rabbi, Solomon B. Freehof, would give brilliant talks about Shakespeare and other secular subjects. Then the Men's Club served a sumptuous brunch of smoked whitefish and bagels with cream cheese and lox. People at Temple welcomed my mother and overlooked the coffee she sloshed on the saucer because her hand was jittery. I went to these events with my parents when I was home. They were pleasant enough, until the Sunday Rabbi Freehof exhorted us all to support the buildup in Vietnam.

By then, I was a confirmed agnostic. And my boyfriend was a *goy*.

AA sent me a letter when she learned I was dating a *goy*. "I don't want to tell you to date only Jews," she wrote, "although as a psychologist I know that marriages work out better if the husband and wife share the same background." But she did want me to read the newspaper clipping she enclosed. The article reported on a medical study. Women married to Jewish men had much lower rates of cervical cancer than women married to non-Jews. The researchers suspected it was because the Jewish husbands were circumcised.

I didn't bother to write back to tell her that, as far as I could tell, most of the men of my generation had been circumcised.

True Colors

Yesterday, because it had rained almost all day and was too muddy for biking, I left my Norcroft writing shed to walk for half an hour along the Highway 61 frontage road. The rain had stopped, but the world was shrouded in mist. The gray sky and flat light made every color stand out: velvet brown on the tiny alder cones, crimson leaves on scrubby bushes growing by the side of the road, young balsams green as a Christmas tree, dried grasses a subtle palette of yellow-greens and golds shading to tans and browns. Some flowers still hung on: the lustrous white pearly everlasting, a purple clover, a few small yellow blossoms on the tip of a mullein stalk. A daisy, love me, love me not.

A few days ago, hiking the Oberg Mountain loop under blue sky, the world sunny and clear, I stood at an overlook and was sad that the color was gone. All I saw were acres of birches, the branches bare and gray.

The world shows its true colors. But which colors really are true? The saturated yellow of a black-eyed Susan in the fog or the drab gray of leafless branches in the sun?

Of course, the concept of "true colors" has nothing to do with sun or mist, bare trees or brilliant blossoms. It comes from the world of navies and pirates, sailing ships, the duplicitous ruse of concealing flags, and war.

Saturday morning, March 1, 1986

March at last! February has been too long for all of us. Slush, ice, the worst kind of winter. At least it is now light until six o'clock, and there seems to be some hope of spring. The Thin Ice signs are up all over the Tenney Park lagoon.

Yesterday I learned that a documentary I produced won an Ohio State Award—a big honor. The station will help pay my way to the awards banquet next month at the National Press Club in D.C.

On the way home, I stopped to get strawberries for a special dessert to celebrate the award and say goodbye to Sara, who has bought a house and is moving out. But at dinner, Stu made a horrible scene. Sara's friend Katie had come to help her move; they were also going to baby-sit David, Eli, and David's friend Andy while Stu and I went to a concert. Katie said she'd parked in front of the garage and would move her car when Stu and I needed to leave. Stu immediately got into his "arrogant boss" role. He ordered Katie to move the car *immediately,* and ranted on and on about how rude Katie was, parking wherever she wished, with no regard to anyone else. Sara was upset, and I was furious, because Stu's behavior was simply inexcusable. (I also felt guilty, because Sara and Katie were doing us a favor, and we were not helping Sara move.)

I blew up at Stu on the way to hear Alexander Lagoya, and I was so upset I could not enjoy the music, even though I love classical guitar and Lagoya was technically incredible. At one point during the concert, when Lagoya was playing an ineffably beautiful, liquid passage, a siren wailed outside. It seemed to me that if I could only maintain the beauty and serenity of life in the face of the tumult Stu creates, I would have achieved a great deal.

Tuesday, March 4, 1986

A dreadful session with B this afternoon. I just babbled the events and emotions of the past two weeks, feeling that I am back to where I was before I started seeing him, terribly conflicted about whether there is any point staying here and struggling. For what? I suggested that maybe I was unable to leave because I was denying how bad things really are.

"No," B said. "You don't seem to be denying. You're just loyal."

Too loyal for my own damn good. I have been having breathing problems again. I thought maybe this shortness of breath was caused by the thyroid medicine I take, but I stopped taking it two days ago. I am beginning to be convinced it is stress.

I can't even be euphoric anymore about "doing something" for my state of mind. I've been doing something for three months now, and although I think I am getting stronger, learning to take care of my emotional state, the prospects for the relationship are, as B put it today, "dim." I felt I was disappointing him, too, describing Stu's extreme defensiveness, his "I can do no wrong" posture.

Oh fuck, I just want to go to bed.

Eli made a needlework sampler that says I LOVE YOU for Stu's birthday, but he hastened to tell me that he would give it to both of us. The worst part about what is going on is what we are doing to David and Eli.

⊛

Sunday morning, March 9, 1986

A complex dream begins with a kind of introduction: I have produced a documentary report for *All Things Considered*. My work has impressed Susan Stamberg. She wants to collaborate on more documentaries.

Then Stu, David, Eli, and I are going somewhere in the van to camp. I think we are in eastern California. When we arrive at the campsite, Stu points out that two tires are completely blown out. We are on the verge of a nasty argument about whether I really took the van to get new tires, as I was supposed to, before the trip. Either the tire store people were liars and cheats, Stu insists, or I am. I am very placating, trying not to anger Stu, although I know I did take the van to get new tires.

It is a weekend, and we are trying to figure out what to do about the tires when a young woman, angular and tall, appears. She suggests that on Monday morning we can go across a river to a town in Nevada to get it fixed. I have important work to do involving Susan Stamberg and *All*

Things Considered, and although it will be very inconvenient, I go out of my way to be nice and agree to get the tires fixed on Monday.

We stay with the young woman in her simple house, and it becomes very obvious that Stu has his eyes on her. He seems to have met her before. He flirts, plays his harmonica, does yo-yo tricks, and is generally charming. By now, David and Eli have disappeared from the dream, and I think—somewhat annoyed—that it would be nice if he'd played the harmonica and done yo-yo tricks for the kids. But they don't even know he has these talents.

I really like the woman, but am very upset by Stu's flirtatiousness. I complain about something Stu is doing, and she takes my side, telling him I am right. Then I ask him if he wants to leave me.

"Yes," he says, "but you won't let me."

"It depends on the conditions," I tell him.

He seems very relieved. "If you don't contest a divorce," he says, "I'll be generous and the conditions will be right."

We discuss where he will live: in California. It is clear that he doesn't care where the kids and I are. I am shocked that he feels this way about the kids, but at least I know that I am free to make my own decisions about where to live. I am sad about this conversation, and suspicious, but relieved.

At about this time, I become aware of a bunk bed in the cabin and of an old man with a gray beard, semi-passed-out, in the bed. I know that this man is the young woman's ex-husband. Stu and the young woman go off to another room, to her bed. I hear him through the plywood wall, bragging about his trip to the Soviet Union in the late 1950s and other past exploits. She is enchanted, entranced. I want to warn her that Stu is an alcoholic, that he is charming her with experiences that are all past, long past. But there doesn't seem to be any point.

I don't realize the stark symbolism of the van with blown-out tires until I wake up. This is our marriage, our life.

⊛

I recorded this dream in the first of the four notebooks that contain the journal I started in December 1985 and kept throughout 1986. I write a tiny, not-very-legible script, and five or six years ago, when I typed the entries into a computer, I found I had written more than six hundred double-spaced pages.

I brought the journal with me to Norcroft on a computer disk. But right away I decided not to "copy and paste" sections into the memoir I planned to write. If I had to retype every word I used from the journal, I would think more carefully about what to include, and why.

Retyping the journal is more difficult than I expected. I know, after all, that things came out OK in the end. But as I read, I am once again the woman in the broken-down van in my dream, addressing my younger self. "Get out!" I say. "You know what to do. Take the kids and leave. Get out now!"

Yesterday, about three o'clock, I couldn't bear it anymore. I had to take a walk, and I wanted to walk on the shore. As I stepped out the door of my shed, I saw a few spatters of wet on the wooden front stoop. It had begun to drizzle. No matter, I was determined to walk.

The rain grew more intense. I dropped my notepad in a puddle; it floated, but I could see the blue ink begin to run. I turned back after fifteen minutes. By the time I reached my Volvo with its two bumper stickers—Question Authority and Love Your Mother (a picture of the Earth)—my Gore-Tex jacket was soaked. Cold water dripped off my bangs and collected in the corners of my eyes.

This morning it is still raining, hard enough that I open an umbrella to walk to my writing shed.

<hr />

Monday morning, March 10, 1986

Stu initiated a discussion of our sex life last night. He complained that I masturbate while we are fucking; he hates that, because when I do it I "go away from him" and he can't stand having me distant. I tried to explain that when I am not fully aroused, I masturbate so I can have some pleasure, but agreed that our sex life is terrible.

"Our first and most important job is to improve it," he argued, "even if it means buying another house around the corner and living apart from each other."

I didn't see how living separately would improve our sex life. "For me, good sex grows out of a good relationship," I said.

"That's true," he agreed, "but it doesn't deny the obverse. Couples who have bad sex split up." Then he "warned" me that when a thought like divorce enters his head, "which it has, repeatedly, in the past few days," he almost always ends up acting on it.

By the time we were done talking, it seemed to me he was holding out no hope (or desire) for staying together. He insisted that the way to "break out of the prison we are in" was to live in separate houses, but not split finances. And he hastened to let me know there would be no dropping in on each other, because he would be sleeping with other women. He refused to get help for the marriage. "We can deal with this between the two of us," he insisted, and used the conversation we were having as a fine example of our ability to solve our problems by ourselves. The conversation ended in an argument. "You are nagging me all the time," he shouted. I fled into the bedroom and slammed the door.

✤

I can be a very slow learner. A few days ago, after lunch, I grabbed my jacket and headed up the Norcroft driveway on foot. I turned east, toward Lutsen, on the gravel frontage road. Walking, I'm always annoyed by the sounds of traffic above the embankment, on Highway 61. It's two lanes, but it's the route to Canada, the only one for hundreds of miles; it carries a heavy load of cars and trucks.

I walked for fifteen minutes and then turned and headed back. The Norcroft drive is one of about ten along the frontage road. They all look pretty much the same, and even though I'd walked and driven the road at least a dozen times, I always had trouble finding the right place to turn.

This time, I noticed that a screen of spruce trees along one stretch of road slightly muffled the traffic roar. When I reached the last spruce, the end of the screen, a very loud truck went by. I looked up and discovered that I was standing in front of the Norcroft driveway.

It had taken me an entire week to see that the trees provided a land-mark by which I could always find my way.

✿

Tuesday morning, March 11, 1986

Yesterday morning, I took the kids to school and ran a couple of errands. When I got home, Stu was reading the *Wall Street Journal* in the kitchen. I tried to confirm my impression of what he'd said Sunday night. "It sounded like you wanted to buy another house and split up."

"No," he said. "All I meant was that improving our sex life is of the ut-most importance. I shouldn't even have mentioned anything else, like liv-ing in different houses."

"For me, good sex is connected to the state of the entire relationship," I said, and suggested again that we see a marriage counselor together.

He listened politely but said, "I won't go to any headshrinker," and added that the idea "scares" him. I suggested that we discuss ways to im-prove our sex life. We agreed we should be more impulsive and more openly affectionate.

"Let's do it now," Stu said.

"In the front hall," I suggested and described a fantasy to act out. So there we were, at ten in the morning, on the threadbare runner, having a great time. Suddenly the day seemed to be going well.

But things fell apart again in the evening, when I came back from a Children's Museum meeting. Stu seemed distracted. "I'm going to prac-tice," I told him, "and clean up the kitchen, and then ..."

"Let's fuck," he interrupted.

"That's what I meant," I said.

After I practiced, he stormed into the kitchen. "Have you seen the folder with the 1986 tax-deductible receipts?"

He was in a complete frenzy because the folder had disappeared and I was "diddling" on the piano while he was looking for it. "Your practicing drives me crazy unless I'm either working steadily on something or just relaxing."

Of course, sex was off.

Today I told B that I want to deal with Stu's alcoholism in some way. I don't think he is able to communicate in a constructive way when he's been drinking, and most of our conversations are in the evening, when he's been drinking. I should have known better than to talk with him about sex late Sunday night, for example, when even though he could be coherent and was not slurring words, he had been drinking steadily.

We talked about how it could be a loving thing to shock Stu into recognizing his need for help, possibly setting up some sort of intervention, or at least a discussion with Helen, with Bill and Linda, and with somebody who's experienced in dealing with alcoholism. Maybe Stu will show up and maybe he won't. But I think we need to confront him.

This is not a new desire. I thought about it last October. But back then I thought maybe I *was* driving Stu to drink. Now I see that I've allowed myself to be put upon for a long time by abusive, demeaning behavior that I won't allow any more. And a lot of that behavior has to do with alcohol.

❀

Sara took me to my first Al-Anon meeting a couple of months after I read all the pamphlets I got at PICADA. People sat around in a big circle of chairs, in a cavernous room with terrible acoustics. Someone picked up a sheet of paper that had been slipped into a clear plastic cover and read a short greeting. She explained that this was a mixed meeting of alcoholics and friends and family members whose lives were affected by alcohol. Then she passed the sheet along the circle, and each of the next twelve people read one of the twelve steps aloud. I stopped listening after step two, "Came to believe that a Power greater than ourselves would restore us to sanity." I was wondering how this stuff could work with people like Stu who didn't believe in God.

The rest of the meeting involved people saying "Hello, my name is ___" and telling their tales of woe. A teenage boy slouched in his chair, sullen and bored. "I was busted for shoplifting," he said. "Me and my friend had a few beers, and then we went out to the mall and lifted a couple of CDs. The judge said he'd let me off if I came here."

A woman who looked a little strange and talked a mile a minute told a complicated story about how she almost hadn't gotten to the meeting. A balding man in a gray business suit described a fight with his wife. Several students said they'd come because the semester was almost over. One said, "I'm a nervous wreck, thinking about exams." Another was scared to go home for Christmas because he'd have to deal with his alcoholic dad.

Before the meeting, a lot of these people had been chatting and laughing with each other. They seemed to know each other pretty well. But during the meeting, no one offered anyone advice. In fact, no one really responded to anything anybody said. I was puzzled, and appalled.

I did like one part of the meeting. At the end, everyone stood up and held hands and recited a prayer. "God grant me the serenity to accept the things I cannot change, courage to change the things I can, and wisdom to know the difference." I wasn't so sure God had anything to do with it, but I knew I could use some serenity, courage, and wisdom in my life.

⊛

Monday, March 17, 1986

This weekend showed promise. David was at Andy Thompson's house Friday evening, so Stu, Eli, and I watched *Willy Wonka and the Chocolate Factory* after dinner; then Stu and I saw a Swedish erotica flick after Eli went to bed. Stu thinks watching porn movies will improve our sex life. I have big questions about these movies, and I cannot entirely separate my physical reactions from my intellectual ones. I think this disappoints, maybe even angers, Stu. And although watching does turn me on, I can't say (in the spirit of the title of this particular movie), "I Like to Watch."

Saturday was a disaster as far as Stu was concerned, but I did not allow myself to get sucked in. I just ignored his obstinacy and anger, which were brought on partly, I'm sure, by the mini d.t.'s, since he has cut back on alcohol consumption, and on Sunday he snapped out of it. The main issue had to do with new space allocations in the house, now that Sara

82

has moved out. We went up to the third floor to see how much painting, floor refinishing, and wallpapering it might need. When we got to the big room, Stu asked if I thought it needed paint.

"It depends on how we're going to use it," I said.

"Let's talk about that."

I said I wanted to move my desk and studio to that room, and he was obviously livid at the suggestion, even though a month ago he *wanted* me to move to the third floor. Now he wants to put the playroom up there, "so I don't have to look at the kids' mess." We went around and around on the issue.

"You've had your own study for the past ten years," I pointed out. "But I've *never* had one." (And isn't it ironic that I am the one who has run a business out of the house all those years? But I didn't say that.)

"It's not *essential* that I have the third floor," I finally conceded. "But I want my own space."

Later, Stu said that the thing that most upsets him about me and the "women's liberation movement" is that, having been held less than equal, we would be looking for retribution: superiority.

"Let's leave the movement out of this discussion," I said. "I can't answer for others. Let me assure you that I don't want to be superior. I just want equality, but I'm going to insist on that for the rest of my life." If Stu doesn't want to live with a woman as an equal, so be it. But it seemed significant to me that he was expressing his feelings about this—fear—rather than slam-dunking me for my behavior.

※

When Stu was in a bad mood, it felt as though he somehow puffed himself up, made himself big enough to fill the whole house. I felt as though I was pressed tight against the walls. The only thing I could do to get away from the feeling was leave the house, or hide in a corner, or try to make myself invisible.

I always wondered whether the feeling was just in my head. Was Stu's anger tangible to other people too? Years after I moved out of the big house on Lake Mendota, I asked our old housemates, Tony and Claire.

"We could feel it all the way up to the third floor," Tony said. And he reminded me of the time Stu kicked Frances's child-sized rocking chair the length of the living room. (The chair was a family heirloom. Stu said it was in his way.) Claire took the rocker up to the third floor and glued it back together. A few months later, she, Tony, and Frances moved out. I was about to leave for California for a month of radiation treatments. Stu was furious. He couldn't understand why they left. "At least Claire could have stayed until you got back from Stanford," he complained. "Now how am I supposed to take care of Eli and David?"

⊛

Tuesday afternoon, March 18, 1986

I'm so happy and so much at peace with myself and just generally *pleased* that it makes me want to cry. I never realized I could be this way again. At my therapy session, I was feeling so smug and happy about my week that I almost thought that B was going to say, "Goodbye, we've done what we need to do, and that's that."

Instead, we talked a bit about what I need to do about Stu's alcoholism. I described how Stu kept coming down to the kitchen late Monday night when I was talking with Rachel on the kitchen phone. He really wanted to find out what I was saying to her; he must have come downstairs three or four times in a half hour to pour himself drinks, and finally he just camped by the refrigerator and started making himself a midnight snack. He's very curious. I think he's scared *and* he's curious at the same time. I just stopped talking at one point when he came into the kitchen, but he still kept coming down and pouring himself more drinks and more drinks and more drinks.

B agreed that the alcohol was going to get in the way of solutions to our problems unless we could deal with it in some way—unless *Stu* can deal with it in some way. He suggested that I talk with a Dr. Santoro, an expert on alcoholism. So tomorrow I will call Santoro and either make an appointment for myself or initiate something for Stu. I'll just have to see what.

84

But I feel so good! Several times in the last week I've done posture checks while I was walking and realized I was standing up straight! And I've become aware that I'm *smiling* at people as I'm walking. I'm aware of the people who smile back and the people who are too preoccupied. I can see myself in them: unhappy people who are unable to reach out. (I mean I can see myself a few months ago. I'm not unhappy now. I'm so happy I could cry.)

When David and Eli were very small, I took them to visit Nana in Florida every spring. After she moved to Philadelphia to be near her only living daughter, my aunt Audrey—AA—the kids and I made regular pilgrimages to Pennsylvania, combining trips to Philadelphia with stops in Pittsburgh to visit my father and stepmother. Stu almost never came with us. He saw my family when he couldn't avoid them: when they came to Madison.

AA visited once, in 1978, not long before Eli was born. I was busy setting up a third-floor nursery. One afternoon, I carried the pieces of David's old crib up from the basement. AA saw me as I rounded the second-floor landing. "Stu should be doing that," she said.

I was a liberated woman, plenty strong, though more than eight months pregnant. "Why?" I asked, indignant. "I can handle it. I don't need any help." I told AA I'd be done in a few minutes. "I'll meet you on the sunporch. We'll have a glass of iced tea."

I walked through the living room with the pitcher and glasses on a tray. Stu stood, arms crossed, in the doorway to the porch. I couldn't see AA, but I could hear her, using her best New York *yenta* accent. She was making a statement, but her voice curled up at the end, like a question. "You don't even carry the crib upstairs for your pregnant wife?"

Stu didn't bother to answer. He turned on his heel, saw me. "She's full of it," he said and left.

Thursday, March 20, 1986

Spring! A beautiful sunny day with a windchill of minus twenty-five degrees. I have spring fever, regardless!

This morning, Eli and David asked why Stu isn't coming to Philadelphia and Pittsburgh with us. I told them, "He doesn't like AA. And I think he has a hard time reaching out to people like Pops and Grandma and being with them on their own turf." Then I said that these were only my guesses, and they should really ask *him* his reasons for staying home.

When I told Stu about the conversation, I got no response. He talked about everything else but. Zeroed in on a newspaper clipping that was on the kitchen table. I'd marked a checklist that is supposed to help you tell if you have a drinking problem. "I intended to give that to you," I said. He made some defensive response but, I think, took it to read.

✿

A big part of our political activity, back in the late 1960s, involved research, and that meant clipping newspapers. We couldn't read a paper without finding an article to clip. The *Wall Street Journal* yielded news of defense company contracts and mergers. The *Palo Alto Times* gave us the official Stanford Press Service view of the anti-war movement. We read the *San Jose Mercury-News,* the *San Francisco Chronicle*—we were on top of what was coming down. But we rarely clipped a paper while we were reading it. Instead, Stu taught me to mark articles with the paper's initials and date (WSJ 6-4-70) and then note the pages on which the articles appeared (2, 5, 14) in the white space above the paper's masthead and to the right. He was pretty particular about how all this should be done.

When I moved into Stu's house, stacks of yellowing newspapers ran all along one wall of his living room. Whenever he had a chance, he'd grab one or two sections and have at them with a tool that held a single-edged razor blade. I clipped papers too.

We never caught up. But what we did manage to clip and file came in handy when we were writing press releases or pamphlets for demonstrations. And the habit stays with me, though now I rarely use a razor blade. I tear articles out of the *New York Times,* producing ragged edges and losing letters, words, sometimes whole sentences. Stu would not approve.

◎

Dane County Airport, Saturday, March 22, 1986

I'm camped in the airport with David and Eli, waiting to get to Chicago. When they needed seats on our 9:45 A.M. flight, I agreed to give ours up in exchange for free tickets anywhere Northwest flies in the United States. Stu had brought us to the airport about 8:15; it was mobbed because both the public school and university vacations begin today. The standing in line and reticketing took about an hour or maybe (at the outside) an hour and a half. I figured it was well worth three free tickets to California (or Portland or wherever—perhaps we can fly west somewhere and backpack this summer), but Stu was livid. "Would you have done this to anyone else?" he demanded.

"Done what?"

"Made him cool his heels while you played games with the airlines."

Well shit. I suspect he was hung over and perhaps hungry, since he didn't have breakfast with us before we left the house. But basically, the situation was out of his control and he didn't like it.

Last night, while I was packing, Stu drank, watched basketball on TV, drank more, and sulked. In the middle of packing, I took time out to read *Marriage on the Rocks,* a book about alcoholic spouses. I needed to be reassured that I wasn't making Stu drink and sulk. At about 12:50 A.M., I was finally ready to go to bed. I asked Stu if I should wait up for him

"No," he said. So I didn't.

We are well away from him for the next ten days.

◎

Philadelphia, Sunday, March 23, 1986

This evening, David and Eli went with my cousin Alan to see battleships, to eat cheese steaks, and to watch a movie. AA and I went to a dessert party given by one of AA's friends for a group of single (divorced and widowed) ladies in their fifties and sixties. A strange subculture. I just sat and observed. One of the women was a terrific storyteller, but otherwise I didn't get much of a sense of them as individuals. But they seemed pretty wry and good-humored about their situations as single women and very supportive of each other. I felt as though I was viewing a possible future, and that it wasn't all bad. These women had their children and grandchildren to talk about and to support them, emotionally and financially, if necessary. I had the feeling that things could be a lot worse for all of them.

***

Tuesday, March 25, 1986 (Nana's birthday)

Although I sent Stu a postcard from Chicago, saying I was sorry to have made him wait around at the airport, I have felt no desire to speak with him. Who knows what mood (or state of inebriation or withdrawal) I'd find him in. Nana suggested calling him before dinner tonight so she could thank him for his birthday card. When we tried, the phone was busy and she asked rather slyly, "Who could he be talking to?" I was just glad it was busy. But I may have David and Eli call from Pittsburgh tomorrow.

***

Stu met my father and stepmother in November 1972. We'd been married a couple of months and traveling in the van since June. The week before Thanksgiving, we headed east from Madison aiming for Long Island, where we planned to eat turkey with Shelly and Patrick. Stu drove as we approached New York City; I navigated. The highway signs said things like Major Deegan Expressway and Lincoln Tunnel and West Side Highway, while the map used numbers like I-35. "Do we want the George Washington Bridge?" Stu asked, and I said, "You want to stay on New York 72." A taxi and three trucks cut in front of the van. Stu's knuckles turned white on the steering wheel. "We missed the bridge," he said between clenched teeth. "We're headed for the Holland Tunnel. What do we do now?" I thought we might get a divorce before we reached Stony Brook.

Shelly and Patrick were engaged in a struggle about who cleaned the bathroom and who cooked dinner and who mopped the kitchen floor. A list of chores, each assigned, in Shelly's handwriting, to herself or Patrick, hung on the refrigerator door. I felt immensely superior; Stu and I shared the van housekeeping without discussion or lists. Every morning, someone siphoned melt-water out of the ice box, someone whisked pine needles off the carpet with a little hand-held broom, we each stuffed our own sleeping bag. We shopped together for food, cooked together over a campfire or on the Primus stove, washed and dried dishes together. We ate in restaurants every few days and often stayed in the homes of friends or family. I couldn't see why Shelly was so hung up on fairness and equality.

But if life in Stony Brook felt a little strange, when we stopped in Pittsburgh on the way back to Madison, we seemed to step into a family saga scripted by Eugene O'Neill. My father and Charlotte had been married for three years, long enough for Charlotte to realize that, by marrying the father of my two youngest sisters, she'd been sucked in over her head. Ellen had a relatively normal infancy, but Bobbi had never known a healthy mother. As a result, she was severely disturbed.

Like Mother during her illness, Bobbi didn't act quite right. But unlike Mother, Bobbi was impossible to ignore. By the time my father married Charlotte, my youngest sister was an overweight adolescent who spoke in a nervous, quavering voice that frequently broke into a whine or annoyingly high-pitched giggles. She lacked ordinary social skills: she couldn't hold a proper conversation; she wasn't always aware when she invaded someone's space. My father had long since decided she was retarded, incompetent. Charlotte agreed, and she soon deemed Bobbi incorrigible, a hopeless case.

Charlotte had raised four daughters of her own. She determined to impose order on my sisters' chaotic lives. She set rules about appropriate behavior and personal cleanliness. She assigned household chores. Ellen gradually warmed to her "wicked stepmother." Charlotte, Ellen realized, was the only mother she had. But Bobbi rebelled. She wouldn't empty the dishwasher; she wouldn't iron her clothes; she wouldn't clean her room. She screamed and cursed at Charlotte. She committed the ultimate crime in our family: she refused to learn. After a year or two, Charlotte gave up. She handed my father an ultimatum: one of us has to go.

My father arranged to send Bobbi to a home for disturbed adolescents in Wilkes-Barre, Pennsylvania. She was to move in the spring of 1972. But that spring the Susquehanna River flooded its banks. The institution suffered structural damage. They could not accept another child. When Stu and I pulled into Pittsburgh at the end of November, the whole family had been waiting six months for Bobbi to be placed in a foster home.

Stu and I arrived in the late afternoon. Before supper, Charlotte asked Bobbi to empty the dishwasher. She refused. She was asked to set the table. She seemed not to know how. After supper, she cleared the table, sullen and glacier-slow. Bobbi and Charlotte fought pretty much nonstop until she was sent to do homework in her room. Stu, my father, Charlotte, Ellen, and I sat in the living room. Charlotte drank highballs and recited an endless litany of Bobbi's sins. Ellen sat on an ottoman, grim faced, waiting to escape to a movie with a friend. My father read the paper. Bobbi crept down the stairs to the landing so she could hear what was going on. Charlotte broke off her diatribe to send her back to her room. She resumed the monologue. Bobbi crept downstairs again. This went on for hours. Eventually, Stu and I excused ourselves to go to bed. Exhausted, we marveled at Charlotte's stamina.

A few days later, as Stu was packing our duffels into the van, Charlotte took me aside. "If you really loved your father," she said, "you and Stu would take Bobbi to live with you."

✿

Pittsburgh, Wednesday, March 26, 1986

Drove a rental car here from Philly today; arrived late afternoon.

Dad, Charlotte, and I had some useful conversation about Bobbi this evening after David and Eli went to bed. I said I've been thinking about trying to reestablish contact with her. "Why?" Charlotte asked. So I talked about my feeling that family's important—even more important than friends.

Dad agreed. "Home is the place that will always take you in," he said. Then he started to talk about his distress at the way Bobbi, her husband, and their little daughter live. They have very little money, and they room with Gary's mother. Dad said he always feels helpless when he pays his very brief annual visit to see them in St. Louis. "I feel sorry for that woman," he said, meaning Gary's mother. "But I never really get a chance to talk to her. She never stays around when I'm there."

I suggested that he think about how we appear to her. We are rich, in comparison; her husband is disabled and she has a very low paying job; and she's the one who feeds and houses Bobbi, Gary, and Marlene. The class perspective seemed to startle Dad, though I have a hard time believing it never crossed his mind.

We tried calling Stu about eight-thirty eastern time and got the answering machine. I had David and Eli leave messages, but I did not. My stomach has been in knots since then. I envision Stu having a grand old time, living out all his fantasies and grinding me under his heels. Why should I care? Worse, why do I even imagine this? Let him fuck Lori or someone else or no one at all. What can it possibly have to do with me, if I am in control of my life and responsible for my own happiness?

＊

I discovered, after college, that my boyfriend was two-timing me. Tom was in Monterey, at the Defense Language Institute, studying Chinese. Some weekends he would drive up to see me in San Francisco; others, he would say he'd pulled KP and had to stay on base. Sometimes he went to see his family in Los Angeles. I knew—because he told me—that he saw Sandy too. When he wasn't around, I dated other people, but I was in love with Tom. One weekend he called at the last minute to say he couldn't come up. He was confused about his love life; he said he was staying in Monterey to think.

The next weekend, he left his checkbook in my apartment. I snooped; as I confessed to my journal, a rather ugly illustration of the petty side of me. The previous Friday, Tom had written a check for cash and scrawled on the stub, "S." Immediately, I wrote, I got suspicious that either a) he went to Los Angeles, and of course, saw Sandy, or b) she came up to Monterey, when he said he was going to think about things.

Tom was a bad liar, with a guilty conscience. Stu was either completely innocent of extramarital affairs or exceptionally discreet. During our years in Madison, I grew jealous of three or four women, but Stu never left solid evidence that he was having an affair with any of them. The first, a lovely graduate student in biology, Stu met in a bar at a conference. She lived in Saint Louis. The spring before Eli turned one, I loaded the kids into the van and joined Stu's sailing partners in a ten-hour caravan down to a regatta at a lake near the Illinois-Missouri border. Stu had flown down to Saint Louis several days early to "talk science" with his new friend. She drove him to meet us at Lake Carlisle. Glowing, they described the gorgeous day they'd had, botanizing together. A month or two later, she came to Madison for a visit. She and Stu went for walks. Then she wanted to talk with me. "At first Stu didn't say he was married," she apologized. "And he didn't wear a ring." (Neither did I.) I told her I felt like a schlumpf, still fat from my pregnancies, focused on my children, unable to talk about science. How could Stu find me attractive? The three of us talked for hours about how to improve our marriage. After that weekend, the grad student disappeared.

Four years later, the year I was sick, Stu spent a lot of time with Kathy, who had lived with us before we moved to the big house on Lake Mendota. She adored our kids. I was pregnant with Eli when we were housemates, and Kathy wanted to see me give birth. Her request made me uneasy, but I didn't want to say no. I know she was at the hospital. I don't remember when she came into the birthing room.

"Kathy gives me emotional support," Stu told me when I confronted him. "Everyone asks me how you're doing. She's the only person who asks me how *I* feel. I need to see her so I stay strong enough to give you the support you need."

I accepted what he said, but I had the distinct feeling that he was trying out my replacement, someone who could be his wife and a good mother to the boys.

And then there was Lori, a writer who exuded an animal sexuality and supported herself by taking on typing. She'd done some work for Stu; he gave her expensive gifts. But I was most jealous when he told me she'd won five thousand dollars in a writing contest.

⊗

Thursday, March 27, 1986

I was anxious all day about Stu. Finally, I called him and hung up as soon as he answered, just to annoy him or to find out if he was home. Then I decided what the hell, I'd call and talk to him. I put David and Eli on first. Then I took the phone. He was very curt and abrupt. "This is a bad time to talk. I just put the hamburgers on."

"Who are you cooking for?"

"Myself."

"Oh," I said, "spattering yourself with grease, are you?" (Ho, ho, ho.) We hung up. Later, very irritated by his abruptness, I decided to take his explanation at face (or car) value and called back. Again, he was barely civil. "Why are you so pissed off?" I asked.

"Saturday morning at the airport was one of the most traumatic moments in my life," he said. "And a postcard is not enough to dispel the trauma." He didn't want to talk about it.

"Have you seen Bill and Linda?" I asked, to change the subject.

"Bill came over Tuesday afternoon to look at the lake."

I pressed him a bit about the weekend, and he wouldn't respond with any information about what he'd been doing. Just got nasty about not needing to report to me. So I said, "Gee, Stu, I was just hoping you'd been living out all your fantasies."

He hung up on me and wouldn't answer when I called back, so I left him a message on the machine about not appreciating his belligerence. Now I'm sure my responses were provocative, but I'm not sure I give a fuck.

I bedded down the kids and went into the living room to read and stew about the phone calls. I wanted to tell Dad what was going on with me and Stu, but every time I started to say something about my life, he changed the subject. Then he retreated to the den to watch Bill Moyers. I was annoyed enough that I decided to tell Charlotte about Stu's drinking. Good ploy. Of course she was very interested, and eventually Dad joined the conversation too. Even though it was hard to get them to pay attention to me, I was not surprised at their supportiveness, once I told my story. They've watched Stu trash me and been trashed enough by him to be amazed that (as Charlotte put it) "you would trade everything for financial security."

I did manage to say that the way I behave with Stu seems related to the way we treated Mother. "I never learned to be honest about my emotions," I said. "There was no emotional honesty about Mother or her illness."

"No," Dad said, "we were honest. We just didn't talk about it."

⊕

I've thought so much about family problems, for so many years, I didn't realize how hard it would be to write about them. Yesterday, sitting in my Norcroft shed, thinking about that trip to Pittsburgh, was especially difficult. And then the trackball on my rented laptop acted up. The cursor wanted to stay on the bottom half of the screen; getting it to move up to open a file took minutes of fiddling.

I shut the thing off in disgust and got in the car. First I stopped at the nearest resort to call a computer store in Duluth. They're going to send up a mouse. Then, even though it was starting to drizzle, I went to Cascade River State Park and walked for two or three hours.

Along Cascade Creek, I followed a trail dedicated to the memory of an Eagle Scout. "Died 1970. Vietnam." The water, brown with tannin and iron, slid down slick dark rock. The footpath was narrow and rocky, not very well maintained. Crossing a plank bridge, slippery with moss and a layer of slime, I lost my footing and fell. Picked myself up and went right on. In another mile or so I came to the Cascade River overlook, a lovely site where three waterfalls the color of root beer drop through steep banks of black volcanic rock. I stared at the lip of the nearest cascade, which drops twenty or thirty feet.

A couple of months ago, I dropped Eli off at college for his freshman year and headed north toward Niagara Falls. That night I had a sense of terrifying freedom. For the first time in twenty-seven years, since I moved in with Stu, no one knew where I was; in fact, probably no one cared. For nearly three decades, I'd been like a whirling tether ball, always tied to a pole. I felt the connecting cord snap. I feared I would turn into a dervish, spinning wildly out of control.

The next day, at the Falls, I discovered that if I stared long enough at a point just where the smooth braids of water dropped over the rock, I felt as though I were of the water myself, rushing downstream, headed over the falls.

Yesterday, staring at the lip of the Cascade River falls, I was in the stream again, dropping over the edge.

Saturday, March 29, 1986

Shelly flew in from Washington yesterday afternoon; Thursday was her birthday, and tomorrow is Dad's. After David and Eli went to bed, Charlotte disappeared into the bedroom, leaving Shelly, Dad, and me to talk about Bobbi, Mother, family life. I was so straightforward that Shelly seemed shocked. I suggested that Dad had withdrawn vital support from Bobbi at a critical age, and maybe he should now offer some unconditional support. He was frank about having wanted something for himself, at last, when he chose Charlotte over Bobbi. "Your mother was sick a long time," he said. "I paid my dues." And he was quite clear that he had tried to do the best for Shelly and me by making our lives as "normal" as possible when we were growing up. "That's why I didn't talk about your mother's problems," he said.

If you ignore the elephant in the living room, it must not be there.

Shelly said that she would be upset to see our marriage fail. "I have a relationship with Stu," she said. "It's not a particularly comfortable relationship, or one of my best relationships, or one I'd want full-time for myself. It's not even a relationship I've always thought was best for you. But I think maybe it's one of *Stu's* most successful relationships."

Oh, I do grieve for David and Eli.

☙

Was I ever unfaithful to Stu? Not, I suppose, technically. I once had a crush on a housemate who played classical guitar. He practiced Bach on the sunporch and my heart yearned for him. He had no interest in me.

I had a few long, intense conversations over coffee with one of the men on the Children's Museum board. We would start discussing museum business and end up dissecting my marriage. He was happily married. He sympathized with my plight, but I think he saw me as trouble to avoid.

Once, I sat in a rowboat, in tears about my marriage. I was facing a friend; we had stopped rowing and were both seated on the bottom of the boat. It rocked gently in the swell. I wore a bathing suit. He started to run his finger along the elastic at the crotch. The finger wormed its way under the elastic, slowly stroked my vulva . . .

I put a stop to it at that.

Was I unfaithful to Stu? I was as loyal as my father, who slept with my mother all the years she peed the bed.

Was I unfaithful to Stu? I loved my children more than I loved him.

Clear Vision

Home again, Tuesday evening, April 1, 1986

I am very upset and sad. Stu is obviously still furious with me. I suspect he wants to split, and I think that I am most upset at the prospect that he will tell me this is his decision without giving me the chance to give him an ultimatum about getting his act straight. This sounds evil and manipulative, but I have the (perhaps unreasonable) notion that if he gets an ultimatum, a real threat, he will wake up and see the damage he is doing to himself and all of us. Especially David and Eli.

I was really very shaky flying into Madison this morning and most terrified that Stu would give me a long letter he'd threatened to write. But he didn't. I did find a page of notes about trying to find a way "to extricate myself from this situation while preserving a modicum of respect for myself and you with our kids (most important), our relatives, and our friends."

Well, if it's respect he wants . . . Frankly, I'm not interested in talking about it with him, though I did confirm my impression that his "worst trauma of my life" at the airport was occasioned by nothing other than his total lack of control of the situation. He became almost apoplectic, talking about the free tickets. Apparently, taking the tickets proves I'm a money-grubbing monster of some kind.

B saw me at my teariest this afternoon. When he asked what he could do for me, I knew: I wanted support, strokes, validation. Even writing that makes me cry. I want those things from Stu, but I'm sure I'll never get them again, though perhaps, B suggested, "someone" might thank me for sticking through all the crap. Today I doubt it, but it does seem important to go through all the possible motions before ending the relationship.

The first thing I bought myself, after I moved to San Francisco and started to work for Ma Bell, was contact lenses. I'd worn glasses since I was eight. I had very thick lenses and a square jaw that looks especially awful with the jewel neckline, pixie haircut, and dark-rimmed cat-eye frames I sport in my Rodef Shalom confirmation picture. I knew girls in high school who wore contact lenses, but I wouldn't have dreamed of asking my father for such a luxury. I could tell we didn't have much money. My parents were always screaming at me to turn off the lights if I wasn't using them. ("Or do you want to pay the electric bill?") Nana sent clothes for Shelly and me from Alexander's, the discount department store on the Grand Concourse in the Bronx. She swore they were stylish, up to the minute. But in Pittsburgh, no one had ever seen yellow slickers trimmed with brown corduroy collars and cuffs.

Every now and then, Daddy would look around the house, trying to figure out how to save money. One day, he hit on the idea of cutting back on magazine subscriptions. Why did Mother need *McCall's,* the *Ladies' Home Journal,* and the *Woman's Home Companion?* She should be able to get by with just one of them. Did Shelly and I really read *American Girl,* the Girl Scout magazine? Ellen and Bobbi could have either *Highlights for Children* or *Jack and Jill,* but not both. Mother put the end to this scheme when she asked which subscription Daddy would keep, the *Atlantic Monthly, Harper's Magazine,* the *New Yorker,* the *New Republic,* or the *Saturday Review?*

Thursday, April 3, 1986

I should have written yesterday evening, when I was in a fairly calm and philosophical mode. I had gone to work, biked with David and Eli after Eli's piano lesson, reviewed the keyline for my new business letterhead. After dinner, I wrote a short note to Dad and Charlotte, entered all the trip expenses on the computer, and practiced for a while. Then as I was coming upstairs, planning to write in my journal and go to bed, Stu waylaid me.

He wanted to show me his assets spreadsheet. It was a revealing display, though I'm not sure why he chose to display it to me last night. He said it was because he's going to talk with a broker about investments in a couple of days, but I think it was also a not-so-veiled threat or, perhaps, an appeal to my baser instincts. "Be nice" (as he pleaded with me in the morning, not having been nice to me for two weeks) and I'll share the goodies with you?

Anyway, the figures show non—real estate assets in the six figures. Maybe, because this is now a community property state, half of these are mine. But when I added up the assets in my name alone, they came to a small fraction of the total. Stu said that he figured our marriage had about a fifty-fifty chance of surviving the next six months. "Because those aren't very good odds," he said, "even though I told Mother that I would give you half my inheritance from Wayne's estate, I'm going to find a way to keep that money separate." (Wayne, Helen's brother, died a year ago.) Stu estimates "that money" will be another couple of hundred thousand dollars.

I found the discussion a bit weird. Except for Stu's comment about Wayne's estate, we didn't talk about what would happen if we split. The conversation was mainly about investments and Stu's feeling of increasing responsibility and—his word—"oppression" at having so much money to manage.

This morning, Stu (who was sleeping on the porch) was awakened by the coach of the University of Wisconsin rowing team, shouting instructions to the crew. So he renewed the vendetta that he began last summer. He got up and tape recorded the noise, took notes, swore he'd have them arrested for disturbing the peace. The noise isn't very loud, and Stu's crazy behavior—his paranoia—really upset me. I slipped out to take a walk. My emotions had just about settled down by the time I got back. Stu was making coffee, and I started to make the kids' lunches.

"Why don't you use white bread?" Eli asked.

"There isn't any," I said.

Stu got angry. "I was *instructed* to get whole wheat bread when I went shopping," he told Eli.

"This isn't whole wheat bread," I pointed out. "It's just 'dark bread.'"

"Do your own shopping if you're going to be so inflexible," Stu snarled and clearly implied that I had cockeyed notions of nutrition.

"Yeah," David chirped sarcastically, "she only likes food if it's good for her."

I got furious about being trashed. Stu and I had a screaming argument in front of the kids, who thought it really was about bread. As far as I can tell, what it's really about is that in terms of food, as well as everything else at home, I am doing what I please and what pleases me—still, I think, with due consideration of other people's schedules, desires, etc. And Stu cannot tolerate this new "inflexibility." I am paying the price for years of walking on eggs, doing things around the house primarily in reaction to his demands, out of fear and a desire to maintain the peace. And it is driving him berserk.

⊗

I first saw Stu's paranoia after I moved in with him. I was involved with a group of people studying land use on the San Francisco peninsula. We planned to write a booklet that linked Stanford and its industrial park tenants to the destruction of the environment, racism, and the war in Vietnam. One day, the land-use researchers met at our house in Redwood City. We divided into committees, each responsible for a single chapter. One group sat at the kitchen table. Two huddled in opposite ends of the living room. Several people gathered in Stu's study, the room in which Hal slept.

Stu came home, discovered people in his study, went ballistic. Ranting about "intrusions on my privacy," he herded the group out of the room. Within a few minutes, the land-use meeting broke up. Everyone left.

I didn't understand Stu's rage. "Did you think they were going through your files?"

"No," he said. "I just don't want strangers in there. Hal's dirty underwear is all over the floor."

These "strangers" were the people we called our comrades, people we'd joined on picket lines, at rallies and demonstrations, in antiwar strategy meetings, people we'd partied with. Some of them, I knew, suspected that Stu was some sort of undercover agent. How else could he go for so long without a job? "Your irrational rage is going to feed those stupid suspicions," I told Stu. I didn't know which was worse, his paranoia or theirs.

⊛

Late evening, Thursday, April 3, 1986

After I wrote the last entry, I told Stu that I was available to talk and suggested a one-hour limit. We talked for something like three and one-half hours, and I'm not sure it accomplished anything except moving closer to the end. It's clear that he feels totally battered and bruised by my assertive behavior. He came close at one point to saying that he'd see a marriage counselor. But then he backed off.

He seemed to have no hope or desire to stay together, but did two about-faces from earlier positions. First, he insisted that I should move my desk and studio equipment to Sara's old room on the third floor. "But it's a waste of money to fix up the third floor," he added.

Second, he insisted, "We need to learn to cooperate in work and play before we attempt to have sex." (It was March 10 when he said, "Our sex life should take primacy over everything.")

By the time we were done talking, I was very sad but ready to leave. I actually went out driving around the neighborhood. I found some nice-looking houses with For Sale signs and stopped at a real estate company to talk with a Realtor.

All of this makes seeing Santoro tomorrow about Stu's drinking somewhat superfluous. I know that any sort of intervention would absolutely infuriate Stu. He gets very upset when I "drag our friends into this" by telling him that Bill and Linda are also concerned about his strange behavior. "I realized how resilient I am when you were gone," he told me today. "I was able to limit myself to two beers a day because you weren't around."

He said he thinks he'd be happier if we split. "It would be better for

David and Eli too," he argued. "They would see us both at our best, instead of tearing each other to pieces."

Well, perhaps. Stu does seem to realize that he's been very hard on the kids. At dinner, out of the blue, he told them, "I've decided that I'm not going to nag you to clean up your rooms anymore. If they're dirty when Betsy comes to clean the house, she just won't vacuum them." I think David was flabbergasted. Later this evening, in front of the kids, Stu said to me, "If we're going to have things David and Eli don't like for dinner, like smelt, you should make them hot dogs." I'd fried the smelt as a special treat for Stu.

Meanwhile, he spent most of the afternoon writing poison pen letters about the University crew to the sheriff's lake patrol.

I wonder, really, about his grip on reality and his sense of proportion.

❦

I've been at Norcroft working on this memoir for two weeks now, and my writing shed can best be described as an organized mess. The cord for the new mouse snakes over a rat's nest of computer disks, scrap paper, a tablet, a roll of stamps. Reference books lean at a crazy angle against an untidy stack of back issues of *Poets & Writers* magazine. Another resident says she naps on the floor of her shed. How does she find room? My floor is cluttered with boxes, a plastic milk crate half-full of slumped-down file folders, the case for the laptop. Music tapes spill out of a canvas sack with a Pittsburgh Pirates logo. Once or twice I've used the little red vacuum to suck up some of the leaves I tracked in, but I see that the floor could use a good cleaning again.

Long ago, I learned to ignore messes of any size. I don't know what I looked at as a kid, but I know it wasn't the little sliding-door chest in the living room, its unfinished top stacked high with sloping piles of homework papers, picture books, and magazines. (That particular mess annoyed my father. If I appeared to notice it, he'd tell me to clean it up.) I ignored all the dolls and toys on the floor. I didn't focus on my father's awkward home improvement projects: the raggedy edges of red Formica mounted on plywood to make a drop-down table for the kitchen wall; the crooked rows of gray

102

plastic wall tiles in the powder room he built for Mother under the back stairs.

Not looking gets to be a habit. It's not hard: you just narrow your vision. I don't see the mess inside my shed. I just look over the laptop screen, out the window at the birches and the balsams and the grasses that glow green-gold on a sunny afternoon.

⊛

Saturday, April 5, 1986

Saw Santoro yesterday afternoon. He agreed to chair a confrontation with Stu and set tentative dates, April 22 or 24. Then this morning he called to say he'd talked with B, and they decided we had not yet come to the point of confrontation—that being the Final Step. Santoro thought we should try to get Stu to meet with me and B and then with Santoro. If Stu refuses, it will be time for confrontation.

I had already mentioned the confrontation to Bill Lange, and he'd immediately raised objections. "Is this a good technique for someone who is already a bit paranoid?" he asked. "It pits all his friends against him."

The whole thing made me feel cold-blooded but at the same time teary and upset. I was relieved about the postponement.

Stu was angry today because I spent the afternoon on the west side, doing some volunteer work for the kids' school while Eli was at a birthday party. While Eli and I were gone, Stu and David had a row about work and cooperation. "David has a bad attitude," Stu told me. This meant that David preferred to watch a video of *Used Cars* for the nth time rather than sort glass for recycling or rake the yard. But I'm sure Stu's fight with David was caused by his displaced fury at me. "You seem to be home less and less," he complained.

"I'll be happy to stay home when it's a pleasant place to be," I said, but I added that I planned to work around the house tomorrow.

He wasn't impressed. "If you'd rather look at houses for sale, go ahead and do it."

⊛

Sunday, April 6, 1986

Spent much of the day putting edging around the flower bed on the left side in front of the house. I did the right side two years ago. My hand is too stiff to fit easily around the pen.

Skipped out to look at three houses: one across the street from David's friend Andy, one around the corner from here, and one I drove past that had an open house sign. Came back confident that I will be able to find a house I like and could afford—if necessary.

Stu tiptoed around me today, but he came down hard on the kids. David said that yesterday Stu spent a good deal of time bitching that no one helps around the house. "He told me you admitted that you stay away from home on purpose," David said.

This morning, the kids and I took a nice long bike ride. I wish that our bike rides and story-reading sessions (*The Phantom Tollbooth* these days) could ease their nervousness about Stu and me. Eli has too many stomach aches. David picks on Eli and says, "Why can't we fight if you do?"

※

Last night, about midnight, I walked down to the shore of Lake Superior. The full moon hung directly above, very small and cold, but casting such a bright light that I could see my shadow on the rocks. Huge waves, pushed by the thunderstorms earlier in the evening, crashed and swirled at my feet. Moonlight reflected off the foam; it dazzled, luminescent white. Back in my room, listening to the roar of the surf through the open skylight, I scrawled in my little notebook, "How would it be, to live in this beauty constantly?"

I remind myself that I know what it's like to live on a lake. Lake Mendota's a scrap of a puddle, compared to oceanic Superior. But I loved standing on our shore, watching storms come across from Maple Bluff. Lightning slashed the northern sky, wind whipped up the whitecaps, rain sheeted over deep water, and we prepared to run for shelter—into the boathouse/garage or back to the big old house. In the winter, we watched for the day the lake closed up—magically, on a still, cold night. Each spring, we waited for ice-out, checking

104

daily as the lake's surface, for months a white glare of snow, puddled with water and darkened with rot. One year, when the ice went out, a strong wind blew the crystals onto our shore; they piled as high as the boathouse door, tinkling like a chorus of tiny bells.

Was it Stu who made living on the lake into a chore? Or is it simply a lot of work, taking down the snow fence, changing the storm windows, cleaning the screens, setting up the pier and hoists for the boats? Every September, when it got so cold that we had to weatherstrip the windows and turn on the furnace, I wished we still lived in California. All winter I looked forward to the time when we would move outside again. But as early as May 1981—the second spring we lived on Lake Mendota—I wrote on a scrap of paper that Stu's "angers and obsessions" over spring chores filled the house, . . . pushing Claire and Tony to the third floor, making David and Eli cling to me. I thought of calling Hal and Julie, to see if I could move into their house when they left Madison for a summer of sailing on Lake Michigan. I wondered whether it was feasible to leave Stu—either financially or from the point of view of Eli and David, who were only three and six.

❁

Monday morning, April 7, 1986

After I wrote in my journal last night and got ready for bed, I allowed Stu to pull me into an hour-long discussion of what we should do on the third floor. It began, innocently enough, when he asked, "What shall we tell the painter about the estimate?" He urged me, again, to move my studio to Sara's old room, and I was just beginning to feel comfortable with this idea, thinking that perhaps he really wouldn't hold it against me, when he said, "I used to think that big room would be a great bedroom for us, but I've changed my mind about that."

"Why?" I asked.

"We need two bedrooms," he said. "I think you should take over the big room on the third floor. It'll be your room. You can have a study up there, and your bedroom."

"Where will you sleep?"

"I'll stay where I am," he said, meaning he'd take the sleeping porch spring, summer, and fall and our current bedroom in the winter. "Before we can share a bedroom, we need to learn to coexist. This is my route to coexistence. You have your own bedroom, and I have mine. I don't want to be under any obligation to sleep with you. I only want to do it if I feel positive about doing it."

I really find this suggestion intolerable.

When I stop to figure out why, I have several thoughts. Stu sleeping elsewhere (as he often does when he's angry) drives me crazy, I think because Dad never left Mother's bed, even when she was incontinent. I know this was ridiculous, but nonetheless, it defines marriage for me. Also, I want to be able to cuddle, to express in touch what one cannot in words, even if we don't end up fucking. But mostly, I think this is Stu's ploy for ultimate control: he decides when he will sleep with me. This isn't a two-way option. If I refused to allow him in my bed when he wanted to be there, he would experience it as the ultimate rejection, and he'd get hostile. Likewise, he won't let me decide that I want to sleep with him. I'm not allowed to join him in bed on the porch. This puts him under "obligation," he says; he leaves and sleeps elsewhere. My reaction to all this is, if he wants separate bedrooms so badly, he can have a separate house. I will not be controlled in this degrading way.

Stu seemed to have resumed drinking last night, and I should have known better than to be drawn into a discussion that lasted from midnight to one in the morning. Even he knew better. He said, "I think you're too tired to talk." This annoyed me, and I kept talking. Not good.

Just now, I tried to explain to him why I didn't like the idea of two bedrooms. "It seems like a no-win situation for me. It's like our sex life. When I take the initiative, you maintain the right to say 'no.' But *I* don't have the right to say no to you." Somehow we got into a discussion of female orgasms.

"Your idea that your orgasms are clitoral comes from reading too much," Stu maintained. "Your real problem is a deep-seated fear of rejection. That's what you have to deal with. And the best way for you to deal with it is for us to have separate bedrooms."

He insisted that he likes me to initiate sex. "All of my fantasies revolve around you taking the initiative," he said. "I want you to tie me to the bed and show me what a loving person you are. I want you to show me how much you love me, to shower me with affection and loving attention."

"Yes," I said, "but those are your fantasies. If I do exactly the right thing—exactly what you want me to do—then it's OK because you're still in control. But if I assert myself and tell you that what I need for my satisfaction is something different, that's not acceptable to you."

This whole thing is so ludicrous I can barely write about it.

It's also ironic. A couple of days ago, it occurred to me that I should find one area that Stu could control and just let him be in control in that area. And I thought sex could be that area. But I don't respond "properly" (that is, the way he wants me to). In fact, sex is probably the hardest area for me to allow him to control, because my body simply isn't there and doesn't oblige, no matter what my mind says ought to happen.

⊛

My father and Charlotte came to visit in June of 1981, that second spring we lived on Lake Mendota. I was still trying to figure out how to escape from Stu's anger and obsessions. Now he made himself as scarce as possible. He disappeared for hours without any explanation. He stood up in the midst of a conversation and walked out of the room. I wrote myself notes complaining about his "brutal egomania and insensitivity." I recorded a dream: I have decided to commit suicide and check into a hospital where it will be done to me after an overnight stay. In the morning, I see Eli and change my mind; I manage to escape from the hospital before I am killed.

The body knows so much more than the conscious mind. Five months after that dream, I was diagnosed with Hodgkin's disease. The date is easy to remember, because in the fall of 1981, I decided to keep a journal for the first time in twelve years. I bought myself a blank book bound in navy blue cloth. The entries start October 16, two weeks after I turned thirty-seven: At last—my birthday present to myself.

Leafing through the book, I find the entry for November 3.

Maybe the strong urge I had to keep a journal had a purpose. Went into internal medicine clinic yesterday for a checkup. . . . The nurse called about a half hour ago to say that the blood tests were all good, but the X-ray was not.

The clinic visit was exactly fifteen years from next Saturday, the last day of my residency, the day I will leave Norcroft.

⊛

Monday evening, April 7, 1986

Despite the wretched conversation this morning, I have been "up" most of the day. I edited a lecture for the Sexuality tape in the *Marriage and the Family* course; took Eli to his piano lesson; and then shopped for clothes to wear at the Ohio State Awards banquet, with Eli tagging along. (He said shopping was "peaceful and relaxing.") Later, Sara came over and we had a reasonable, not-too-tense dinner; then Stu and I went to see *Sugar Baby,* while Sara did her laundry and stayed with the kids.

Since we got home, I have been trying on clothes and selecting things to take East. I have quite a pile for four nights and five days! I am in such a good mood that I wonder why I even have to see a therapist or contemplate leaving. Stu is friendly, but I suppose we will sleep separately.

⊛

The body knows so much more than the conscious mind. How Stu sneered at ideas like that!

I am reminded of this by a letter I find in my file folder, a letter I wrote a few months after I was diagnosed with Hodgkin's disease. Picture me in January 1982. I am recovering from surgery to remove my spleen, biopsy my liver and lymph nodes. I have started chemotherapy. On two consecutive Tuesdays I am given nauseating infusions of mustard gas, vincristine, and procarbazine; every day I swallow prednisone pills at home. The intravenous drugs make me horribly sick. They alter my sense of smell. Everything—the bed sheets, food, my own breath and skin—exudes a nasty metallic stench. For a full day after each treatment, I do nothing but lie in bed or rush to the bathroom to puke.

Unlike the intravenous drugs, the steroids pump me up. The doctor says he's had patients on prednisone who got up at three or four in the morning to vacuum the entire house, clean the bathroom, and mop the kitchen floor. "Don't you do that," he tells me. "You need to conserve your strength." I laugh. The white tornado isn't quite my style.

But I am only on prednisone for a month. My energy level crashes. I am still in charge of a big house and two small children. I take a leave of absence from the Children's Museum, but I continue work on a radio project funded by the National Endowment for the Humanities and on my resume-writing business. One day I sit down at Stu's IBM Selectric. I feel that you would be perfectly happy to see me sleep through the entire day, I write to Stu in frustration, so long as I could still carry my load of cooking and child care and run the household efficiently. I plead for his help with the housework and children so that I can continue my other projects. I need to do significant, involving work outside the house, I type. I need it perhaps even more, now that I am sick, than I did before. The ability to do that kind of work confirms, for me, that I am still an intelligent and reasonably active human being, not some sort of sick lump who can't accomplish much. And in despair I ask, If I can't get help when I am undergoing chemotherapy, how can I expect to have some permanent change in the way our household is structured so that, after I am well, I can stay well?

The letter shakes Stu up. He's afraid I'm losing my mind. "There's no scientific proof," he tells me, "that stress can make you sick."

❀

Tuesday morning, April 8, 1986

I was quite provocative last night. Because I was in such a good mood, I decided to state my rejection of Stu's "separate bedrooms and I get the porch" pronouncement by simply going to sleep on the porch. I did think it might be a nasty thing to do since I planned to set the alarm for 6:00 A.M. so I could get to a 7:15 meeting this morning. What I didn't thoroughly think through was how he would be outraged by the whole act of intruding on his turf.

Anyway, there I was on the porch when Stu went to bed. He didn't retreat, and we didn't make love; we just lay together, cuddling. But of course, the alarm woke him up, and now he is furious.

❧

Wednesday morning, April 9, 1986
O'Hare

Between planes, on my way to D.C. Writing (thinking) about domestic crisis feels like an awful intrusion, but I do need to fill in.

Last night Stu, extremely hostile, asked, "Have you gotten any additional insight into what is driving you to attack me at a continually intensifying level?"

"What do you mean?"

"I assumed that you were in my bed because you wanted to make love. But you didn't." That was especially provocative, apparently.

I tried to explain why I couldn't accept his demand that we sleep in separate bedrooms. Then I said, "I want you to take some responsibility for your drinking and your attempts to control me and everything else."

He didn't deny a problem with alcohol, but blamed me for it entirely. "I drink to ease the pain," he said, "and you cause the pain. You seem to have developed a new vocabulary as a result of your work on that sociology course, and you're trying it out on me. You're determined to push me into some mold you've read about." He called me "bookish" and "like someone who has joined a cult." And then: "I've set up the small bedroom on the third floor for myself. You'd better not set foot in it or even stand in the doorway." If I did, he said, he'd be physically abusive.

I was shaken enough after the conversation to run to one of my books for reassurance that no one can cause someone else to be an alcoholic. But while he was talking, I was mostly able to listen, respond levelheadedly, and let virtually all he said roll off my back because I knew that in a day or two he will get a letter from B suggesting that he see Santoro as a way of allaying my fears about his alcoholism and his controlling behavior. B composed the letter in my presence yesterday afternoon, after saying that he did not want to see Stu and me together. "If Stu came to a session, he would be defensive, tell me all about how awful you are, and insist on hearing the details of your psychopathology," B said. "It's a classic situation and one I avoid since I'm not a masochist."

B said he was designing the letter to appeal to Stu's desire for control and dominance over me. I don't know whether it will get him in to see Santoro. But I think I will be finding myself an attorney next week, just in case.

I am rather astonished by my degree of detachment from the whole situation. It is only when I speak or think about David and Eli that I get shaky. B asked why, and I didn't have a good answer. But after I left his office, I realized that I am scared that somehow, by leaving Stu, I am doing to them what my parents did to me. Abandoning them, somehow.

❀

Stu and I stand in the laundry room in the basement of our first house in Madison. He raises his hand and slaps me, hard. Why? Are we arguing about the layer of lint on the dryer? Is he angry because there's laundry detergent caked around the rim of the washing machine? Or has he already taken over the job of washing and drying and folding clothes? Did I follow him down the cellar stairs when he went to put the wet clothes into the dryer? Did I want to continue an argument? Did I scream at him about something that had nothing to do with clothes? What I remember: my stinging cheek.

❀

Friday afternoon, April 11, 1986
Amtrak en route to New York

Arrived in D.C. about three o'clock Wednesday. Too late to do any sightseeing, but I had to stretch my legs, so I took a longish walk toward the

111

White House after checking in at the hotel. The late afternoon light was spectacular against threatening skies. Fortunately it didn't rain. Went back to the hotel, changed, and took myself in all my finery to the National Press Club for the awards dinner. I was very apprehensive: how does one cope when one knows no one? But I made it through and even enjoyed myself by practicing flirting.

I suspect Stu has gotten B's letter by now. I am very nervous about his reaction. I think if he would begin to deal with his problems, to take responsibility for his 50 percent of the relationship's problems, I could compromise on coexistence in separate bedrooms, at least with a definite time limit. But it all seems so up in the air.

⊗

In the house on the lake, we stand in the kitchen, arguing. I am stirring ham-and-split-pea soup with a wooden spoon; ten quarts of viscous green simmers in the big aluminum pot. Stu is making himself a drink. A quart of Jack Daniel's sits on the counter; at the sink, he breaks ice cubes out of a plastic tray. Are we arguing about alcohol? Or why I didn't clean the playroom with David and Eli? Is Stu angry because the onion skins are still on the cutting board? The argument grows intense. Stu moves toward me. I say something. He swings. The plastic tray cracks against my right forearm. A simple law I learned in high-school physics: for every action, an equal and opposite reaction. A glob of pea soup flies off the end of the wooden spoon. It hits the white ceiling over the stove.

My arm reddens and swells. I go to the hospital. "How did this happen?" the resident asks.

"My husband hit me with an ice cube tray. It was an accident."

He shakes his head. He says the arm's not broken, but maybe I should talk to the police. He gives me a sling to wear. I put it on and go home.

The soup hardens on the ceiling. It is still there, a small dark splat, five or six years later when we sell the house.

⊗

Saturday, April 12, 1986
New York City

I am not sure this trip was such a good idea. I came up to New York to
see Shelly, who is at a conference, and my old friend Gwen, who came up
from Philly to talk and go to museums. We used to do that in Chicago
after we both moved from California to the Midwest. She'd take the bus
up from Indiana. I'd leave the kids with Helen and take the Greyhound
down. We'd spend an hour or two at the Art Institute and then find a coffee shop where we talked the rest of the day. I remember those trips as
great fun. But I think I'm simply too much up in the air now to let go and
just have *fun*. This seems like a bad example of what the single life is like.
Too much uncertainty, too much depressing talk about me and Stu. Gwen
said, "Maybe Stu will have an epiphany, you'll develop incredible respect
for him, and you'll all live happily after." I'm afraid I rather more expect that
I will go home tomorrow and find him outraged and hostile because of
B's letter. I *am* ready to go home, though, and face whatever awful music
there is to face.

⊛

I almost always got tense returning from a trip, coming home to Stu.
The pattern began before we were married. I picture myself on a bus
pulling into a Greyhound terminal, on planes landing with a bump
and starting to taxi. I have no children with me; or David, who has
spilled 7-Up all over my good gray slacks; or Eli, who has nursed
contentedly through every takeoff and landing. I am returning from
visiting Rachel in Los Angeles, from a summer working for the
Christian Science Monitor, from a day in Chicago with Gwen, from
taking the baby to visit Nana and Poppy in Florida, from my annual
spring pilgrimage to Pittsburgh with David and Eli. Stu will meet
me at the San Francisco airport, at the old Madison Greyhound station. He will be in his light blue '66 Volvo, parked in the Memorial
Union lot, waiting for the bus from O'Hare. My heart thumps, my
palms sweat, I have butterflies in my stomach. I'm never sure why
this is.

Monday morning, April 14, 1986
Home again

Two dreams: a very complex crisis dream in which Stu threatened suicide and refused to see Santoro and then a dream about sex.

In waking life, a strange return. I was very tense and untrusting; Stu seemed cordial and relaxed. B's letter, marked "received 4/11" was on his desk. On my desk, I found a Shere Hite article from an old *Penthouse,* arguing that women's orgasms are clitoral, not vaginal, and a note from Stu asking me to read the article and consider whether we can discuss it nonbelligerently.

I unpacked, helped Stu move the canoe to its summer position on the lake front, took a bike ride with the kids, made a salad. We picked Helen up at the airport, tanned and in great good humor after her trip to Indonesia, and brought her to our house for a steak dinner.

Later, Stu took her home. When he came back, he retreated into his study. I went in to say, "I have a Children's Museum board meeting tomorrow evening."

He snarled, "That doesn't surprise me."

Rather than drink himself into a stupor, he got ready for bed at 10:30, grabbed pillows from our big bed, snarled when I said goodnight, and went out to the sleeping porch.

Monday afternoon

I asked Stu, "Were you angry with me last night?"

"No. I was trying to avoid a donnybrook, so I avoided you."

"I read the Shere Hite article. It's very interesting, and I'd be happy to talk about it."

"Discussing that isn't a high priority," he said, which surprised me. But he added, "When we're ready, I think it would be useful to read it aloud and discuss it line by line."

※

Monday evening

Stu has clearly been affected by B's letter. He's trying to cut back on alcohol. He waited until after six o'clock to start drinking today and just had one beer before dinner.

He also suggested that I buy a seven-year-old white Volvo wagon that our friend Dan has for sale. "One of the things we should work on is making you feel less like 'used goods,'" Stu explained. "I think replacing your beat-up orange car would be a good place to start."

"What makes you think I feel like 'used goods?'"

"You. You told me that."

I don't remember ever saying that, and how a used car would make me feel less like "used goods" is beyond me. But I think he's scared. Or at least concerned.

※

Snow flurries dance outside the window of my writing shed, tiny bright sparkles adrift against branches of evergreen. The snow and the sun come on the back side of a storm. Yesterday evening, rain battered my umbrella as I made my way back to the lodge. The wind tore open a casement window I had left unlatched and howled through the open skylight, chilling me first from the east, then the west as I huddled under the quilt. The surf roared. Waves broke without pause, without any soothing rhythm.

By this morning, the rain had stopped and the temperature dropped so low I wished I had my mittens for the short walk down to the shore. I pulled the gazebo door open against the wind. I sat in the white wicker rocker, writing in my journal, my hand stiff with cold. Bare branches tossed high above the roof, and far out on the lake, the ruffled, wind-dark water broke white. But the rocks at the shore were sheltered, the waves in the little cove not nearly so high as I have seen. And then a sudden gust: the gazebo windows shuddered, wood creaked, dried grasses shook and bent parallel to the ground.

Tuesday morning, April 15, 1986

Stu was in the kitchen at breakfast, lobbying once again for me to buy the white Volvo station wagon. "You have the money," he told me. "I looked at your assets. You have five times the cost of the wagon sitting in cash accounts right now."

"I'm aware of that," I said, "but I'm also aware that I might have to buy a house and support myself. I'm not sure I want to buy a car now."

Stu was surprised. "It never occurred to me that you would buy a house by yourself."

"You're the one who suggested that I find a house and move out."

"I figured that if you found a house to live in, we'd buy it as a joint investment."

"Oh. I thought you wanted me to move out so we could live separate lives."

"Even if we separated formally, you would have half my assets," he said. "Of course, if you don't want them, you don't have to take them. But that's what I've always assumed."

"I guess I'm just looking at the worst-case scenario," I said. "I don't think I can be sure I'd have half your assets if we were divorced."

Tuesday afternoon

A nice session with B. We talked about my feelings about David and Eli, and he used the image of a sword that cuts both ways: they'll get hurt, but maybe leaving Stu is something I have to do. He said, "Maybe the reason you've tried so hard to stay with Stu is because you want so much to give your children something you didn't have."

"What do you mean?"

"I think you want them to have a normal family," he said. And he's right. I want to make it work for them. But it seems to me that in trying to make a normal life for David and Eli I've become a model for women—and men's relations with women—that I really don't want to be for my sons.

⊛

Tuesday evening

A little while ago I asked Stu if he'd gotten B's letter.

"Yes," he said. "It was pretty foolish. I suspect that he was just doing your bidding."

"So you won't see Santoro?"

"I'll deal with my drinking problem my own way," he said. "I drink too much after ten PM., and it's because wondering whether or not we're going to have sex puts too much stress on me. So I propose that we change our schedules and have sex earlier in the day, if we're going to have it at all."

I was flabbergasted. I said, "I'll consider changing our schedules if you see Santoro and he says you don't have a drinking problem—or that it's something that can be dealt with that way."

"I'll tell you right now that I won't go to see Santoro. I don't see any reason for it. You're the reason I drink. And if you want me to prove it, we can try a one-year separation."

Then he said, "I'm not going to take any ultimata from you. For the past seventeen years, you've watched me resist Helen's attempts to manipulate me. You, of all people, should be sensitive to the fact that I will refuse your much less subtle attempts to tell me what to do." This little speech was quite striking, because earlier today B and I had talked about how Stu, having grown up in a family of autocrats, was going to resist all attempts to "mold" him.

This afternoon, I asked a friend on the Children's Museum board to recommend a lawyer. The lawyer—Carol Madsen—is in court until late this week, but I don't feel a big rush. I do need to ask her what separation and divorce mean, legally, and how long it takes to get a divorce. Things like that. I will be damned if I will adjust my life and schedule to suit Stu's drinking habit.

❀

I thought about divorce long before I ever called a lawyer. For example, late 1982: I have suffered through three rounds of chemo and two of radiation. I am getting ready to go to Stanford for the final month of radiation. I fill the freezer with spaghetti sauce and chili, mark a calendar with carpool details, note David's sleepover plans and the days we're signed up to bring treats to Eli's nursery school. I fight with Stu, who insists that I welcome his blossoming relationship with Kathy. I read about Simone de Beauvoir and Jean-Paul Sartre. Their relationship was "primary and essential," but not exclusive. I berate myself: Why can't you accept something like that?

I am trapped, I fume in a two-page diatribe. I appear jealous, which only shows my "immaturity"; or I appear mature and understanding and *moderne,* which only underscores my helplessness. In either case, you fuck (or don't fuck) whom you please, and I am left to stew in whatever real feelings I can sort out. I write that Stu would be pleased if I died, but say I don't propose to solve his moral dilemmas like that. I suggest that I might take off—and then call that an idle threat. . . . To prove what? That it is fun to be alone and cancerous? That health starts when the divorce papers are signed?

I file the letter in a folder. I never show it to Stu.

❀

Wednesday evening, April 16, 1986

At breakfast this morning, David and Eli complained that there was no cereal.

"Stu decided not to go food shopping this week," I explained.

Eli said, "Yeah, all he cares about is whether there's enough gin in the house."

In the car on the way to school Eli began to ask about Stu's drinking. I explained that alcoholism is a disease, not something Stu does because he's being mean.

David said that he never noticed Stu drinking, and that it didn't bother him. He said, "Stu naps after dinner, but that just seems normal."

We talked about denial—Stu's denial and my own. Eli said, "Maybe David's doing the same thing."

"What do you mean?" I wondered.

"Maybe he's denying that Stu has a problem. But that doesn't mean there isn't one."

"This conversation is boring," David said.

I spent much of the afternoon filling Helen in on what is going on. She was obviously upset, but was very supportive of me—and anguished over "what went wrong" with Stu. She was astonished at Stu's notion that a new used car would improve my self esteem. "Doesn't he have any idea how he might have affected your self esteem?" she asked. She wants to come with me to talk with Santoro, and I will set that appointment up for next week. She also offered me financial help if I need it. What a lady!

Stu has been occupying himself all evening by listing all our magazine subscriptions on the computer and organizing them. This seems to me like a frantic effort to exert control over *something;* to create order where there is none. Oddly, I do not have any of this impulse. I will let everything play out and create order in the new house, if there is one, or in my new space in this house, if that is what I get.

I've spent the day thinking about obsessions: Stu, tracking every penny, creating databases to catalog magazine subscriptions, his record collection, all the books in the house. Me, writing obsessively in my journal, three and four times a day.

In the late afternoon, I drive to the mouth of the Cascade River and sit above a rocky beach, looking south across the lake. Waves come at me, over and over. I seek solace in the waves, find comfort in the unceasing swell, the patterns of foam, the rhythmic pounding and roar. The water thins to translucence at the back of each curl; the leading edge breaks in a tangle of foam and lace. Waves crash on enormous rocks, shiny basalt and gabbro, oozed from the earth's core a billion years ago. The tongues of the biggest waves lap the foot of the wooden staircase where I've made my seat. The bottom two steps are soaked, a rich wet brown. The next two, splashed and spotted. I sit on the fifth step from the bottom, thinking, This is obsession, these waves crashing endlessly, day after day. For ten thousand years, since the last glacier, against the intransigent rock.

And as I watch, the waves start to pull tiny stones from the beach. Shiny black chunks smaller than charcoal briquettes mix with the water, toss high in the foam, fall back to the lake. Again, a wave tosses stones in the air; they shower down with the surf. And again. And a big wave crashes onto the beach, onto the tumbled pile of billion-year-old rocks. Most of the tiny stones wash back into the lake. A single pebble, tossed high, drops on a rock and bounces, two times, three, scrapes off a few molecules, rolls back into the lake.

⊛

Friday, April 18, 1986

This afternoon, Eli and I went over to Dan and Jeanne's house and I tried the white wagon. It drives very nicely, but I am still not certain I need to buy another car right now. I gave Jeanne a thumbnail sketch of what is going on, and she came right out and said, "You've probably done all you can do. It sounds like it's time to bail out."

When Eli and I got home, Stu, Bill, and Linda were at the picnic table by the lake. "Looks like summer," Eli said, and that prompted me into a crying jag. I'm afraid summer this year will not look much like this, and I realize that when I look at houses, I must really focus on the out-of-doors and the nearness to parks. I think about regular picnics at Vilas Park on the west side, Eli and David getting their "lake fixes" when they visit Stu on weekends.

Bill and Linda stayed for dinner and dominoes (which I took *enormous* pleasure in winning by scoring repeatedly on Stu). While we played, I looked at the furniture in the lake room and tried to decide what is important to me and what is not. I wonder whether domino games are important. I will be able to see much more of some friends (like Claire and Tony) without Stu, but much less of the Langes.

While we were playing dominoes, Bill said that his two-year-old nephew had recently pointed to a dead grasshopper and called it "Linda." Bill, Linda, and I roared with laughter. Stu was mystified.

"Don't you remember?" Bill asked. "You called us grasshoppers one time when we went cross-country skiing in December. It stuck. We call ourselves 'grasshoppers' when we go out to play."

Stu couldn't remember calling us grasshoppers and got quite angry. He remained very quiet until Bill and Linda left.

I read some old journals this evening. They are revealing, and appalling. I have been thinking of splitting for at least six years. And I have been thinking explicitly about *how* for a year. I think a year, or six years, is really long enough for thinking. I feel as though I have just awakened from a very long sleep — or perhaps have just torn a blindfold from my eyes.

⊛

I went to pick up my new contact lenses late one afternoon, the winter of 1967. I worked at the phone company until 4:30, so I was pleased to get the last appointment. Raindrops spattered my glasses as I walked up Market Street. The receptionist was gathering her purse and gloves as I stepped into the waiting room. She worked until 5:00; after she checked me in, she put on her raincoat and left.

The eye doctor stepped into the waiting room. "Judith?" he asked, and I nodded. He showed me back to an examining room and turned out the hall lights. "No one here but us," he explained and closed the door. I sat in the patient's chair, staring straight forward at the big *E* on the chart.

"You must be happy to get these," he said, taking a lens out of a little bottle. "Your glasses are pretty thick."

I nodded. I was happy. "Boys don't make passes at girls who wear glasses," Dorothy Parker said. Besides, in a few weeks I was going to Los Angeles, to Tom and Sandy's wedding, and I needed to look as good as possible.

He had the lens on his finger, his hand against my cheek. He pulled gently on the bottom lid of my right eye. "You'll see much

121

better with these. And I think you'll like the way you look." The lens was in. With my left eye closed, I could read small letters several rows below the *E*.

He leaned forward, barely brushing my breast, to put the other lens in. I blinked. He stepped back and smiled. "You really are a very pretty girl."

I got up to go, but he wasn't through with me. I had to learn to take the contacts out and put them back in again. He had me sit on a stool at the Formica counter. He handed me a small mirror. I felt his thigh, a slight pressure against my own. The dark hall, empty waiting room, seemed suddenly ominous. I squirted solution on the left contact, pulled my own lid down, popped the lens into my eye.

"You're a quick learner," he said. He patted me on the shoulder. His palm lingered on my back. "Can I buy you a drink to celebrate?"

I looked at the clock next to the eye chart. Nearly six. "I don't think so," I said. "It's late. I have to get back to work."

He raised his eyebrows. "I stayed later than usual so you wouldn't have to go back."

I shrugged. He didn't pursue it. I wasn't that appealing, even with contact lenses.

He opened the door. I grabbed my coat, rushed through the dark hall, through the waiting room. Outside, the sun had set. The wet pavement glistened. A light rain fell, or maybe a heavy mist. I felt it on the backs of my hands, on my forehead, on my cheeks. And then I knew something had changed. It was raining, and my vision was clear. It was raining, and I could see drops!

Standards of Performance

Saturday, April 19, 1986, 2:45 A.M.

As I was preparing for bed, Stu barged in—unable to sleep, he said—to demand conversation. We talked for about an hour and a half. "Do you think you'll ever be able to be loving toward me?" he asked.

"I don't know," I said, "but certainly not unless you deal with your alcohol problem."

Ultimately, he said he could give up drinking for one month. "Will that be enough?"

"No," I said. "Not unless you've had at least one meeting with Santoro." He refused, and I said, "Then I will see a lawyer next week."

"A lawyer's not necessary," he told me. "I'll give you an article on arbitrators that I clipped out of the *Wall Street Journal*. They're cheaper."

I backpedaled. "Helen and I are going to see Santoro next Friday, and I'll withhold judgment on your solution—giving up drinking for a month—until then."

Saturday, early afternoon

Stu is in a rage about my "demanding" behavior. This morning, he scaled down his "offer." "I'll cut back to two beers per day for ten days," he said.

He is hostile, sniping, throwing barbs. He insisted on clearing "our" possessions out of the bedroom (which he now calls "your room") and took away a photo of one of our old cats, which has been on my desk for years. That pushed a button: I reminded him that "coexistence" on his terms is absolutely out of the question for me, and we were off again, on a round-and-round hate spat.

⊛

Saturday evening

Hideous day. Stu is intent on proving he does not need to drink. "I want you to ask Santoro how long I have to go without alcohol in order to satisfy him that I'm not physiologically addicted. Two months? Six months? I hope not that long."

He is hostile and abusive, eager to press his point that my "sexual inadequacy" is the root cause of his drinking problem. This evening, he suggested that we talk. "The next thing we have to deal with," he announced, "after I prove I don't have a drinking problem, is your profound difficulties with sex and anger. I think you should enter a new round of intensive psychoanalysis, preferably with a woman, several hours a week."

"Why?" I asked.

"Because I'm not going to be able to wait if you go only once a week." (This from someone who is outraged that I asked him to see Santoro once.) He had other messages too:

"I doubt we'll ever sleep in the same bed again."

And, "Let's coexist until August 3."

"Why August 3?" I asked.

"I remember that as the date David was conceived," he said and described a passionate all-night orgy eleven and two-thirds years ago that was, according to him, "the last time we had good sex—maybe the only time." Then he said, "But that's three-and-a-half months away. I don't know if I'll stay here that long."

And often, when I opened my mouth to respond, he interrupted me or looked at his watch and complained, "You're using some of my precious time."

This is all using too much of *my* precious time, and I plan to end it, soon. I will miss the lake, the promise (rarely fulfilled) of intimacy, the cats. But I will not miss Stu.

The summer after eleventh grade, Uncle Al got me a job at a family resort in the Catskills. The owner, who must have owed Al a favor, hired me and another girl to run the "day camp." I think we were supposed to play croquet with the kids so the mothers could sit on folding aluminum lawn chairs and gossip and do their nails in peace.

My day-camp duties lasted less than a week, the amount of time it took Rusty, the waiter in the children's dining room, to calculate that he'd never pull together his college tuition if he spent the summer with us. We're not talking Grossinger's. This was a shabby, lower-middle-class resort. As soon as I showed up, I learned the pecking order for tips: waiter-in-the-main-dining-room, busboy-in-the-main-dining-room, chambermaid, waiter-in-the-children's-dining-room, busboy-in-the-children's-dining-room, day-camp counselor. "But," a main-dining-room waiter smirked, "once they tip us, there's nothing for anyone else."

Rusty left, but not before we followed someone's directions to get to the beach at midnight for a goodbye campfire. The water seemed pretty far away, and by the light of the fire, we could see the flag for the fourth tee of the local golf course. We were on a sand trap, but it didn't matter. Rusty had a guitar, and he knew Kingston Trio songs.

The owner promoted Rusty's busboy to waiter in the children's dining room; I became the busboy. It didn't matter that they didn't change the title. Within a week, this waiter also left for greener pastures. I was a waitress. Dinners were pretty easy. All the kids trooped in at once, but there were only three choices: meat, fish, or dairy. In the morning, kids straggled in throughout the breakfast hour. They all ordered different things, but since only two or three kids showed up at any one time, I had no trouble keeping the orders separate. (We couldn't write the orders down. It wasn't "professional.")

Lunch was the worst meal of the day. The kids came all at once, and they came with their parents in tow. A toddler would ask for something she liked, like blueberries and sour cream. "What? This is a lunch?" her mother would say, looking at me. "Does this sound healthy to you? Bring her a little egg salad, dear. The blueberries and the egg salad. And herring. She likes herring." The mother turns to her daughter. "Or you want tuna instead?" To me: "Herring, and tuna too. Fresh air gives a good appetite." Multiply this by twelve, or twenty, however many kids happened to be in residence, and it's no wonder I treated myself to a Hershey's semi-sweet chocolate bar as soon as I went off duty each afternoon. As predicted, I didn't get any tips.

But I did get an education. One night before Rusty left, several of us gathered in his room. He played "Hang Down Your Head, Tom Dooley" and sang the ballad of poor Charlie, trapped underground when Boston raised the subway fare. People passed a bottle of something. Maybe I had a sip. Maybe not. I lay down on a bed cuddled up to some college boy, and in his warmth, purring like a cat, fell asleep. When I woke, this boy was pretty angry. "Don't ever do that again!" he said.

I had clearly done something bad. But what? What could be bad about falling asleep?

🐚

Sunday, April 20, 1986

From Stu's desk notepad (always left where I can see it when I turn the computer on), the following list of qualities:

Feminine:	playful, warm, flirtatious, inquisitive, seductive (come hither), self-loving, confident, open, sincere, trustful, discrete [sic], imaginative
not:	bellicose, carping, pouting, nagging, rancorous, sharp-tongued

Presumably I am the "not."

In a dream last night, I showed an oncologist friend how Henry Kaplan, the Hodgkin's expert at Stanford, used to check for enlarged lymph nodes on my neck. The friend felt my neck and identified enlarged nodes—or perhaps just the remainder of nodes zapped by radiation. Graininess, radiologists call it. It does make me nervous to think that the stress I am under could make me sick again. It makes me want to forget all the talk-talk with Stu, which I don't think will lead us anywhere good, and just split.

❧

A hard frost yesterday, record-breaking cold, utterly changed the North Shore landscape. Mud froze into a pattern of ruts and foot-prints on the trail to Leveaux Mountain; my boots cracked the sur-face of puddles-turned-to-ice, my hiking stick skidded and slipped. I rushed up to the top and back, racing dusk, alone on the icy trail. The hanging fuchsias on the porch, beautiful healthy plants in the morning, froze by midafternoon; the leaves curled and drooped, a sick glazed green, the blossoms and buds went hard. But the fuch-sias, so far as I know, are the only tragedy. Last night, the ground, dusted with snow, gleamed in moonlight, ethereal. At the beach, ici-cles hung from the rocks like walrus tusks; the waves transformed low shrubs into glistening castles, ice-slick fantasies.

❧

Monday, April 21, 1986

Feeling groovy! I blew up at Stu before dinner. I was so tired of his hostil-ity and pigheadedness. I told him that I was not going to let him malign my sexuality any further; I was tired of being blamed and made the cause of all our problems, including his drinking. He said, "Oh, you mean you don't buy the cause and effect theory?"

"No," I said. "I don't. If there's any cause and effect relationship, I'd say that our sexual problems are caused by both of us. By *my* anger at *your* behavior. All day you've been acting furious, slamming things around, and I have no idea why. But you've been making me angrier by the minute. I think you have problems, too, and you need to admit that."

"I don't have any sexual problems that couldn't be cured by another woman."

"Fine," I said. "This morning I made an appointment to see a lawyer. I'm going to file for divorce next week. You'll have ample opportunity to have your problems cured by many other women."

He came down to the kitchen while I was making dinner. Practically pleading, he asked me if we could talk this evening after I come back from the Children's Museum.

"We can talk if you can overcome your tendency to blame me for whatever went wrong. And I don't want to discuss *my* sexual problems, although if you'd like, we could talk about *our* problems."

He was like a pussycat. "I don't want other women," he said. "I want to make it with you."

※

Monday night

Came back from copying addresses onto mailing labels at the museum and had a long talk. Stu very friendly, we both very civil. He clearly wants to preserve the marriage, and he insisted that I *do* affect his behavior. "In the last six days, I've only had two beers a day. It makes me angry, but I'll continue to drink no more than that at least until next Sunday. I'm not making any promises after that."

"I didn't ask you to limit your alcohol consumption. I asked you to see Santoro. What will you do if Santoro tells me that the only way he can judge whether you're physiologically addicted is by seeing you in person?"

"I won't go."

But the whole tone of the conversation was conciliatory, even friendly (as enemies at truce may appear to be friends). I was almost seduced into thinking there is hope. In retrospect, though, I think of Stu's insistence that we don't need a marriage counselor; his announcement that he has decided we should not have any sex "until we have talked a lot about sex."

This is all such bullshit. Really, he is maneuvering me into a position in which I will look as though I am at fault (unwilling to stay and work things out; impatient to mold everyone into the proper shape) if I leave.

Just went through some files and found notes dating back to 1975, expressing my discontent, if not anger, with our relationship.

Would leaving be the first time in eleven years that I've really done something for myself?

※

One afternoon, a guest at the Catskill resort invited me to go out on the lake in a rowboat. His stomach pudged over his belt, he wore a white short-sleeved sport shirt and dark pants, he didn't seem the rowboat type. But I didn't have the money to rent boats, and I loved being out on the water. Only the summer before I'd spent two weeks at an all-states Girl Scout camp, learning the rudiments of sailing, running whitewater in a canoe.

He launched the rowboat after dinner, after I finished wiping crumbs off the children's tables. I stepped into the bow and moved to the stern, holding the gunwales, keeping my weight centered and low. He stepped in after I sat down. The aluminum boat rocked wildly as he walked to the center seat, standing as straight as he would to stroll down a city street. It steadied when he sat down, facing me, his back properly to the bow. At least he knew that much. He dropped the oar pins into the oarlocks, leaned forward, pulled on the oars. We moved through the calm water. The sun rode low in the west.

He rowed us out to the center of the lake. (Really, it was more like a pond.) "This is a good spot," he said.

I looked around. A few lily pads, muddy water. "As good as any," I agreed. I expected him to ship the oars, rest them along the gunwales on the inside of the boat. But he let them drag in the water. I started to say something, then shut my mouth. Boys didn't like girls who told them what to do.

"Let's get comfortable," he said. He unlaced his black street shoes, pulled them off, rolled his socks down his ankles and tugged them off by the toes. Sparse black hairs bristled on white skin. He rolled his cuffs up a few turns, then stood up suddenly. The boat rocked; the oar pins jounced in the oarlocks. He sat back down on the bottom of the boat, hairy legs stretching in my direction, leaning against his seat.

"Come over here," he said. "You can rest your back on me."

I crouched low in the boat, pivoted, sat practically in his lap. I made myself comfortable, reminded myself not to fall asleep. He circled my waist with his arms. A breeze rippled the water. We bobbed gently with the swells. The sun set. His right hand inched toward my breast.

How far had we gone when he decided to stretch out? "Ooch down, baby," he said and moved his butt off-center. The boat dipped violently to starboard. I heard metal scrape on metal as the oar pin rode up in its hole. Then, splash! The oar fell into the lake.

He managed to fish it out, but the moment, the momentum, was lost. We sat back up on our seats and he rowed to shore.

I never saw him again. This didn't make me sad; just curious. What would have happened if he'd really known about boats?

⊛

Tuesday, April 22, 1986

Sad session with B today, in which he practically broke down at the same time I practically broke down, talking about Stu's defensiveness and his off-the-wall reaction to me and the way I'm changing. We also talked about security: why I feel uncomfortable about having a need for security; why I feel uncomfortable looking for security from a man; why I feel uncomfortable thinking that monogamy is OK and looking for security in monogamy.

I said that Stu and I argued about monogamy, especially when I was being treated for Hodgkin's disease. "They were philosophical discussions, really. My sister Shelly says she thought Stu's behavior back then was cruel, but I think that word is extreme. I wasn't all that interested in sex while I was being treated. And as Stu said, he needed to get emotional support from someone else so he had the energy to give me emotional support."

B said, rather dryly, "There are other places to get emotional support. I can see how Shelly might have thought he was cruel."

Tonight, David and Eli were squabbling so much that I couldn't read to them. They are both edgy, worried. David complained that we don't have vacation plans. Why aren't we going to Europe (or wherever) like his friends' families? What he clearly meant was why can't we take a family vacation, all four of us. He even asked, "Why do we have to go camping? Why can't we do something that Stu likes to do?" He said he'd rather go to Great America than on a camping trip—I think because he realizes that Stu doesn't want to camp.

"One reason we don't take family vacations in the summer is because Stu races his boat every weekend," I said. "But you could ask Stu why he doesn't want to come on vacations with us. I'm sorry we're not a family that takes vacations together. It makes me very sad." I hugged David and began crying—which made him cry.

Meanwhile, Stu is back to his "I'll be friendly and this will all blow over" mode. I swear, David and Eli have a better idea of where my head is than Stu does. We can't just kiss and make up and go off about our separate lives.

✦

There was one more lesson in the Catskills. I met the guy in the casino. He was tall and thin, good looking, in his mid-twenties or maybe even older He took me in his arms and we swayed to the schmaltzy three-piece band. It was a weeknight and pretty slow, only a few couples out on the floor. Some of the guests, middle-aged couples with kids who ate in my dining room, sat at little tables, drinking Cokes and watching us.

The guy was a local. He took me home so we could continue dancing after the band packed up for the night. He had two rooms: a big kitchen/living room and, beyond French doors, a room with a mattress on the floor. He switched on a gooseneck lamp set next to the mattress. A tangle of sheets blanketed the unmade bed. He angled the light into the kitchen. It cast long shadows as we danced to the radio. He held me close; we slowly circled the kitchen table to a couple of tunes. Then he steered me through the French doors, bent down to turn off the lamp. He tilted my chin and kissed me, exploring my mouth with his tongue.

I closed my eyes. When I opened them, we were sitting on the mattress. Moonlight streaming in the window brightened the rumpled sheets.

"Uh," I said, "what time is it?"

He wasn't sure. He said it must be twelve-thirty or one.

"I have to go," I said, standing up. "I have to be in the kiddies' dining room at six."

I could tell he was pretty unhappy. Still, he followed me out to the car. Was it a Mustang? I sat in the bucket seat on the passenger's side. He got in, slammed the door, put the key in the ignition. Then he leaned over to give me another kiss. I backed away.

"C'mon," he said. "Just one more. You kiss so good."

"If you don't start the car, I will," I told him. "I know how to drive a stick." He swore, but he turned the key in the ignition and jammed the stick into reverse.

The next weekend, Nana came up for a visit. She said everyone was worried when I left the casino with "that man." It bugged me that anyone knew, much less cared. "Nothing happened," I told her. "I know how to take care of myself."

At school, a few months later, I heard someone called a "prick tease." I could tell it wasn't a compliment.

⊛

Thursday evening, April 24, 1986
Passover

This afternoon I suggested to Stu that we discuss the Shere Hite article. So we began reading it line by line, discussing it as we went. We got through two or three paragraphs and talked for about two hours, until the kids came home from school. It was quite a good and honest conversation, I think, and made me positively buoyant and hopeful that perhaps we can get someplace in this way. But it was all about sex—and really, the nitty gritty details of sex. And while I think Stu did hear me when I said that, for me, physical responsiveness is directly related to mood and emotional state, I'm not at all sure that he understands that he is directly responsible for much of my anger.

He did accept some responsibility for our problems. He said he'd had a "dumb" perception that the female orgasm was caused by penetration and an "unhelpful focus on standards of performance." He seems to accept the idea that I am totally turned off when he comes to bed drunk. And I think that he was able to understand that I feel cozy and secure in bed with him, whatever we may or may not do, and that I want to sleep with him the majority—the great majority—of the time. But I am left, ready to see Carol Madsen (the lawyer), with not much idea of whether this is an example of pussycat behavior prompted by my announcement that I was going to see a lawyer or an indication of real progress.

This evening we had a formal non-Seder, which I found minimally acceptable (and I'd guess Stu found minimally objectionable). I made a chicken, set the dining-room table with candles and the cutwork linen tablecloth Nana made, put out matzo and a Seder plate. We talked about the holiday's meaning as we ate. David and Eli hunted the *afikomen*, and it was perhaps the only relatively tension-free meal we've had in a week.

※

My last morning in my writing shed. I leave Norcroft tomorrow; we move out of our sheds tonight. I am sad to be leaving, but astonished at how much I have accomplished in three weeks. I'd set myself a goal of seeing whether it would be feasible to turn my 1986 journal into a memoir; if not, I would abandon the project and move on. But I think I have found a workable shape, one that pleases me enough to keep working on it at home. And last night I printed out a revised version of my poetry manuscript. The work feels stronger than the version I sent to contests all last year, and it looks beautiful, printed on the rented laser printer. So I leave having done what I set out to do.

Yesterday, as I printed out my poems, I remembered the first one I ever published. I wrote "First Storm" when I was fifteen. I can still feel the moment of its conception. It is dark, early evening, March or early April. I stand just outside the French doors, in front of the glassed-in porch. I am watching a thunderstorm. My sick mother, my oblivious father, my squabbling little sisters inhabit a different world. Only I know the power of this moment. A screen of evergreens shields me from the rain that pelts the sidewalk, rushes down the potholed street, but I hear the crack of lightning, see the sky light up like day. I taste ozone in the air; smell the earth as it opens, the soil preparing to welcome seed.

I rush to my third-floor room; write down what I've seen, what I feel. A few days later, I show it to Miss Cathon at Carnegie Library. I've known Miss Cathon since I was a little girl waiting in the children's room for my parents to finish their grocery shopping and come to pick me up. She has gray hair, a pronounced hunchback. Our old housemate Sara's lover, Liz, once told me that Miss Cathon had a formidable reputation among librarians. John Hersey used her as the model for an important character in his novel *The Child Buyer.* But when I am fifteen, I know only that she likes to see what I write. She sends "First Storm" to *The Horn Book,* the professional journal for children's librarians. By the time they publish the poem, it is 1961. I am a high-school junior. *The Horn Book* sends me a check for five dollars. My father takes the check to work, to copy it on one of those new Xerox machines.

I wrote "First Storm" in 1960. I had been writing poems for years. I still have the lined copy book into which I inked my best poems, in a loopy child's script. On the mottled brown, shiny-paper cover, I titled the book: "My Poems, JLS."

I wrote "First Storm" in 1960. I was fifteen. And then I froze. I didn't write another poem until 1986.

Selective Attention

Saturday evening, April 26, 1986

It feels like the first night of summer. Very hot. Stu is randy; he actually changed the sheets on the porch (putting on the polyester "satin") and tried to lure me to bed with a bear hug. But I am exhausted from four and a half hours of sleep last night, talking to Santoro and Carol Madsen, and doing a lot of outdoor work today. And I am planning to get up early tomorrow for a long bike ride with Bill, Linda, and the kids. So I turned him down— feeling obligated and rejecting, ergo a "bad wife."

Santoro was a disappointment. He was supportive but patronizing with Helen and, I think, left her (and me) with a sense that he might not be able to help Stu even if Stu went in to see him.

Carol Madsen encouraged me to try to make the marriage work. I thought this was strange for a divorce lawyer. But I decided that I am going to make a decision on my mother's birthday, June 1, about whether I'm leaving this summer or staying. From now until June 1, I will try to be pleasant, upbeat: to encourage positive conversations, not destructive ones. (That means only in neutral territory, before ten o'clock.) On June 1, I'm making my decision based on a number of variables including: resumption of sex relations; sharing a bedroom; Stu's willingness to deal with alcohol problems; my general feelings about how things have gone, day-to-day (and I'm going to keep score on a day-to-day basis); my feelings of anger toward Stu; Stu's attempts to control me and others; and finally (for now, anyway), Stu's changes in behavior around the house and with the kids. Today he suggested that he could go shopping with them to buy shorts.

Put the boat hoist in today and ate outside: brats and potato salad.

When I got home from Norcroft a few days ago, I found a card from a man I've flirted with, off and on, for most of the past ten years. We met through work. He lives thousands of miles away. Once, not long after the purple and yellow faded from my eye, he came to Madison to work on a radio project. We were in my car, on the way to a meeting. I had to stop by my house to pick something up. I invited him in to see my brand-new life. He refused, waited in the car. But after he left Madison, he kept up a correspondence, sending clippings, notes, unprintable limericks, occasional letters, a tape he thought Eli might like.

Stu used to bully me: "Who will love you the way I do?" Who indeed? In ten years, I have had one flirtation and two lovers. One lover, really, unless you count a friend's ex-husband who couldn't get it up. One long-distance affair that lasted three nights, maybe four.

Once I asked Paul Bergeson how long he thought it would take for me to find another man. He looked at me speculatively. I said, "Tune in, in two or three years."

"No," he said, "I don't think it will take that long."

Stu knew better.

Celibacy, it turns out, is not so difficult. You just ignore sex, as much as possible. You focus on something else.

Sunday, April 27, 1986

Stu, rejected last night, turned brutal and abusive. When I went downstairs this morning, trying to be loving and demonstrative, he practically took my head off. In his hostility, brutality, anger, he said, "I've never read your journal, but I might burn it. You have a habit to break."

It didn't help matters that he knew I was about to ride around Lake Monona with David, Eli, and the Langes. And later at dinner, when I tried to describe how beautiful the bike ride was—all the bulbs and the fruit and nut trees at their peak bloom—he simply refused to let me talk about it. I shut up. He asked me a question to which I could only reply with more about the bike trip—and he bore into me, interrupting and being very nasty. I picked up my plate and fork and left the deck. I went into the kitchen to finish eating. Eli followed me, and David came in shortly after. I am not interested in being brutalized, even in conversation.

I could write much more, but it hardly seems worth it. I talked with Dad and Charlotte this evening and told them I would be making a decision in early June.

Today it is hard to imagine a decision other than to leave.

※

I am not happy to be back in Madison, reentering my ordinary life. The never-ending work and lack of time for writing overwhelms me. Yesterday I put up storm windows, paid bills, restocked the fridge and the pantry, but I didn't finish unpacking. I never even managed to empty the dishwasher.

I did go for a walk. At Hoyt Park, three little boys, eight or nine years old, marched single file through the woods. The leader sang, "The bear went over the mountain . . . Sound off!" His troops called out: "One." "Two." "The bear went over the mountain . . ." "One." "Two." They stopped when they saw me, ducked behind the crest of the hill. I continued up the road and arrived at the overlook about the same time they emerged from the woods. The leader opened his khaki knapsack and handed out Fig Newtons. I tried not to scare them off: looked straight out over the city, pretended they weren't there. The boys hoisted themselves up to the stone wall and sat, dangling their legs, looking over the leafless trees at the sprawling expanse of Hilldale Mall; the houses set on tidy plots; the state office building where, in a few years, they will take their driving tests. The city sparkled in the sun. "This is so cool," one of them said, and the other two agreed.

Tears welled in my eyes. I thought of Eli and David, about the age of these boys, just after we moved off the lake. They used to explore the "woods" near our new home, a scraggle of second- or third-growth oak, maple, and beech. What did they call the secret hollow where David once told me his runaway friend had taken up residence? Nearby, someone had rigged a rope from a tree branch so it could swing out over a gully. I have a vague memory of David, Eli, other kids running back to our house, blood running from Eli's nose, or was it his mouth? Did we go to the emergency room? You would think this would be seared into my brain. But I was working, I was shopping, Helen was coming for dinner, I was going to school conferences, taking the kids to soccer. . . . Taking care of so much.

The boys in Hoyt Park made me cry for the past I no longer remember, for the little boys who grew up. And for me. Now I take care of myself.

❦

Wednesday evening, April 30, 1986

Tonight Stu proposed a family activity: "Each of us should choose a bird to find in a particular habitat and go for weekly bird hunts. And since your schedule is so tight, I'm willing to sail only on Saturday *or* Sunday. We can use the other day to look for birds."

"I can find time for canoe trips or hikes during the week," I assured him.

But I don't like the birding aspect very much. Why do we have to make up excuses or rationalizations to be together? Or maybe I am annoyed because Stu can identify a lot of birds and I can't. Still, it seems petty to argue with something that looks so much like concession. I've been upset for a long time because he spends so much time on the boat.

❦

I walk to work along an abandoned railroad spur. Houses back onto the right-of-way. People have planted gardens where flat land borders the tracks, but mostly, steep embankments slope up to the back-yards. I walk below the houses through an urban woodland, like a long, skinny park full of high weeds and scrubby trees.

A few hundred miles, one or two degrees of latitude, separate Madison from the North Shore of Lake Superior. Coming south has been like winding the season back a couple of weeks. Bleak November, the bare black-and-brown that comes before the snow, hasn't quite settled in. A few days ago, I looked for birds along the tracks. I focused my eyes and ears.

Immediately, the ragged caw of a crow. A chickadee swooped past; I saw its black cap, the white feathers in its tail. In the trees, a twittering, hard to hear against the distant traffic noise. Sparrows? Or chattering squirrels? In the bushes, some dull-colored, robin-sized birds. So many birds! Usually, when I walk to work, I don't see the birds at all. I am thinking of other things, the program I'm producing, what I'll ask in an interview. I'm remembering that I want to call the phone company, to disconnect call waiting. I'm looking at the ground, watching for dog shit and mud.

"Selective attention" we call this.

Once, years ago, I met Paul Bergeson walking his golden retriever along the railroad track. He didn't see me at first; he was looking up at the trees. I had stopped therapy, but Paul remained with me, a little homunculus residing in my brain, helping me figure out what I felt and what I should do about it. When he appeared on the tracks, life-size, gazing into the trees, he was trying to identify the evergreens, to separate white spruce from red, black from Norway, on the basis of shape, cones, bark, and needle length. Paul told me he'd been reading Goethe. "Goethe knew the importance of minute detail."

I couldn't have cared less about detail. I wanted Paul to pay attention to me.

※

Thursday evening, May 1, 1986

One month and counting. Woke up this morning knowing what bothers me about Stu's great concession, his willingness to give up one of the sailboat racing series. It's a trap, and a rather crude (if perhaps subconscious) trap at that. Where would I be if I encouraged him to give up sailing, even one day a week? I could *never* live down the consequences!

Tonight Stu dropped on my desk his newly revised asset sheet, which separates my assets from his. But the spreadsheet he gave me showed only my assets and our joint assets. When I asked for a copy of the spreadsheet with his assets, I got hostility rampant. "See a lawyer," he said.

This afternoon B said, "It's quite clear that Stu is willing to love you so long as you are willing to let him guide you." For example, I can have his love (and he will spend the day with me and the kids) if he can be the guide and we can find birds. But I don't want a guide; I don't need a guide. Or rather, I need a guide whom I can respect, whom I trust, who respects me. And I don't get that from Stu. All I get is his desire to exercise authority. His "God complex," as B called it. "He thinks he's better than everybody else, so he can be everybody's leader and guide."

But it's terribly easy to be taken in by Stu's charm; by his sense of command when he's in control. Helen was taken in by it on Tuesday when Stu asked her out to lunch. She was delighted that he wanted to talk. But then he showed up thirty or forty minutes late and took her to a crowded, noisy burger joint where you can't have a decent conversation. Helen said, "I realized afterwards that it made me angry because I had the wool pulled over my eyes."

Friday evening, May 2, 1986

Spent most of the day working on the Sexuality tape for the *Marriage and the Family* course. Got home about three and had a thirty-seven-minute "conversation" with Stu. I told him about my June 1 deadline and demanded—yes!—that he change. He got very defensive and angry and refused to let me respond. I screamed, "Shut up and let me talk!"

"You talk too much," he said. Yes, and truth he doesn't like to hear. He was so stubborn, arrogant, controlling that I refrained (barely) from splashing hot coffee in his face, but as I started to lash out, he hit me, smashing my glasses across my nose, breaking the frames. I felt incredible rage, but then an amazing calmness. I drove to the optician, picked new frames, and decided I'd get contacts before I left Stu. Certain I would leave.

We had planned to take the kids out for dinner, but Stu refused to go.

He explained to David, "Judy hit me this afternoon during an argument, and I hit her back in self-defense. I don't want to sit across a table from her."

David and Eli asked where I got my new glasses. "Did you pay for them from the household account?" David asked.

Eli said, "If you had the number of one of Stu's accounts, you should have used it."

Too sophisticated for their own good.

After David, Eli, and I got back from the restaurant, we watched *Raiders of the Lost Ark* and sent the kids to bed; then, right there in the lake room, I stripped and we fucked on the couch. My initiative. Stu was surprised, but apparently pleased, though he said, "I got no emotional release." I feel in control and where I want to be. Not certain I will leave: maybe I've made my point and things will turn around. Stu made "a generous one-time offer": he will buy me contacts if I get them before June 1.

Is this what happens when I stop doubting myself? I felt that I was taking control away from Paul Bergeson, too—though I used his image to pull me through the evening.

⬦

My San Francisco ophthalmologist said I had the most amazing reason he'd ever heard for giving up contact lenses. I'd worn hard lenses for three or four years, long enough to change eye doctors, quit the phone company, start graduate school, get involved in the antiwar movement. Long enough to meet and move in with Stu. Long enough to discover the problem with the lenses: they changed the shape of my cornea. I couldn't take them off, put on a pair of glasses, and expect to be able to read or drive.

I could wear the lenses all day. I put them on as soon as I woke up and took them out the last thing before bed at night. But, as I told the ophthalmologist sometime in 1969, I worried about tear gas.

"Tear gas?" This was a new one on him.

"In demonstrations," I said. "I go to a lot of protests, and I'm afraid the cops might use tear gas to disperse the crowd." I couldn't just switch to glasses when I thought it might be politically prudent; it took my corneas too long to get back to their normal shape.

The ophthalmologist prescribed new glasses. The next time I saw him, he told me my case had amused a lot of his buddies at an ophthalmologists' convention.

I didn't say that I was willing to go back to glasses because I'd finally caught a man.

⊛

Sunday, May 4, 1986

This evening, Stu went by himself to the yacht club's spring banquet. The kids and I had pizza and pasta (cooking for only three will be difficult to get used to), then took a bike ride and ended up at the Ice Cream Shoppe. I felt very much like a single parent this weekend, especially tonight and Friday evening, when I took David and Eli out to eat. It's not my favorite feeling. I wonder if one grows into it?

⊛

When I came home after taking Eli to college, I sensed his absence in the house. It felt tangible, something in the density of the air, or the way sunlight moved across the living-room wall. The house felt qualitatively different than it had when the kids were away at camp, or visiting Stu in California. I could feel it, the absence, in the same way I used to feel Stu's angry presence pressing into every nook and cranny of the house on Lake Mendota.

You could say, I suppose, that it's all in the brain, this sense of Eli's absence, or of being crushed against the wall by Stu's malevolent presence, or of being a single parent, alone in the world with two young sons. But it has nothing to do with reason. It's deep in a primitive part of the brain, a part that harbors the sixth sense and third eye and second skin. The part that tells a wife that her husband is sleeping with someone else, that lets a mother know her child's mood when he's a thousand miles away.

The reasoning part of my brain tells me I can stay in my sweats, ignore the mess in the house, and write all day on Sunday because I have an empty nest. The reasoning part tells me that a man who stood five-eleven and weighed less than two hundred pounds could not possibly fill up every cubic inch of a four-thousand-square-foot house. The reasoning part allowed me to comprehend, long before I left Stu, how under certain conditions, being a single mother could be easier than being a married one.

The fall after Eli was born I pushed him in the carriage to pick up David at nursery school. We waited with other mothers and babies in a tiled hallway painted beige. One day a friend pointed out one of the waiting women as a paragon of motherhood. I knew this woman as the mother of a Down's syndrome child. But my friend said the child was only one of a dozen adopted and foster children the woman cared for and loved. Each child had a different physical or mental disability.

One day I got up the courage to approach this modern-day heroine. "How do you do it?" I asked her. "I only have two children, both completely healthy, and I can barely get through the day."

"It's easy," she said. "I don't have a husband." I must have looked astonished. "What I say, goes," she explained. "I don't have to discuss my decisions with anyone. And when the kids are finally in bed, my time is completely my own."

Tuesday evening, May 6, 1986

I asked B today for a devil's advocate view of what is going on. "What do you see?"

He said, "What impresses me is not your dominance, or your 'Jewish motherness'—all these things Stu sees in you—but rather your diffidence with regard to men." What he called "your unwillingness to make demands." He pointed out that I was even nervous about asking him to give me his reflections on my situation. "After all," he said, "you hired me. You'd be free to ask advice and make demands of a plumber. You should be free with me."

B insisted that "Stu's reaction to your slightest demands—his retreating, running off—is a little boy's reaction to a big overbearing Amazon mother. It doesn't have anything to do with you, Judy." In fact, he repeated that twice. He said that he's come to think that Stu is very weak and "brittle" in his control. Very easily threatened by what B thought were really relatively minor statements or demands.

When I got home, Stu showed me two wire in-baskets—"his" and "hers"—on the bookshelf in the hall between his study and the bedroom. "With this setup we can control each other's communications," he explained. "We can write each other letters and read them at our leisure. I don't want you to leave any more of your notes—splat!—on my desk."

Thursday, May 8, 1986, David's birthday, 1:00 A.M.

Just got off the phone after a wonderful hour-and-a-half-long phone conversation with Rachel. I had just read Stu's nine-page response (deposited in my in-basket) to my explanation of how I will decide whether to stay or leave. A ludicrous document. Stu turned my criteria into "our strategies" for staying together. We are going to make the decision jointly; that's his tone.

The most incredible part is his rejection of sociologist Sara McLanahan's equation of intimacy and vulnerability in the sexuality lecture I've been editing. (I thought the tape was so interesting that I gave it to Stu to listen to a few days ago.) He wrote, "I heard Sara yesterday equate being intimate with being vulnerable. I emphatically reject this idea. This is an anachronistic 'women's notion.' If we don't explicitly reject our protracted attempts to make ourselves mentally (emotionally) vulnerable to each other, we have no hope."

I don't even want to respond. I don't have anything to say, except that if that's the way he feels, I might as well buy a house tomorrow, if I possibly can.

I feel remarkably good and in control. Rachel said I was like Halley's Comet.

"What do you mean?"

144

"It seems like you've been far away, in a depression, for a long time, and now you're turning a corner and coming back."

❦

One of the women who was at Norcroft has sent a Christmas card and enclosed a snapshot of me. I am standing in Norcroft's pine-paneled kitchen, at the cutting board, wearing my blue sweatpants, red fleece pullover, white socks and slippers. I have been cutting vegetables; you can see a sliced red onion and the half-rounds of a yellow summer squash on the board. My back is toward the camera, and I have partly turned to face Elise, who has just called my name. I have taken off my reading glasses, and I'm holding them, along with the knife, in my right hand.

I wear a wide grin. I have no bags under my eyes. I glow like the golden knotty pine.

❦

Thursday evening, May 8

It has been a long time since I felt as wonderful as I did most of today. Went to work in the morning to revise a grant application, and just felt positive. Certain that we would divorce; certain that we could be friends and co-parents; certain that we would not be lovers again. I felt that I was flying.

After school Stu took David for a haircut. Eli and I wrapped presents; then I took him to soccer and, later, to Helen's for David's birthday dinner. I was flying high until the party, when Stu was quite belligerent (on two Jack Daniel's) and took several very pointed swipes at me. For instance, he gave me a bouquet of flowers when I got to Helen's. I was touched, and Helen was clearly impressed. Then I read the card: "Congratulations on your new baby." I knew at once that the gift was a dig. Stu was getting back at me for telling him B thinks he acts like a child with a big demanding mommy.

The whole thing pissed me off and brought me down—and also made me determined not to drag things out until June, because I'm afraid the possibility of friendship will disappear if we interact repeatedly as we did

145

at Helen's. So after the kids went to bed, I suggested we talk and proposed that we move toward separation and/or divorce instead of reconciliation. I thought I was quite clear about this; in fact, I thought that I would be able to remember that we'd made the decision to divorce on David's birthday. But although Stu seemed to agree, he could not let me make the decision. He kept following me around the house with questions and comments, mostly focused on reconciliation.

"I think we should get involved in some sort of political campaign as a family," he suggested. "It would be a way of turning our anger outward. And it has a precedent, since we met doing politics."

But at the same time he was suggesting "togetherness cures," he got very nasty. "You're going to have to fight for every penny," he told me. And he suggested that we make a complete inventory of our furniture and other property.

He is ambivalent. I am not.

⌖

Saturday evening, May 10, 1986

After dinner, Stu had about three of his bourbons in a row and began to play the "Is There Any Hope?" theme. After I bedded Eli down, I went into Stu's study to talk. The notion finally registered on him that I really was going to leave and didn't think there was any hope. He freaked out, going into a screaming frenzy fueled by lack of sleep and too much to drink. Eli crept to the study door to listen.

"Hello. What are you doing?" I asked.

"You said I shouldn't worry about divorce, and now Stu is yelling, 'I want a divorce,'" Eli said. I put him back to bed and went to pick David up from a party.

When I got back, Stu attacked me with hugs, pleading, "Come to bed with me." We made love; he was hard, demanding, needy. I stayed the night on the porch; in the morning, Stu got up and left, slamming the door.

⌖

Sunday evening, May 11, 1986

Bad scene when Helen came for her Mother's-Day-and-birthday dinner and for the "three-way talk" to which Stu had invited her. In the middle of dinner, Stu tried to introduce his current "solution" to our problems— CPC (which stands for Courtesy Politeness Civility).

"I don't think that the dinner table is the appropriate place to deal with this particular agenda," I objected. But Stu continued to command virtually all the conversation at the table, instructing Helen on Indonesian politics, David and Eli on table manners, . . . whatever.

After dinner, we really got into it. Stu gave Helen an impassioned monologue about the course of our relationship, my diffidence and dependence on him, and my need to overcome the diffidence and become strong and assertive.

"You know, you can help me," I said. "You could encourage me to be assertive instead of retreating from me when I am."

He called up the new bogeyman. "You're asking me to act like your sweet, ineffective Poppy," he said. "I won't have it. I won't let you push me around the way Nana pushed him around."

In his eyes, I am an ogre ready to devour him if he accedes to my smallest "demand."

☙

By the time Stu met my grandparents, they lived in Florida. Poppy retired in the early 1960s from his job selling flashlights and transistor radios; before I graduated from college, they moved to a small apartment on Bay Drive in Miami Beach. The building was a short walk from the fancy hotel where Nana's brother Al and his wife Frances spent the winters. Poppy hated Florida. He wrote me a funny letter about his neighbors, bored old men and gossipy *yentas* whose days revolved around the mailman's visits. Before the mail arrived, they waited eagerly, sitting in their deck chairs out by the pool or hanging around the lobby, discussing who was due for a letter from a child or grandchild. When the mail came, they rushed to retrieve it and then hurried back to their apartments, carrying little stacks of bills and bank statements. Later in the afternoon, they gathered around the pool again, lying about the letters they said they'd received from loved ones up North. Sunday, Poppy reported, was a special misery: no mail, nothing to live for. And every day, the unending, ungodly heat.

"Only my love for your dear Nana," he wrote, "keeps me sweltering in this sun."

Stu and I arrived at Bay Drive in early February 1973, a few months after our marriage. We'd driven the van straight from Madison, stopping only to tour the Jack Daniel's distillery in Lynchburg, Tennessee. I drove most of the way from Atlanta to Miami Beach; Stu had a bad cold and the trip south did not improve his health. He dropped me off at Nana and Poppy's apartment, staying only long enough to have supper, and then left to crash with his aunt Martha, who wintered in Coconut Grove.

✍

Monday, May 12, 1986

Tonight, I agreed to discuss the six paragraphs on sex or, as Stu put it, "Touching Our Bodies," in his nine-page missive. (He wrote that he wasn't much interested in cuddling. "Climaxes, then cuddles," he insisted. He proposed that we set up a "cumlog," a notebook divided into sections where we'd each record our orgasms, the date and approximate time, and whether we "came" together or by masturbating. Then he proposed that we set a goal for increasing my orgasms and that we accomplish this goal not by having intercourse, but by making appointments to masturbate in front of each other, with me always going first!)

"I'm willing to work on improving our sex life," I told him. "But your suggestions are demeaning, and they ignore my emotional needs. I'm much less interested in whether I have an orgasm than I am in feeling close, loved, taken care of. Cuddling does that for me."

We talked, making no progress, for about an hour and a half. Stu kept insisting that he is changing. "I even hugged Eli yesterday," he said, very proud.

When we'd run out of words, Stu hugged me and asked, "Are you angrier now than you were before we starting talking?"

"Yes."

"Do you feel more vulnerable?"

"Yes."

He felt me up, asked for a kiss, had me cop a feel of his hard-on. "We don't need to do more. It's OK to be tired." So cuddling is now OK? This represents how he has changed?

Am I cute when I'm angry?

I hung out with Nana and Poppy for a week, window shopping in thrift shops, eating in fast-food restaurants, observing the nasty clash of loud, demanding, elderly New York Jews with the tired, poorly paid, and often rude blacks and Puerto Ricans who waited tables, bussed dishes, made change, and stocked the shelves in grocery stores. Nana's friends had all moved to Florida or spent winters there. She said she sometimes felt as though she had never lived in The Bronx. To me, Miami Beach seemed a lot like a warm and humid Bronx, trimmed with palm fronds and painted in pastels. I didn't like it. I wondered whether Poppy was the only transplanted New Yorker who saw Florida as I did, a Jewish geriatric ward, a place where old people killed time while they hung around waiting to die.

Eventually, Stu said he was well enough to see me, and I took the city bus—three buses, actually—down to Martha's bungalow. Coconut Grove seemed rich, tidy, quiet; not at all like The Bronx. Stu and I wandered through Fairchild Botanical Gardens, admiring the cycads, stealing a taste of ripe star-shaped fruit with translucent yellow skin that had fallen from a tree. A day or two later, we drove up to Nana and Poppy's, collected my suitcase, and left for the Florida Keys.

Later in the month, we went back to Miami and flopped in a ten-dollar-a-night motel. We had dinner one night with Nana and Poppy and Aunt Frances and Uncle Al at the Alamac Hotel which, Al assured us, "used to be real high class." We took Nana and Poppy out to dinner at McDonald's—that's where they insisted they

149

wanted to eat—and spent an evening with them, watching television and washing our clothes. A few days later, Nana made a birthday dinner for Stu: steak and birthday cake and cheap champagne.

I recorded all these details in the log I kept the year we traveled in the van: typed, single-spaced pages snapped into a green vinyl notebook. The log records facts: where we went, what we saw, what we did. It is remarkable mostly for the complete absence of comments about my feelings. I remember feeling great anger at Stu for disappearing to Martha's, but it's not in the log. I remember Nana's bewildered questions: what's wrong with Stu? Doesn't he want to stay with us? I remember being very upset because he didn't call me from his aunt Martha's house. Was he too sick to use the phone?

The details I did record are revealing. I don't remember taking three city buses to Coconut Grove, but now I wonder why Stu didn't come to pick me up in Miami Beach.

How much time did Stu actually spend with Poppy? A couple of hours when Nana and I went to a luncheon at the Montmartre Hotel, a fundraiser sponsored by the Ladies' Auxiliary of the Sunshine Lodge, Knights of Pythias. A supper at McDonald's, a supper at the once-fine Alamac, the birthday supper Nana made for him.

My grandfather died in 1978. That birthday dinner in 1973 was the last Stu saw of the man he scorned as "sweet, ineffective Poppy."

❀

Tuesday evening, May 13, 1986

With B today, began to consider why I feel one can't make the same sorts of demands in a family that one would make in business.

"This is interesting," he said, "because this diffidence is your problem, not Stu's. Why does it make you so uneasy to set demands with consequences on Stu?"

I don't know, but it makes me so uneasy that my eye tics when I act on the consequences—when I make appointments with lawyers or Realtors or financial planners.

"Do you think your demands are extreme?" B asked.

I had great difficulty thinking of anything that Stu might find less threatening than my demand that either we see a marriage counselor or he get some psychological help. Of course, this is an enormous demand, but he seems to think even my smallest requests are enormous demands. And suddenly I was certain that he needs to respond to this demand if I'm going to stay. Unless he's willing to meet a *big* demand like this, I don't have any confidence that we'd be able to compromise on all of the other issues in our marriage.

After my session with B, I talked with Stu about getting outside help.

"Why can't we just talk to our friends?" Stu wanted to know. "Why can't we talk to the Langes?"

"A marriage counselor can provide objectivity and experience that none of our friends could offer," I said. "You know, even you agree that professionals have something to offer. Paul Bergeson was the one who called me 'diffident,' and you think that's very important."

Suddenly, Stu slammed his fist on the wall, hard. If it had been wallboard instead of plaster, he'd have gone right through.

"All right. I'll see a marriage counselor."

I was taken aback and not very pleased.

"You see, I do acquiesce to your demands," he said. "Since I'm in such an obliging mood, do you have any other demands? What other biggies can you come up with?"

All I could think of on the spur of the moment was a monthlong trek in Nepal.

"OK. You go to Nepal for a month in the fall and go someplace warm with me for two weeks in February. I'll exchange that for marriage counseling."

"I want to take a vacation with David and Eli in August," I said.

"How about circumnavigating Lake Superior?" Stu asked. "And how about coming to Manitowoc with me next weekend?" (There's a motel on the shore of Lake Michigan he thinks would be great for a romantic tryst.) "I'll give up sailing to be with you."

All of this dizzied me and made me uncomfortable and suspicious.

And I think I still want out, but may now be trapped by my own demands.

151

I'm still close to Stu's mother. It's not just that Helen is David and Eli's grandmother; she and I love and respect each other. In the two or three weeks since I came back from Norcroft, I've seen her several times. Yesterday the Pro Arte Quartet played Beethoven and Schubert at the Elvehjem Museum. It was cold and rainy; the concert seemed like a good place to spend a Sunday afternoon. I called Helen to see if she wanted to join me, and she was enthusiastic. But a few hours later, when I picked her up, she'd forgotten where we were going. "We're going to a concert at the Elvehjem," I reminded her.

Fifteen minutes later, sitting in the Brittingham Gallery, surrounded by Old Masters, she said, "I'm confused. I don't know where we are."

Helen has probably been in the Elvehjem hundreds of times. She's an art lover and a collector; she was a good friend of the professor responsible for getting the university to house its collection properly in a modern teaching museum. But something has attacked her memory. The last time I took her to the Elvehjem, about a year ago, she disappeared. We were visiting an exhibit of late-nineteenth- and early-twentieth-century Russian Jewish art. She lost interest quickly, and I saw her leave the gallery. I figured she had gone to see her favorites in the permanent collection. But when I looked for her, a half hour later, she was nowhere to be found. I talked to the guard at the security desk. Could he see an elderly woman with a cane in any of the monitors? He said he'd seen her a short while before, but now, he assured me, she'd left the galleries. I checked the ladies' room, the gift shop. She wasn't there. Maybe she was having a cigarette, waiting for me outside. I checked the back door. Not there. I ran around to the front entrance. No Helen. I happened to look down University Avenue, toward the bus stop—and there she stood, talking to a graduate student. I rushed up to her.

"I'm glad I found you before the bus came!" I said.

"So am I," she agreed.

"I hope you don't think I would bring you to the Elvehjem and then abandon you!"

"Well," Helen said, "I didn't know. I think I was confused."

Yesterday, at intermission, she studied the nearest oil, a luminous Christ child in the center of a dark, velvety canvas. "This room seems so familiar," she said. "I think I've been here before. But I don't know where I am."

✿

Wednesday evening, May 14, 1986

Just walked very rapidly around Tenney Park to ease the knot in the pit of my stomach I felt as bad as any time in the past five months. I really had managed to convince myself that I had demanded too much—that Stu's extreme hostility today was a consequence of too severe an assault on his tender ego and that I was a bad person. On the walk, I decided that I was simply uneasy because I'd made such a big demand. In fact, I felt like I did when I created the non-Seder: guilty and afraid. And I realized that Stu responded with incredible hostility because he—in his words—"acceded" to my "demands." He has just made quite clear that he is not *willing* to see a marriage counselor; he has simply acquiesced.

"You'll pay 100 percent of this indulgence," he said.

When I told him that I would not go to a marriage counselor under those conditions, he said, "You tell Helen." I said I would, and he suddenly began pleading with me to "be reasonable." Mommy is quite an ally against the widdle boy.

✿

Helen's short-term memory began to fail several years ago. But not long before Eli left for college, I realized her long-term memory was going too. She had come for dinner.

"New York is a wonderful place," she told Eli, suddenly animated. "I lived there, all over the city, for four or five years in the 1930s."

Eli nodded. Helen had talked about her years as a New York

153

working girl every time we'd seen her in the months since he'd decided to go to Columbia.

I thought I could get her to tell a different story. "You lived in New York later, too, didn't you?" I prompted. "During the war, when Richard was in the Navy?"

Helen frowned slightly and shook her head.

"I don't remember where he was stationed," I said, "but you told me he taught at a Navy school somewhere near New York."

"He did?"

"And you and Stu went to live in Manhattan."

"I'm puzzled," she said. "I don't know."

"You used to tell me how you and Stu looked for an apartment to sublet." Her puzzled expression vanished. She looked eager, interested. She wanted to hear about this.

"You said you'd been looking all over for apartments." I launched into one of Helen's favorite stories about Stu's intelligence and sensitivity as a little boy. "During the war sublets were very hard to find. It was 1943. Stu was only four years old. Finally you heard about an apartment owned by an elderly woman, and you and Stu went to see it. It was full of antiques and delicate bric-a-brac. You said that Stu sat very still while you talked with the woman. He was very quiet and polite. And then, after you left the apartment, he was very solemn. 'Mother,' he said, 'I don't think we would be happy here.'"

Helen laughed as though she'd never heard the story before.

⊛

Thursday evening, May 15, 1986

David's teacher took me aside when she saw me this afternoon and said that David (who has been pretty good at home) is completely out of hand at school, and she is having to play police. I explained that Stu and I are having problems — and that they're pretty intense right now. Perhaps this will help somewhat. I also suggested to David that there are better ways of dealing with his anger at us than destroying himself at school and suggested he could talk with a therapist or even with a friend whose parents separated a few years ago.

When I tried to talk with Stu about David's problems, he said, "David would be fine if you'd get off his case. You just nag him too much about homework."

⊛

David was our miner's canary—a child who responded with great sensitivity to the poisonous family atmosphere.

Every fall, from the time he started nursery school, we'd get the same phone call. His new teacher would report problem behavior. She would ask, is this a problem child?

I didn't think so. Challenging, yes. Creative, certainly. But not a problem if you knew how to handle him.

When I was pregnant with David, Stu and I wanted a bright, inquisitive kid who took nothing on faith. We bought the unborn baby a metal political button with a pin on the back and a straightforward message: Question Authority. We stuck the button up in the nursery, which I had decorated with a hand-painted chest, a wicker bassinet lined with denim and lace, and handmade rainbow curtains. We took the button back when David was a year or two old. He'd taken the message to heart.

As the mothers who drove the nursery school car pool discovered, David tested every grown-up who tried to tell him what to do. He had a built-in shit detector. If a grown-up was inconsistent or unsure of herself or tried to buy his cooperation, David rebelled. He responded best to adults who were willing to explain why he should act a particular way.

"Tell him that if he makes too much noise, you'll stop," I told a car-pool mother. "Tell him you can't concentrate when he's yelling, and it's too dangerous to drive."

She was appalled. "But what if it doesn't work?"

"Pull over to the curb and stop. Say you'll start again when you think it's safe."

155

At first, she wouldn't follow my suggestion. Instead, she tried rewards for good behavior. David got louder and louder. She played books-on-tape. No one could hear them. David got the other kids to join his high-volume chorus. She tried yelling at all of them. Nothing worked. She complained of headaches every time she drove. After a couple of weeks, she gave up. She parked the car three times in one ten-minute trip. The third time David told the kids, "Shut up, or we'll never get home."

I laughed when I heard the story. I prided myself on knowing how to handle my difficult child. For years, I brushed aside his teachers' concerns. I knew David wasn't a problem. It took me much too long to understand that Stu and I were.

※

Saturday, May 17, 1986

Rainy all day; no question of having David's birthday party at a county park. Instead, seven eleven-year-old boys are crashing around on the third floor, after an afternoon and evening of bottle rockets, movies on the VCR, dinner at McDonald's.

Woke up this morning understanding why I am depressed by this marriage counselor business. It fits right into the old pattern: when Stu acquiesces to my demand, he trashes me and demeans my point of view. He has been telling me that I am being sucked into a "new thing," taken in by "the doctors of mind control." This is not much different than his increasing criticism of my abilities as a mother (I bug David about homework too much—that's why he's upset in school; I make too many demands of Eli, and he should not have to take piano lessons anymore) as he increases his involvement with the kids. Or his attacks on my menu planning and ideas about nutrition as he takes over the shopping and some cooking. I am left with no areas in which my ideas are respected and my authority is unchallenged.

B said on Tuesday, "You don't have the fundamental tools necessary to be married: the conviction that you can make demands and bring consequences to bear within a domestic relationship." But when I do make demands and they are accepted, the ground shifts so that I no longer have the authority to bring the consequences to bear. Or perhaps I just *feel* that way. I need to let Stu know that simply doing what I ask is not enough. He needs to do what I ask without undermining my authority to continue acting in that realm of our lives.

※

Back to writing again after a wonderful Thanksgiving vacation, a weeklong trip to the east coast to see David and Eli in what has become their natural habitat. The prospect of the trip filled me with joy; intensified, really, the joy I have felt for the past two months, starting in early October when I arrived at Norcroft. And the euphoria continued in New York. The sky was clear, the air crisp, the city thrilling in its noise and bustle. I spent hours at the New York Public Library, looking at an exhibit called *The Hand of the Poet*. The room was full of manuscript drafts of work by Elizabeth Bishop, Adrienne Rich, Marianne Moore, Robert Lowell, E.E. Cummings. . . . I don't know which was more affirming, to study the work in the glass cases or to feel the presence of dozens of others in the room, studying the work. To see: this is what poets do, these crossed out words, these lines scratched on whatever napkin or newspaper came to hand; this is what I do; I am a poet, though of course not nearly so good a poet as these. Or to know: these people who've passed the marble lions and climbed all the way up to the third floor, these are all lovers of poetry.

※

Tuesday, May 20, 1986

Last night, I asked Stu for his perceptions of the past few days. And the realization came crashing in that I have been deluding myself, thinking that, because he allowed me into his bed one night and fucked me twice and said he'd see a marriage counselor, things were much better and I could/ should stay. He was hostile, overbearing, demeaning of my sexuality. Barely allowing me to get a word in edgewise, he told me, "I have nothing but scorn for your idea that a third party has the potential to help us, but I'll give it my best" (surely a contradiction in terms).

I felt quite murderous.

Today, a helpful session with B. He told me a proverb about the mountain that labored mightily and produced—a mouse. We talked about why saying "no" to Stu (who, like the mountain, labored mightily, but produced a mouse) might make me feel like a bad girl. That is, why do I struggle so against my instincts to leave, feeling that it would be terrible to hurt him? Perhaps because I really do want to hurt him: to kill him. These are very similar feelings to those I had (have?) about Mother: terrible to hurt such a weak person, but wanting terribly to make her suffer as much as I did, or do.

I told B about a dream in which Stu appeared, his normal shape and size, but with tiny little feet, teetering in ridiculous little high-heeled shoes. I don't like to think of him as helpless, weak, female, someone I can blow over with one breath. But that *is* how he appears to me, and I guess to B, too, who asked me some sharp questions about Stu's behavior just before I left: "Does he have a weapon? Does he have a history of psychosis? Have you ever feared that he would physically harm you?"

⊛

Those questions startled me. What was B thinking? Stu didn't own a gun. He'd never been psychotic.

Had I ever feared that Stu would harm me physically? He'd slapped me around, more than once. His ice cube tray attack sent me to the emergency room. He knocked off my glasses and broke them. I didn't like this stuff when it happened. But it didn't happen very often. And really, it was never serious. I was puzzled by B's questions. Why was he asking? What did he expect?

Was I afraid of Stu? Not really, I told B. And I told myself, *I'm not a battered wife.*

Tokens of Love

Thursday, May 22, 1986

Pleasant enough day; if it weren't for the fact that we now communicate via in-baskets and written notes, live in separate parts of the house, and speak very formally to each other, one might almost think Stu and I were getting along quite well. He has now assumed a very paternalistic attitude toward me. He wrote Bill Lange a letter chastising him for inviting me to join Lange-ian grasshopper activities last weekend and telling Bill, "it is necessary to avoid tempting Judy with preplanned programs, because she has to learn to take the initiative to do things herself"! Stu left a copy on his desk in front of the computer terminal, presumably knowing I could not avoid seeing it when I turned the computer on. Whether Bill got the letter or not, he proceeded to invite me to bike with him, Linda, and some other friends tomorrow afternoon and have dinner with them afterward, and proposed canoeing Sunday afternoon.

Meanwhile, Stu wrote me a formal note yesterday, asking my weekend plans. When I wrote back saying I planned to clean the kids' rooms, he offered to help and immediately began to tell me how it should be done. I declined his offer of help. He proposed that we see an Altman movie; I proposed *The Color Purple;* we will do both. I suggested doing something as a family on Monday; he suggested canoeing. I said I planned a long bike ride with the kids one half-day or full day; fine with him. I said I would not sail or go to the after-race party. Et cetera. Ad nauseam. As I was brushing my teeth this evening, I realized that I don't care whether I ever sleep with him again; this in itself should be reason to leave.

A few nights ago, Hal, Julie, and I gathered in Helen's living room to trim her Christmas tree. I missed David and Eli, who used to love this ritual. They were still back East, finishing up their finals. While Julie sorted the ornaments and untangled chains of tiny packages wrapped in red and gold, Helen paced restlessly, silent and vacant eyed. When I told her that David and Eli would be home from college next week, she looked at me vaguely. "Where are they now?" she asked.

I have spent a good part of each of the last three weekends thoroughly cleaning their rooms. I sorted through all the clothes Eli has abandoned and bagged them for Goodwill. I threw out (with his permission) all the duplicates in his collection of plastic cups from tourist attractions and basketball stadiums. I dusted every surface. I vacuumed and made both beds. I have spent more time on the third floor this month, cleaning, than in the entire ten years since we moved here.

When I went east for Thanksgiving, I saw Eli's cramped dorm room. I stayed overnight in David's house, with its scruffy couches. Cereal boxes slid down a shelf hung deliberately slant; a crust of bread lingered under an overstuffed living-room chair. I know how oblivious they are to dirt and disorder. Why does it matter so much to me that their rooms be spic and span?

Saturday, May 24, 1986

Very heavy day. This morning I felt quite angry with Stu. I'd had no opportunity to talk with him about his letter to Bill or about his telling the kids, a few days ago, that he wanted to help clean up their rooms but I wouldn't let him. (He'd decided to "help" by telling me the "proper" way to do it, when he's never done the job himself.) Stu knew I was mad and thought he'd make everything lovey-dovey by preparing eggs Benedict for breakfast. But I had planned to go to Farmers' Market, and when I got up at eight-thirty, I went, with David and Eli. I knew this would disappoint Stu and probably piss him off, but I *had* told him on Thursday in a written response to his written question about my weekend plans, that I was going to the market. *And* I had no appetite for eggs Benedict or anything else he might serve up.

When I came back, I found a copy of a long letter from Helen in my in-basket, with a note from Stu suggesting that we could talk about it. (In the letter, among other things, Helen pleads with us to "be more fair minded" and "get rid of the basic premise that the Other is the offender") It was eleven o'clock, substantially before time for the afternoon sailboat race, so I said I was available to talk briefly about Helen's letter or anything else.

"No. Bill is here to help put in some pier sections."

So, OK.

A few minutes later, I tripped going up the stairs, fell, and knocked my head against the wall. That released a lot of tears. Stu looked into the bedroom to ask if I was all right, but he was about the last person I wanted near me. I was/am *not* all right precisely because of him. I am trapped in a situation that I cannot stand to stay in, and yet I am afraid of the consequences of leaving.

I took Eli to the Children's Museum to volunteer about twelve-thirty and then worked all afternoon cleaning the playroom, part of the time with David.

After the race—and an after-race party—Stu came home and offered to make dinner. I continued cleaning the kids' bedroom. About seven-thirty, when I came down to dinner on the deck, I realized he had hit the bottle hard while cooking steak.

"I think we should buy a video camera," he said, while we were eating.

"Really? Can we get it tomorrow?" David was very excited.

"Why are we suddenly getting a video camera?" I wanted to know.

"To record your angry face." Stu turned to David and Eli. "Don't you think that's a good idea?" He was belligerent, slurring his words, taunting.

David and Eli finished eating and left the table. Stu said, "Judy." I looked up—and he hit me, hard, on the face.

I was stunned. "Why did you do that?" I asked.

"To show affection," he said.

I went upstairs, shaking and trying to figure out what to do. He called up the stairs, "What are you doing? Bawling your head off and feeling sorry for yourself?"

"I'm packing," I said, and I did. Then I went out to round up the kids to go to the Ice Cream Shoppe. David was at the end of the pier, and when I went out to get him, Stu came out and blocked us from getting back to shore. The neighbors were out on their pier, watching the sun go down. We put on quite a show for them.

"Let me by," I kept saying, and Stu finally let David and me off the pier.

"Isn't Stu having ice cream?" Eli wanted to know, as we got into the car.

"Stu hit me," I said, "and I don't feel like being with him right now." Then at the Ice Cream Shoppe, I explained that I would not stay home tonight if I thought it was dangerous.

"Where would you go?" David asked.

"To Helen's. She's in Door County. Or to a motel. If you want to come with me, you can."

"If you go, I'm going too," Eli said.

David said, "I'll come with you if you think it's dangerous for me to stay with Stu. He tries not to drink, but sometimes he pigs out."

"He pigged out tonight," I said, and David agreed.

David also said, "You just think he's a drunken slob, but he has feelings too."

"I know he does, but I'm not going to allow myself to be put in a dangerous situation by his feelings. If he's so angry that he hits me, I have to get out of his way."

David said, "But you got angry a long time ago."

When we got home, Stu was gone. He left me an incoherent and almost illegible note that said he'd gone to see *The Color Purple*. Full of remorse: I love you, I want you, we can still make it, etc. Also full of anger that I didn't spend last night with him after he'd spent the evening at the movies groping around, feeling me up.

I suppose I should be overwhelmed that he's crazed because he's going to lose me, but I don't think it has so much to do with me as it does with him and his shaky ego. And my own survival instincts tell me that staying here, with him, is stupid. After he hit me, Paul Bergeson's questions poured in on me.

Will the man really turn psychotic if I leave?

⊛

This afternoon—possibly at this very moment—Eli is taking the last final exam of his first semester in college. David will pick him up tomorrow, and they will head west in David's car, a black Saab that has clocked 250,000 miles.

It makes me think of the start of Christmas vacation, my freshman year at Reed. A boar's head procession makes its way through a darkened dining room. Students and professors, all male, all wearing long, dark brown robes, slowly circle the tables. Four of them carry a roasted pig's head on a large plywood platter festooned with evergreens. The rest carry candles. They all chant, in harmony, "The boar's head as we understand / is the fairest feast in all the land . . ." I am wearing a black velvet dress with a full skirt, a fitted bodice, a low-cut scoop neck, and tight three-quarter sleeves. Nana bought me this dress at Alexander's when I was in junior high school. I think it is beautiful. It doesn't matter, really, whether it is or not; it is the only thing I have that is close to appropriate for a Christmas formal. It is the first time in months that I have worn anything but jeans.

Outside the dining room, wet snow, falling fast, has carpeted the city. Tom holds me by the arm of my turquoise corduroy coat as I negotiate the snow in nylons and heels. The coat, fully lined with white synthetic fleece, keeps me warm. But my shoes, it is clear, will be ruined. I am more concerned that the snow will delay my train. I am leaving for Pittsburgh tomorrow afternoon.

The train ride from Portland takes two and a half days. We creep through the Columbia River Gorge in the gathering dark. I make my supper from a grocery bag full of crackers and cheese, cookies and juice, apples and oranges. To sleep, I recline the seat, pull up a metal bar for my feet, and cover myself with my long, heavy coat.

In Denver the train stops for twenty minutes. The hairs freeze in my nostrils in the time it takes to walk the length of the platform. I

163

buy a candy bar and hurry back to my seat. That night, I eat my only dining car meal: rainbow trout and steamed potatoes. The table is draped with starched white linen, set with heavy silver plate. The window reflects my face back from the cold dark night.

I change trains in Chicago. The Broadway Limited approaches Pittsburgh in the middle of the night. The conductor wakes me. I collect my belongings. We slowly cross a river on a lattice-work railroad bridge. Up river, the steel mills flare.

Am I excited? I haven't been home since early July, when I left for Europe on an American Friends Service Committee travel seminar scholarship. I haven't seen my family since early September, when they met me at Idlewild Airport and took me to the Bronx. We stayed overnight with Nana and Poppy. The next day, they took me back to the airport and I flew off to Reed.

I am eager to tell my friends about the AFSC trip to Europe, about college, about my new, grown-up life. I want to see my sisters, Shelly especially.

Am I happy to be home? I don't remember.

I am happy to be off the train. I do remember that.

My father unlocks the front door. The house smells terrible. It smells of my mother's piss. It's dirty. Not just messy. Filthy. I see it, I smell it, as I have never imagined it. I've been away six months, and now I see how my family lives. I'm embarrassed to know that I brought high-school friends home to a house like this. But I remind myself that things could be much worse. I remember the AFSC work camps, apartments with holes in the walls and torn linoleum, cockroaches swarming a kitchen counter in a slum tenement.

✺

Sunday, May 25, 1986

Stu came home about twelve-thirty this morning and tried on three separate occasions to get me to make love, coming into the bedroom, hugging and kissing me tenderly, telling me he loves me. The first two times, I didn't respond—even when he lay down with me on our big bed for what must be the first time in two or three months. Finally, the third time, I said, "We can make love after we talk."

"I think that's our problem," he said, bitterly. "We always talk first and act later." But then he left me alone.

⊛

The house smells of hot oil and onions. I spent the day — Christmas — making *latkes* for my annual solstice party, which comes on the 29th this year. David and Eli spent the day at Hal and Julie's, with Stu, who has come to visit from California, and Helen, and Julie's kids.

I haven't really been part of the Kingsley Christmas since 1985. Some years, I'm invited to a scaled-down present exchange before or after Christmas day. But mostly, I'm left out. I can't say I miss the traditions: tenderloin on Christmas Eve, Christmas morning eggs-and-sausage followed by an interminable unwrapping of presents, one by one, so everyone can see what everyone else received.

Of course, the traditions have been modified. Helen hasn't been able to host brunches or dinners for several years. The cooking and entertaining have fallen to Julie and Hal. There are no small children, up since dawn, shaking every one of the brightly wrapped packages spilling out from under the tree. Helen no longer shops for presents or even wraps the few items others buy for her to give. She can't remember who has given her gifts, even just after she has opened them.

This year I sent a few wrapped packages to the Christmas festivities along with David and Eli. But I wanted to put something directly into Helen's hands. In a gift shop, I found a charming gray plush cat dressed in a lace-trimmed bonnet and velveteen gown. Helen is devoted to her pet cats, and long before she began to sink into dementia, she took a fancy to certain stuffed animals. The plush cat reminded me of Unicorn, a creature she bought years ago, ostensibly for David, and kept in her Door County bedroom. I imagined

Helen cuddling the cat, in her second childhood. I wrapped it and brought it to her house early this evening, after I knew she was back from the Kingsley Christmas festivities.

Mai, the woman who lives with Helen, answered the door. She was very happy to see me. She was worried about Helen, who sat on the couch in her bathrobe, looking exhausted and dazed.

"She doesn't seem right," Mai said. "I think she should see the doctor. I've been trying to reach Hal, but all I get is his message machine."

I didn't know where to find Hal, but I told Mai that Stu was with David and Eli, visiting an old friend. We looked up the phone number. Mai said she'd call after I left. I said I wouldn't stay long.

I gave Helen her present. She thanked me and set it aside. "I don't have anything for you," she said, upset.

I explained that she'd already given me a present. "I opened it at home."

"Let's see what Judy gave you," Mai said, and urged her to unwrap the package. Helen tore at the ribbon, but she couldn't untie the bow. Mai helped and took the paper off.

The gift made no impression. Helen barely looked at the cat before she set it aside. "I'm so tired," she said. "I think it's time for bed."

❀

Thursday, May 29, 1986

This afternoon, we saw a marriage counselor, Martin Shapiro. He was impassive, but clearheaded (at least he asked good questions and tried to get Stu to answer them). I was quite straightforward about wanting out. Stu described three issue areas (sexuality, treatment of kids and each other, work around the house) in which he thinks Martin can help us. But since we came home, we have been arguing about how to pay for counseling. The insurance I get through work only covers nine hundred dollars of psychotherapy charges per year for each family member. Martin suggested that, since I have already used my coverage seeing B, he could register Stu as the "patient" for insurance purposes. Stu absolutely refused to sign the necessary form.

After we left Martin's office, Stu tried to explain why. "We need to struggle against the idea that there's such a thing as a free lunch," he said.

"I think most people know there's no such thing as a free lunch," I said. "Most people would perceive a 'free lunch' as inheriting so much money that you can ignore your health insurance and pay out nine hundred dollars for marriage counseling without even blinking. I'm not willing to contribute anything toward counseling bills until we've used the insurance coverage that I've already worked hard to get."

"Fine. I'll pay the full nine hundred dollars myself."

"That's not acceptable either. So long as we're married, I'm affected by what you do with your assets, and it's a waste of money to throw away nine hundred dollars in insurance benefits and pay the bill yourself."

It's clearly an issue of control, and I'm not giving in. I'd rather get a divorce than go back to see Shapiro on Stu's nine hundred dollars.

In the late afternoon, Stu gave me a letter announcing that I have three presents coming. He gave me the first present at Helen's this evening, when we had dinner with Hal and Julie: a beautiful (and expensive, I'm sure) lapis lazuli necklace and matching earrings. The letter stressed that these are tokens of love (for "Darling Judy"). I wish they didn't feel quite so much like public bribes.

⊛

Helen was admitted to the hospital with internal bleeding a few hours after I left her on Christmas night. In the emergency room, she had a heart attack.

I don't like hospitals very much. But it is only Hodgkin's disease that has made them bearable at all. Before I was sick, every particle of my being rebelled against visiting hospitalized friends and relatives. I went because it was the proper thing to do. But I wanted to leave the minute I arrived. I could not stand the smells, the sounds, the sight of people in beds. It brought me too close to Mother. It brought back a fuzzy childhood memory: a darkened hallway, a smell of ether, of antiseptics, of fear. A visceral memory of my mother, hospitalized. Unless it is a memory of my own tonsillectomy.

When I had Hodgkin's, I went to the hospital to get better. I wouldn't say I liked the too-hot room where, behind a partition, an elderly woman lay dying. I didn't like the nurses who interrupted my sleep to check vital signs, the chemotherapy drip, the fumbling resident who couldn't pull a bone marrow sample and pierced my hipbone three times. I didn't like hospitals. But I finally understood that good things could happen in them. Patients could walk out, regain their health, resume ordinary lives.

Yesterday, when David, Eli, and I went to see Helen, the hospital again seemed a place of misery, cold, unfriendly, hostile. Helen lay very still, eyes closed, face obscured by an oxygen mask. "Take my hand," she whispered, and I recoiled from the gnarled, age-spotted claw she extended, the skin purple with subcutaneous bleeding. Someone had taped a red call-button to her palm. Eli moved past me and held her hand. He spoke to her. He understood her words, garbled and muffled by the oxygen mask. I prowled the room with David. We read all the signs, examined the posted Pain Scale, from 0 (none) to 10 (most intense). I saw the emergency button marked in big letters, Dr. Blue.

***

Friday, May 30, 1986

Up until one-thirty this morning, alternately talking, lying in bed, arguing with Stu—not my choice, any of these, but his. He was desperate to understand why I won't let him pay for marriage counseling. "My position has changed so much in only seventeen days," he whimpered. "I refused to see anyone at all, and now I'm willing to pay 100 percent. Why won't you let me?"

"I work so we can have health insurance," I said for the umpteenth time. "If you refuse to use it, it makes me feel as though you don't respect my contribution to our financial security."

He admitted, for the first time, that my health insurance is important—that is a step, I guess—but that he simply refuses to be the "patient" in this case.

This afternoon, I found a letter from Stu with a check for $1,000 on my desk. "The money," he said, "can be viewed as nine hundred dollars for Shapiro plus mad money; as a down payment on a trip to Nepal . . . or whatever." I thought about what to do with the check for some time, then tore it up.

A little while ago, Stu asked if I wanted to talk. When I agreed, he kept pressing me to make love.

"I can't," I said.

"Of course you can. You only have to try to love me a little. Why do you keep fooling yourself? Why won't you accept my gifts as tokens of my affection? Why are you being so hard on me?"

Finally, I fled to my room. He followed, and I had to ask him on two different occasions to leave, which he did with ear-splitting slams of the door.

For several years, I've taken Helen to an annual New Year's Eve concert by local singer-songwriters Lou and Peter Berryman. Peter plays the guitar. Lou plays the accordion and sings funny, ironic lyrics in an unforgettable nasal soprano. They used to be married to each other, long, long ago, but now they each have a different spouse.

Once, after a Berryman concert, Helen and I got caught in the traffic around Capitol Square. We wanted to see the midnight fireworks that are set off from the roof of Firstar Bank. We're both passionate about fireworks, but it didn't make sense to park the car and walk to the capitol lawn for a good viewing spot. The night was too cold and Helen would have had trouble walking from wherever we might park. We crept along in the traffic. It took half an hour to traverse three sides of the square. And then, just as we turned onto Main Street, finally facing the bank, the fireworks began. Big, brilliant balls of fire exploded right in front of us; traffic stopped; and we watched the whole show from front-row seats, through the windshield of my car.

Last night—New Year's Eve—even though Helen was in the hospital, or maybe because she was there, Eli and I decided to go to the Berryman concert. As we drove across town to the Madison Area

Technical College auditorium, I remembered driving Helen there last year. She was confused, not certain where we were going. I reminded her that we'd often heard the Berrymans play a concert on New Year's Eve. "They used to play at the botanical garden," I said. "But so many people come that they've moved the concert to MATC." I reminded her that we'd heard Eli play at the MATC auditorium with the Wisconsin Youth Symphony Orchestra.

After we found seats, she looked around. "I think I've been here before," she said. I reminded her again of Eli's concert. The Berrymans came on stage. "I think I've seen those people," she said. I said yes, we'd gone to their concerts together for several years. And then she said, "I don't see Eli. When will he play?"

Tonight, after the concert, Eli dropped me off at home and took the car to go out to a party. I went next door to spend the rest of the evening with neighbors. We played a game. We snacked on herring, cheeses, smoked whitefish. We drank nearly a bottle of champagne. I stayed until one in the morning. When I got home, I found two messages on my machine, one from Hal, asking me to call whenever I got home; the other from Julie, inviting me to soak in their hot tub, but to call before I came.

I knew what had happened. I called; Hal answered. "Mother died this evening," he said. He urged me to come, to be with them, to bring my bathing suit.

I had had too much champagne. I was too tipsy to drive. I was relieved to have an excuse.

Diffidence

Sunday evening, June 1, 1986, Mother's birthday

The last two days went by in a haze. I spent a lot of time reading back over the journal I've kept since last December and studying the chart I started in late April on which I scored our day-by-day progress on issues like "control," "help around the house," and "sex." Stu and I talked. He apologized for the door-slamming. I did *not* apologize for tearing up the check. We made love. I felt very warm toward him, having begun to realize, reading the journal, how far I—and perhaps even we—have really come since December. We talked again about bedrooms. Stu described his new notion: the study would be his room, the third floor, my room; and our old bedroom would be transformed into our room for reading, sleeping, and relaxation. He seemed much less intent on mere "coexistence." This really had me elated. Last night we had carp for dinner, a carp that David netted off our pier and Stu slaughtered. "A sacrificial carp," Stu said.

This afternoon I wrote Stu a letter reporting my decision to stay with him. "I know, and I know that you know, that you would be terribly hurt if I left," I wrote. "You *are* vulnerable, and I treasure the lapis necklace and earrings because they are physical manifestations of your love and your vulnerability." I wrote that I felt I had grown more strong and independent, able to recognize and express my own needs and insist that they be met. And I concluded, "I am much more excited by the prospect of renegotiating our relationship out of my new-found strength and your new-found vulnerability than I am about packing up and moving to the west side."

Then I went to look at another house for sale. Not a great house (I'm happy to say), but when I was there, I ran into a friend. I found myself explaining why I was staying and why I was not sure this was a final decision. She said she knows someone who is taking a sabbatical next year and wants to rent his house. Which made me feel there is an out, if I need one in the next few weeks.

⊗

Monday morning, June 2, 1986

Stu drank too much last night and tried to cajole me into bed on the porch. I refused. I told him, "I won't stay because you're drunk."

He got up, opened the door to my room, growled like an animal, said, "If you won't be with me when I'm drinking, I'll drink some more," and went downstairs for another full glass. Nonetheless, I am *not* going to give him affection when he is drunk: it is too hard on me. Decided this morning that I will make a monthly decision about staying or leaving.

⊗

Two weeks before Helen died, I took her to Walrus, the century-old women's club to which we both belonged. Karen Olsen, the hostess, served delicate Christmas cookies with ice cream and fresh raspberries over meringue. We met in her great room, looking out over a snowy and tranquil yard. Karen had decorated her table and buffet with evergreen boughs and dozens of candles that cast a warm glow over the room. After we ate, we moved to the sitting area for the evening's program.

In the middle of the illustrated lecture, Helen got up—awkwardly, because she was a little stiff—and left the room. I could see her go into the bathroom and then come out and stand uncertainly in the hall. I went to her and showed her the way back to the group. We both sat down. A few minutes later she stood again and went down the hall, looking into several doorways. I thought she again had to go to the bathroom, and I went to show her where it was. "No," she said. "I'm tired. I think I'll go up to bed."

"You can't go to bed yet," I whispered. "Your bed's not here." I took her arm and guided her back to the group. But again she stood

172

and wandered off down the hall, looking for her bedroom. "This is Karen's house," I told her, "not yours." I had never seen her so confused. I took her back into the great room, seated her near Karen, and stood in the doorway to the hall. The speaker continued her talk, and everyone stared at the slides. Helen started to rise from her chair. She looked toward the hall, saw me, and turned toward the buffet. "I'll just blow these candles out before I go to bed," she said.

"Karen will blow them out after the talk," I whispered and gently pushed her back into the chair. "Then I'll take you home." She ignored me, stood up, and started to move toward the buffet.

"I'll blow them out, Helen," Karen said. "I'll blow them out right now." And she snuffed all the candles on the table and the buffet. The room darkened. The slides of Winterthur, the Du Pont mansion in Delaware, came into sharper focus.

⊛

Thursday morning, June 5, 1986

Dream: I am trying to deliver a letter requesting a Children's Museum contribution —a letter he expects—to the loud-mouthed appliance store salesman who advertises on TV. I go to the address listed in the phone book. From the street I can see only a high hill, a steep driveway, and a little shack at the top. As I start to walk up the hill, a young woman warns me not to go any farther. "This is all private property," she says, "and the owner's wife will get mad if you intrude on their privacy." She points out a mailbox across the road.

As I put the letter in the mailbox I say, "So the rule is, you don't get off the road?"

"No," she says. "The rule is, if you're going to make any encroachment onto the property, you don't let anybody know."

I interpret this in two ways. First, if I'm going to make any changes in Stu—who is obviously this obnoxious, heavily defended, secretive person—I have to do it without his knowing. And second, if I'm going to make any changes myself, I have to be secretive about it. I can't telegraph my punches. I'm just going to have to go quietly about my business, and when I'm ready to leave, I do. But no big discussion in advance. I make it a surprise.

✿

A couple of nights ago, I dreamed that Helen, clear minded and lucid, was lighting a great many candles. In the dream, I understood the symbolism; I remembered her distress over the lit candles at Karen's house, and I knew she was trying to tell me that now she was OK. But just in case I didn't get it, she showed me a Christmas card she'd received, one of many sent by artists. This one, on glossy paper the size of a sheet of newsprint, was hand illustrated and signed by Robert Motherwell.

Mother well. This morning, I noticed that the snapshots of my own mother, tucked into the frame of my dresser mirror, have curled so badly that I can't just glance over and see her image anymore. Years ago, someone suggested that I had never grieved for my mother. She had been dead more than twenty years. I wondered if I could induce mourning, or remembrance, at least. I made a little shrine on my dresser. I dug three small black-and-white snapshots of Mother out of my boxes of unsorted photos and wedged them between the mirror and its curved wooden frame. For a long time, I kept a fresh red rose—her favorite flower—in an Orangina bottle on the dresser. Buying a weekly rose seemed a great extravagance, especially since I didn't like roses very much.

After six or nine months, or maybe a year, I grew to love the rose buds, but at the same time, I no longer felt the need for a shrine. I stopped buying flowers for the dresser. The snapshots stayed, tucked into the mirror frame.

Since Helen died, I have lit a beeswax candle every night at bedtime. I have never lit a candle to commemorate my own mother's death. I suppose I could start now, with *yahrzeit* candles, but I don't know when she died. She was born June 1, 1920. She died in 1968. I can never remember the date. Sometime in early September; that's as close as I can get.

174

Diffidence

Friday, June 6, 1986

Crappy day. Stu decided that he didn't want to go out to lunch with me because I said I wanted to talk about summer child care. "There's nothing to talk about," he said. "We'll divide our time with them fifty-fifty, just as if we were divorced."

"I want to talk about how we'll help them organize their time," I said.

But he refused. He thinks adults and children should be treated the same way: "Leave them alone and they'll figure out what to do."

This discussion occurred this morning between 8:15 and 8:30, when I went off to see Susan Margolis. She gave me a good notion of my financial situation and said it doesn't much matter whether I rent or buy a house. But I was brought up short when I realized that the bastard now has it set up so I am responsible for 50 percent of our household expenses, although my assets are perhaps one-sixth of his, and he has reserved *all* his income (which is from inherited assets) for himself, while under the state's new marital property law, half of *my* income is legally his. I came home in a foul mood, knowing that a marital property agreement would be necessary if we did not get a divorce.

When I got home, Stu all of a sudden was in a good mood, after four-and-a-half days of intense hostility. But I was not having any, and told him why.

"I will repeat what I have always said," he responded. "So long as you're married to me, you don't have to work." And proceeded to tell me how much he disliked my June 1 letter, both because I said that he was vulnerable and because I only committed myself to staying with him "for a while."

I could not figure out how to respond, other than to break down and cry when he finally left the house to go grocery shopping. I did say, "I don't need you."

He said, "Of course not. All you have to do is want or desire me."

But I have always needed him more than I wanted or desired him—so

175

all I am left with is leaving. I began thinking about renting as a reasonable—and perhaps faster—alternative to buying. It is hard to see how I could stay, though of course now that Stu sees that he has distressed me and I may be thinking of leaving, he is quite cordial. He brought home a porno movie for the evening. I told him he could watch it himself; he said, "I plan to."

⊛

Helen wanted a daughter; I wanted a mother. Our relationship filled important needs for both of us. I don't know when Helen's yearning for a daughter began, but I'd been looking for surrogate mothers since I was a child.

Summer 1958. My mother is sick, but far from dead, a frowsy, unhappy woman who screams all the time—at me, at my sisters, my father. I escape into books. I find a name for her: she is a "harridan." I avoid her as much as I can. I am thrilled to leave home for two weeks at a Girl Scout camp.

My tent mate, Robin, lives in the suburbs, in a house on the side of a hill. After camp, she invites me to visit. The house is new, modern, architect designed. I have never seen anything like it. You enter on the bedroom level and walk upstairs to the living room! All the furniture matches. Some of it's teak, Danish modern; the rest has been built-in. Robin's mother, Mrs. Mathews, keeps the house very clean.

December 1960. Mrs. Mathews likes kids, and she has a lot of energy. She's a Quaker, and she knows about seminars and work camps for high-school students, run by the AFSC. During Christmas vacation, the year I'm a junior, Mrs. Mathews invites kids she knows to a weekend at the Friends' Meeting House. Twenty or thirty of us listen to grown-up experts talk about the Cold War, about the dangers of nuclear weapons. We head downtown to gather man-on-the-street opinions about the Soviet Union. (On the streetcar we interview Santa Claus.) We stay up, late into the night, sitting on the counters in the big meeting house kitchen, talking about *ideas*.

We are seduced by the grown-ups who take us seriously; by the knowledge that there are other kids like ourselves; by the freedom to stay up late. Before the weekend's over, we've formed Discussion

Group, a "moveable feast" of adolescents who read a lot, idolize Woody Guthrie, talk about politics. Mrs. Mathews has changed my life. I go to Discussion Group every Saturday night. We play guitars, talk, make out in neighborhood parks. Joined by a few Negro teens, we go to AFSC work camps and paint kitchens in the slums. We learn about civil rights at AFSC seminars. We march to Ban the Bomb in 1961—a few of the hundreds of thousands who mass on the bridge across the Potomac, headed from the Tomb of the Unknown Soldier to hear Norman Thomas address a rally at the Washington Monument. Back home, faced with petty censorship, we start *The Forum,* an alternative high-school paper.

December 1962. I am home from my freshman year at Reed. Discussion Group meets at the Mathews'. Because it's also a Christmas party, the food is elegant. I taste the roast beef salad: savory, well seasoned, unlike anything my mother would ever make. I ask Mrs. Mathews the secret. Thinly sliced onions, she says, and capers, and meat grilled very rare. Be sure to use tender beef. Marinate it all in red wine vinegar, herbs, and olive oil. (It's 1962. Few Americans have heard of olive oil.) She shows me the recipe in *The Blueberry Hill Cookbook,* from a famous inn in Maine.

I never make rare roast beef salad. But I remember that dish, the conversation, Mrs. Mathews—healthy, sophisticated, savvy—talking to me woman-to-woman. She felt like more of a mother than the pathetic one I had.

※

Saturday, June 7, 1986

This afternoon, I drove past an interesting house for sale. The kids began talking about how they would like to split their time. "Maybe we could live with you, near Wingra, during the school year," David suggested, "and at Stu's house on the lake in the summer."

"Or," Eli said, "we could spend one week at one house and one at the other." He explained he's been talking with friends "who have divorces" and observing how they live.

David said he's also been discussing his life with two of his friends whose parents are divorced, asking them what it's like to live with only one parent, and learning how the courts create compromises with which no one is perfectly happy.

I was somewhat reassured by this conversation.

Stu, meanwhile, continues his behavior of the past few days, which consists of either not speaking to me or taunting me with barbs about vulnerability. "Do you wear a seat belt because you feel vulnerable?" he asked when we got in the car to go out to dinner. And then, as I was getting out of the car, he tapped me, hardish, on the head. "Here's a love tap," he said. "Want another?"

I know he's furious because I won't warm up to him, but what has he done in the past week to make me want to come to him? Today he told me he loves me. If this is love, I think I'd prefer hate.

※

I am at Reed, in my best friend's dorm room. Rachel has put Mozart horn concertos on her KLH portable stereo. We are drinking Earl Grey tea out of oversized mugs. She is talking about her boyfriend. I am trying to listen, but mostly I am wondering what it would be like to have a mother like hers, a mother who sends care packages full of marzipan, Scotch shortbread, tins of Earl Grey tea.

I meet Flo when I go home with Rachel over spring vacation. I see her often after that. She gives me *The Joy of Cooking* as a graduation gift. She never sends me care packages, but she definitely takes care of me. After college, whenever I travel to Los Angeles, Flo feeds me her chicken soup, chopped liver, lacy cottage cheese pancakes served with sour cream. It doesn't matter whether Rachel is home or not; when I visit, Flo is in her sunny kitchen cooking or sitting at the varnished pine table, a sympathetic ear. She's there when Tom dumps me. She offers tea and cookies and listens to my tales of life as a working girl. She teaches me to make sauerkraut strudel and encourages me to apply to graduate school.

Flo buys oranges by the case. She has an electric juicer, and whenever I stay at her house, she has me cut a dozen oranges in halves and press them onto the whirling grooved dome until juice runs down the plastic spout. We put the spent skins down the disposal. "Citrus is good for it," Flo says. "It makes the disposal smell fresh."

Rachel called a few weeks ago to say that Flo had died. I think of her, almost every meal I cook. I compost vegetable waste: tomato seeds, apple cores, rice soaked from the bottom of the pan. Grapefruit skins, lemon rinds, orange peels go down the disposal, to make it fresh.

When I write about mothers, I make trip after trip to the kitchen. I scour the fridge for things to eat, nuke leftover rice with margarine, fry up an egg with leftover baked potato, come back to the computer with bowls of salted popcorn, mugs of hot chocolate. When I am writing about mothers, I will eat anything in the house. It makes me hungry to write about mothers, all the mothers who have died.

✤

Monday, June 9, 1986

After being a real hostile bastard for the better part of the week, on Saturday Stu realized — because of a message a Realtor left on the answering machine — that I was once again looking for houses, and he suddenly changed. All day yesterday he was really quite pleasant. In the afternoon, I looked at several houses, including a historic bungalow near the zoo that I've admired for years. And yesterday evening, when I was out, Stu took a message about the house that is for rent. After the kids went to bed, Stu said, "Can we fuck first and talk later?"

I was pretty reluctant, but we made love and then spent two or three hours talking. Stu was very ardent and very pessimistic. "I think there's probably a 5 percent chance that we'll be married in a year," he said. "But I want to struggle to make that 5 percent." I thought he listened to what I had to say in a way that he doesn't usually listen. "I've decided that if there's only a one-in-twenty chance that we're going to be together, I'm not going to let myself be threatened by your leaving or devastated if you do leave," he told me. "You don't get devastated by not winning against such odds." He was not even quite so defensive about vulnerability as he has been recently. He helped me make my bed, hugged and kissed me, and said, "I hope you'll be willing to keep on struggling."

I could cry, he's got such a knack for jerking me around. He said, "I think you've probably already decided to leave, and maybe it's necessary to make you strong and independent, and the best thing for you to do. In that case, I understand, and you should go."

"That's a pretty paternal attitude," I told him, "and I don't appreciate it. Why can't you ever say that you're wrong and I'm right: that you're willing to capitulate to me, rather than insist on some sort of dialectic synthesis of our supposedly opposing positions?"

This evening, I looked at the house that I could rent. I was very excited on my way to see it: it's a good price, the right size, available August 20 on a twelve-month lease with a possible option to buy. But once I saw the house, I felt differently. Because it is furnished, it is not a house that I could work on making mine, and even though it has a nice kitchen and dining room, it feels cramped. It's not a house I'd ever want to buy.

It occurs to me that no house will ever please me, so I will be stuck here by my inertia. But the house I live in *now* didn't really please me, and I have never really liked living in it; I don't want to make that mistake again.

⸙

Helen served generous portions of bloody beef and lamb; salads of Boston lettuce and avocado, drenched in vinaigrette; an intense, mousselike dessert, *chocolade;* and *seviche,* a raw-fish appetizer, recipes she'd gotten from an old friend who lived in Peru. Meals at Helen's always began with cocktail hour, when we would sit in the living room, each of us absorbed in a magazine, drinking Jack Daniel's or Tanqueray and eating appetizers. When I first knew her, Helen sometimes made complex hors d'oeuvres like broiled stuffed mushrooms or softened cream cheese with a dab of caviar and a slice of pimento on crackers. Later, she usually served herring or honey-roasted nuts. She put out bowls of Pepperidge Farm cheddar cheese goldfish for David and Eli; they washed down the tiny crackers with glasses of ginger ale. They loved goldfish and begged for them at home. But Helen asked me not to buy them any. "I want goldfish to be special, something they only get when they visit me."

For the most part, Helen refrained with great grace from commenting on my parenting skills and style. I know it appalled her when David scribbled with Magic Markers all over the smooth blond wood tracks for his Brio train. I'm sure she thought I should teach the kids to put away one toy before they took another out. But she didn't criticize. Only twice did Helen make comments that astonished me.

Once, when David was a baby, she told me not to blow on his belly and tickle him. "You don't want to overstimulate him," she warned. This seemed very Victorian. I thought it might explain a lot about Stu, that he was never tickled lovingly. Later, several years after Eli was born, Helen said accusingly, "You love your children too much." I had Hodgkin's disease, and she'd offered to take the kids for a weekend, or maybe a week. I didn't want them to go. I think she was trying to say that she needed to help, that I should welcome her assistance, not cling to Eli and David.

But her accusation stung, and at the same time it seemed to come from another realm. How could I love my children too much? How could any child be too much loved?

Helen always treated me as a daughter, even after the divorce. She didn't side with Stu, unquestioning, flesh-of-my-flesh, blood-of-my-blood. Did she think she could love her child too much?

⊗

Wednesday, June 11, 1986

Yesterday Stu and I got right down to it on the question of money. I said I'd like the second-floor bathroom to be decent enough that I could take a bath in it and feel comfortable. The room is ugly, with really old fixtures, decrepit wallpaper, and peeling paint. Right now we use it only to brush our teeth and bathe the kids. Stu always takes showers on the third floor, and I usually do. And of course, we've had the third-floor bathroom painted.

I realized that one of our unspoken assumptions has been that I would not make major expenditures of Stu's money, and that I would not even suggest a major expenditure unless I was sure Stu would also think it was a good idea. Thus, I could suggest buying the house on the lake because I knew Stu would like to have his sailboat in the backyard. And conversely, it was an act of defiance and assertion of power when I bought a new TV last year when he was sailing with Hal and Julie. (And he has frequently told me that I was wrong to buy a JVC on sale instead of a full-price Sony.)

Now I would like to fix up a bathroom Stu doesn't care about. But I'd also like to use some of the money we have (if indeed *we* have the money) to help my sister Bobbi, who is really struggling. Until now, I haven't been able to tell Stu about either of these desires. But I had to sit quietly at dinner last night when he told Helen how important it was to contribute to the campaign to enter a Midwestern yacht in the America's Cup race!

I want to say to this woman, go already. Leave. It's tedious, coming back to the computer again and again to find that you are still stuck in a relationship that is obviously abusive, obviously past time to end. It's embarrassing, knowing that readers will see how stuck you were, how, even when you knew better, even after seven months of weekly psychotherapy, you stayed. Why did you try so hard?

The *Capital Times* just ran a big spread about battered women, how hard it is for them to leave. I have read plenty of articles like this. Books, too, plenty of books. They all give the same old explanations: these women don't know if they will be able to support themselves and their children; these women are afraid that their husbands or lovers will come after them; these women are trapped in a psychological web. I know all this. I have felt all this, have written obsessively about it. I still don't really get it. I still want that woman, that younger me, to close her journal, to just shut up and go.

Diffidence

Ninety degrees in Saint Louis, and humid. The past day and a half went better than I expected and gave me some insight into my own behavior—but still leaves me in a daze.

Came here because Dad asked me to join him on his annual visit to see Bobbi. Arrived about 8:20 A.M. yesterday, met by Dad, who'd arrived on an earlier plane. Immediate indecision about where to stay: Dad was supremely diffident, and I deferred to his diffidence rather than insist on my own wishes, which were to stay downtown. I thought that downtown we would at least find diversions when we were not with Bobbi. But he was afraid downtown hotels would be too expensive, and since I didn't have any information about hotel rates, I shut up and watched him wander from ad to ad near the baggage carousels. Finally he decided to not decide. We rented a car and went off to Bobbi's.

Bobbi, her husband Gary, and Marlene (who just turned four) live with Gary's mother in a small house that appeared less desperately impoverished than I expected. Still, there certainly was evidence of money problems (for example, in the bathroom, where the plastic tile had all come off the walls). All I really saw of the house were the living room, dominated by a color TV, always on; a dining room with a matched table, chairs, and hutch, looking very unused; and the bathroom. A few months ago, Gary's brother-in-law was laid off, and the bank foreclosed on his house. So now he, Gary's sister, and their four children also live with Gary's mother. Nine or ten people, sitting around talking and watching television most of the day, as far as I can tell.

Almost as soon as we arrived, Dad suggested that we go to Sears to buy toys for Marlene, a small, thin, solemn child. "What Marlene really needs is glasses," Bobbi said. So we went to Pearle Vision and Dad paid for the glasses. Marlene's eyes are very bad; she is at the bottom of the scale for single lens correction. She doesn't speak very well; she had constant ear infections as a baby, which delayed her language development. She got tubes in her ears last October, but she has a long way to go to catch up. I brought her a small package of wooden mosaic pieces, brightly colored triangles, squares, and diamonds. She could not consistently identify the colors of the chips—red, yellow, and blue—and I stopped trying to name the shapes because she was getting confused. She loved the game, and was very eager to play, but I kept thinking of my kids, who could name and match colors when they were one and a half or two.

I said I wanted to buy a tricycle for Marlene, whose large motor development is also delayed. At Children's Palace, I was again confronted with Dad's diffidence. "I was planning to buy her a tricycle," he said, a little peevish. But he hadn't mentioned it before. How was I to know his plan, and now what was I supposed to do? I bought the trike. He backed off quickly, but was obviously hurt. Then he bought some preschool Legos, and that seemed to make him feel better.

With the exception of the glasses, Bobbi seemed incapable of suggesting or requesting anything at all. We had dinner at a restaurant Gary suggested; dropped Gary, Bobbi, and Marlene off at their house; got a room at a Rodeway Inn near the airport; and went into the bar for a drink.

I was wiped out. I am beginning to identify this as an emotional rather than a physical state. But Dad wanted to be filled in on my marital situation. I tried to respond, but I was almost incoherent and felt that I could not even complete my sentences. What I really wanted to talk about was diffidence and how Bobbi and Dad himself both personify what I feel is also my problem—and how difficult I find it to know what to do or say around them, as a result of their diffidence. It is very obvious to me, now, how one's own diffidence encourages excesses of assertiveness in other people and how one can grow to resent the other person's decisions and decision-making power. I can see why Stu's apparent ability to know what he wanted to do, and to go for it, attracted me. What I don't see very clearly is whether we can undo this pattern. He is so accustomed to power and so unwilling to do anything for someone else—and I am so willing to accede and defer and so unaccustomed to identifying my own desires and needs—that it may simply be too late. But it was useless trying to talk about this with Dad.

⊕

I spent an hour this afternoon shuffling through two big liquor cartons overflowing with a jumble of snapshots. I was looking for photos of Helen that we might display in a couple of weeks at a memorial gathering. But what really struck me was the more-or-less arbitrary way the snapshots record my life. In a small, square, black-and-white print I am hanging upside down by my knees on a swing set, my skirt over my head, underpants showing. My father took this shot with the camera he got when he worked for Ansco, just after World War II. A little booklet of blurry photos I snapped with my Brownie box camera: tenting at Girl Scout camp. In an envelope, three or four pictures from high school, taken by Peter Miller, who now sells his prints to museums. Here's Norman Thomas, in front of the Washington Monument. Here's our high school friend Tom Rodd, smoking a cigarette, the drifting smoke a veil against the unknowable future. A few years later, he went to prison as a conscientious objector, one of the first to protest the war in Vietnam.

A few photos from college, taken with my boyfriend Tom's Leica: us in a Portland park, Mount Hood grand in the background; a reflection of Tom in the screen of the console television in his dorm room — his mother's television, inherited when she died.

And then a gap. The Kodak Brownie was long gone. I didn't own a camera until after I met Stu.

⊛

Monday morning, June 16, 1986

Last night Stu said, "I'm jealous. As soon as you got home you started gabbing on the phone about the Children's Museum." (I had made two phone calls.) He said he wanted to hear about Saint Louis. But he wanted me to lie down with him on the porch and tried to cuddle as I talked about Dad and Bobbi.

I said, "Saint Louis and cuddling don't mix."

He grilled me with questions about the weekend. No sense of support or empathy, "just the facts, ma'am, just the facts." After an hour or so of this, he accused me of wanting "to kill off both your mother and your husband. You're trying to go back to the first twenty-four years of your life instead of continuing to live in the present."

"No," I said. "I'm trying to integrate both parts of my life." I said I needed his support to integrate the past and the present. "It would help if you could change your attitude toward my family." He clearly dislikes most of my relatives and conspicuously ignores them.

He said he *has* changed. "When was the last time we spent two hours discussing your family?"

I slept by myself and dreamed realistic, angry, and upsetting dreams, including one in which I was responsible for a fluffy yellow chick falling out of the nest and being tramped on.

⊛

After I moved in with Stu, he let me use his Nikon. We took slides when we went on trips because Stu thought they were better than prints. He took pictures of oil refineries and California's vast corporate farms. I focused on patterns of kelp and tar (after an oil spill) on a Santa Barbara beach.

When we started to travel in the van, we bought two more cameras: a Nikkormat with a macro lens that permitted extreme close-ups, and a little, lightweight Rollei for backpacking trips. We arrived in the Southwest in March 1973, a really wet spring, the first after ten dry years. The desert was a riot of color. Wherever we looked, we saw flowers: waxy, brilliant blossoms on every cactus and spiny bush. Stu took pictures of rock formations and Anasazi ruins. I specialized in flowers, close-up.

When Stu and I split up, I took the slides and had them duplicated. I bought two metal storage boxes and organized some of the slide collection, maybe half of it. Then I lost interest. I was fed up with slides. I didn't have a projector, and I didn't want to buy one. I wanted to take pictures of people, and I wanted to look at the pictures without a lot of fuss and paraphernalia. I bought myself a camera, a little point-and-shoot. I took snapshots on color negative film, got duplicates for anyone who showed up in the prints. I stopped

186

worrying about framing the pictures properly, about image quality. All I wanted was to record the trip, the people, the event. I dumped the snapshots and negatives into liquor cartons, sometimes labeled, sometimes not. Lots of out-of-focus people whose names are beginning to fade.

Names and faces too. Stu was quite right when he insisted that we take slides. The crimson cactus flower I shot a quarter-century ago looks as though it bloomed yesterday. My much more recent snapshots of family and friends are washing out, on their way to oblivion.

And Stu did take some pictures of people. There's a fading print, made from a slide, that he took in 1972. I am sitting at a picnic table, next to the van. The van's side doors are open. You can see furniture Stu made—a clothes cupboard painted brown and tan—and the orange cushions on the bed. A green twill bedspread covers the picnic table. At one end of the table, to my right, you can see the propane stove we used for cooking. My back is toward the camera. I have swept my long brown hair off my neck and pinned it with a leather barrette. I am wearing Levi's and a sleeveless black turtleneck. My upper arms are firm. My hands are on the keys of a portable typewriter. I am typing the log of the trip.

❦

Monday evening, June 16, 1986

Wretched day. Bummed out about Saint Louis; pressed by work; and fed up with Stu's belittling and demeaning comments. For example, as he is making a big point of cleaning up the kitchen: "This way I'll know it's done to my satisfaction." And later, that the *Marriage and the Family* course, which he called "pop psychology," is a big part of our problem because "you've always been impressionable." At which point I got up and walked out. I told him that the conversation was over because I would not stand for his demeaning my intellect.

He said, "Your intellect is fading fast."

❦

187

At Helen's memorial, Stu spoke about the way she taught herself to compensate for her very bad eyes. He remembered her determination to be a bird-watcher; how she bought records of bird songs and played them over and over, committing the sounds to memory. He recalled how she'd trained her visual memory, how she'd learned, Peterson's bird book in hand, to distinguish the confusing spring warblers. His voice thick with emotion, he praised the grit and hard work with which she overcame adversity.

Sitting in the Art Center gallery, facing a wall of paintings, prints, and sculptures Helen helped select for the museum, I could not help but admire the acuity of her eye. But I also felt the sting. Stu praised his mother in the same terms he'd often used to criticize me. How many times had I said I couldn't see a bird he was trying to get me to identify? And how many times had he responded, "You could see it, if you tried."

⊛

Wednesday, June 18, 1986

At our counseling session Stu and I each described our perceptions of the argument we had when I got back from Saint Louis. Shapiro pointed out that we have different ways of coping with stress. Stu observes and reflects. He intellectualizes as a way of dealing with anxiety. And I get emotional. Shapiro suggested that for homework I write down how I'd like Stu to respond to me when I'm emotional.

It's easy to describe how I'd like him to respond. I'd like him to hear me out—just let me talk about what is bugging me. Other people do that. But I feel very pessimistic about the possibility that Stu will ever just listen, without telling me how to solve my problems.

⊛

Friday, June 20, 1986

Saw a great house yesterday, 2318 Rowen. Prairie style, $89,900, nice woodwork, decent kitchen and bath, oil furnace, nice yard.

In the evening after a movie date, we went to a fancy bar. I asked Stu about his reaction to our sessions with Shapiro. He was angry that I brought the subject up because he'd fantasized a perfect evening. He was very disdainful of Shapiro's ability to know our "coping styles" after only three sessions, and he wouldn't admit that there is more than one appropriate style of coping with anxiety.

If I were a gambler, I would buy the fucking house.

⊛

When we are growing up, I invent a game to play with Shelly. I am about eight. She can't be more than five. We sit face to face, barefoot, on my bed.

"Close your eyes," I say.

She squinches her eyelids tight.

"OK. Tell me when you feel my finger on your foot." I touch my forefinger lightly to the callus on her heel.

"Now," she says, right away.

"My turn," I say. "I bet I don't feel anything."

I shut my eyes. Shelly touches my callus. "Are you doing it yet?" I ask.

"Yes." She presses harder.

"I don't feel anything. Maybe you should use your nail."

She pokes a ragged thumbnail into the callus until it makes an indentation shaped like a sliver moon. "There," she says, satisfied.

"Where?" I ask. I need to show her just how tough I am. "I still don't feel it. You have to do it really hard."

⊛

Sunday evening, June 22, 1986

Eli's eighth birthday. We all drove him to camp after Stu got off the lake. Eli really wasn't enthusiastic about going; worried, I'm sure, about what will happen in his absence.

We got home about half past five, and Stu and I started to clean the refrigerator. We talked about the difference between his method of dealing

189

with anxiety and mine. The conversation escalated into a full-scale brawl, which thoroughly upset David. A friend called to invite him for an overnight, and he was eager to go. I was so angry that I drove him across town and went to look a second time at the house on Rowen. I came back about nine; called Shelly; and then ended up talking another two and a half hours with Stu. Perhaps made some progress explaining why I will no longer tolerate his a) hitting me (which he did after dinner) and b) trashing me verbally. We'll see whether his behavior changes. "If you leave," Shelly said, "you may have to resign yourself to not getting your emotional needs met." But on the other hand, I won't have to listen to someone telling me there's something wrong with me for *having* those needs.

❀

My house seems exceptionally empty in the ten days since Helen's memorial. David and Eli were here a very brief time, just the weekend. I don't know when I will see them again. I sent them e-mail messages a couple of days after they left. Since then, I've logged in three or four times a day to look for their responses. I am frantic to keep in touch.

Every few days I think, It's been a long time since I've seen Helen. I should call her, plan an outing, invite her to dinner at least.

In two days I am going on vacation. While I'm gone, my bedroom will be painted. I have been emptying all the dresser drawers, the closet, the headboard, going through all my clothes, discarding the things I have not worn in years, will never wear again.

To take a break, I went downstairs and read the personals. I answered two ads, one from a "college instructor," the other from someone who described himself as an "atypical male." I called a friend to ask if she could help me move my dresser and take apart my bed. She couldn't. She has a two-year-old and a new husband who works weekends and nights. "It's a little like being a single parent," she complained.

"At least you have someone to talk to," I said. "I have to call someone up. Or talk to the cat."

190

Diffidence

✦

Monday, June 23, 1986

Dream: We (or I?) have a "new" car: an old woody station wagon, beautifully restored. But when David, Eli, and I open the door, it smells terrible.
We look around and find a dead rat.

Stu has made several nasty cracks about psychiatrists, psychotherapy,
etc. I'm sure he hates going to a marriage counselor. But it's too bad. So
long as he continues to work on the relationship, it seems worth my
while to stay. Should he let up, I'm gone, and I think he realizes that.

In some ways, I would just like to ditch my whole life—even David and
Eli—and go be a writer somewhere. In other ways, that's the very last
thing I'd like to do. Stu and I spent some time last night talking about why
I don't have patience with him, with my situation. If I felt I would live long
enough, I could be patient: wait until Eli is out of high school and then do
as I wished. But who knows if I'll be around to see Eli graduate—or how
much longer I'd be around to do as I wish. Besides, I want to live well now.
I can't even get my desk cleared—how can I expect to find time to buy a
house and move?

Somehow, I managed to barely note the fact that last night, when I
wagged my finger back at Stu who was wagging his at me, he slapped me.
He was not drunk. I left the room.

Why is it that despite the day-to-day shit, I am too stubborn to leave?

Another dream: I have to call Stanford to arrange for an operation. Before the operation, I must save melon seeds, a certain number from several honeydews. I have great trouble finding and dialing the hospital's
number, finding out exactly how many seeds I need to save, and so forth.
The house is in turmoil because we are painting rooms or refinishing the
floors. Furniture is stored in a large room that has been cordoned off with
a thick, velvet-covered rope, the kind they use in theaters.

Stu is responsible for the disorder in the house, and he knows what is
stored in the roped-off room. I am disturbed, because I can't get into the

room. I know that the things I need to take to the hospital are not there, but I think that if I could go into the room, I wouldn't need Stu's help to collect whatever I need for the operation. Stu helps me to find the information I need and collect the melon seeds. I think, this is why I need Stu: he is organized and calm in an emergency.

At the very end of the dream, I am at a meeting that's reviewing the information provided for people who are going to Stanford for operations. Someone says it's important to update the price list. I suggest giving information about Palo Alto and how to find housing. This is received as an unusual and creative idea.

⊛

Tuesday, June 24, 1986

With Paul this afternoon, I talked mostly about how I can't decide about leaving Stu until I can get into the roped-off room in my dream. Until I realize that it's just a theater rope that I can easily unhook. I really do need Stu's help—his intellectualizing—to solve knotty problems for me. To help me deal with my anxiety (for example, about cancer).

I realized that I'm terribly upset about the possibility that I'll get sick again. I don't feel that I have much time, and it makes me—very sad. Paul suggested that the ending of the dream, where I cope very well and find a creative solution, is important. I feel good because I'm helping other people cope. That's what I want to do for Stu (and the kids) but I don't know what I'm doing to myself—how much I'm stressing myself and making myself sick—in doing that for them, for our family. I really feel as though I'm stressing myself so much that I can make myself sick again.

"J Jumped for It"

Early March, a little like spring, at last. I took my Standard Walk today, an hour-long circuit over the hill and through Hoyt Park. I wanted to check on my favorite pussy willow, a huge shrub, like a small tree, eight or ten feet high. Each spring, it puts out the fattest, softest "pussies" I've ever seen. Today, its yard was a giant frozen puddle, smooth as a skating rink, and the buds were enclosed in shiny brown sheaths, just a little gray showing through.

I have a special fondness for pussy willows, maybe because they were the subject of my first published poem. (Or maybe they were my subject because, even in second grade, I had a special fondness for them.) I still have the poem, clipped from the mimeographed *Tele-Falk*. But I don't need the clipping; it's the only poem I've ever written that I know by heart:

> Today I looked out in the snow
> And what do you think I saw?
> I saw some pussy willows grow
> Out there in the cold, cold snow . . .

⊛

Wednesday evening, June 25, 1986

There is *nothing* like seeing Martin Shapiro to make me feel I am getting somewhere. Stu is so confused and upset by not knowing how to respond—to Martin and to me—it is a delight to behold. It is about time

193

he realizes he does not have all the answers! I think he may eventually learn something from the experience—and we will all benefit.

Because I felt sorry for Stu and good about myself, I suggested before he went off to race that he not get too tired. He seemed pleased at my taking the initiative, but after the race, he sat in his study, depressed and upset because "you're only interested in making love when we're seeing a psychiatrist."

I said, "I am only interested in making love when I feel we are making progress and I have some power in the relationship." I also said that I'd told the owner of the Rowen Street house that it was the right house, but the wrong time.

⊛

My annual checkup with the oncologist looms, and even though I am now more than fifteen years past my diagnosis of Hodgkin's disease, the anxiety grows as I approach the appointments for blood work, X-rays, the meeting with the doctor. Yesterday's mail brought the latest issue of *Surviving!,* a newsletter for cancer survivors. Just before bedtime, I read an article by a woman who had a miraculous recovery from a particularly virulent form of breast cancer. Later, in a dream, my breasts oozed an ominous, sticky substance that I took to be a sure warning of imminent death.

But I don't need doctors' appointments to remind me of my mortality. In recent conversations, I have forgotten the names of colleagues, the titles of books, the subject of the radio program I produced last week. Maybe the increased forgetfulness—or my increased awareness of the same old forgetfulness—is tied to Helen's death, to the strokes that caused her devastating memory loss. Until I was in my late thirties, I was sure I would get multiple sclerosis, that I would lose physical capacity and even my sanity just as my mother lost hers. Cancer trumped that fantasy. But now I wonder if I'm losing mental capacity, as Helen did.

This afternoon I walked to the drugstore to pick up my prescriptions for synthetic thyroid hormone and for Fosamax. The radiation therapy zapped my thyroid; I have been taking thyroid pills since I finished treatment. The Fosamax treats the bone loss that set in after menopause, induced by chemotherapy when I was thirty-seven.

I refill these prescriptions every month; every month, I remember why.

When I got back from the drugstore, I found e-mail from Norcroft. Would I like to come back for a week in June? Each year they draw the names of four past residents from a hat. Would I like to come back?! Who gives a fig for mortality? I've won the lottery!

⊛

Monday, June 30, 1986

I have spent at least half an hour staring at my bulletin board with the announcements David once lettered for casseroles I made for a dinner party: "with shrimp" and "no shrimp." And the birthday card Shelly sent: a picture cut from an old nursery-rhyme alphabet book, a figure leaping over a candlestick and the words, "J Jumped for It." Which about sums up my current thinking.

Today has been terrible. Stu finally said he does not want to take a vacation with me and refused even to respond to a note I wrote proposing a marital property agreement. I suggested we each keep all our own earned income as individual property and contribute to joint expenses in proportion to our assets. (Currently, I estimate, Stu has about four and one-half times as much wealth as I.)

But all that came late in the evening. Earlier, he spent the day in hostile posturing, getting very nasty about grocery shopping and—what drove me over the edge—assuming control of the aquarium. He tried to involve me in installing a new filter he'd gone out to buy with David. The whole point of this was to show David and me how poorly I take care of the aquarium and how much better Stu could do it. The thing that got me was the symbolism of the act: Stu has effectively destroyed my authority by removing my control over virtually everything in our lives, by offering no support for what I do, especially in front of the kids. Tonight David complained about my menu planning. I had made liver and onions, one of Stu's favorites. When David complained, Stu simply laughed.

After dinner I took a walk and regained my equilibrium. Felt very good, but also very much inclined to see if the house on Rowen is still available and to call Carol Madsen and see about filing for divorce. I told myself to wait. To see what happens with vacation; to see how Stu responds to my note about marital property. And now I have his response.

☺

I visit Helen one afternoon in late June 1986. I wear my all-time favorite dress, a white cotton shirtwaist with three-quarter-length sleeves, a wide webbed belt, and a collar, beautifully draped, that frames a deep V at my neck. Helen brought it over one day in the early 1980s. She didn't often bring me clothes; in fact, she used to tell friends how lucky she was to have a daughter-in-law who shared her disinterest in fashion and shopping. Sometimes, she brought interesting fabrics or ethnic costumes back from her travels. I still (in 1997!) wear a Oaxacan tunic, embroidered in brilliant reds, yellows, and greens, that Helen gave me shortly after we moved to Madison. It's very old and shabby, the embroidery threads pulled and snapped. I can't bear to throw it out. I wore it eighteen years ago, over maternity jeans, to the Fourth of July pig roast we hosted at Hal's cottage two weeks after Eli was born.

Helen gave me the white dress because it looked "too young" on her. It makes me look young, too, and it brings out my summer tan. When I wear it, people say I look good. The dress makes me feel attractive, like someone who might be able to find another man.

I sit with Helen on her screen porch. She rocks gently in an old glider. I'm in a canvas chair near the hanging geranium. The petals, a muted coral, echo the salmon highlights of the glider cushions. Helen has a fantastic eye for color. In a store, she can look at a paint chip or carpet sample and match it exactly to the tone, held in her mind's eye, of my upholstered couch or the curtains in her dining room.

We drink iced tea. I feel sad, but strong. I have just told Helen that I am leaving Stu.

Helen says I look very good. She agrees that I have done everything I can; that, unless Stu changes, my situation is impossible. "I wish he would see a therapist," she says, but she knows he won't. "I wish I knew why he resists. But you have to leave. It's better for you, for the children, maybe even for Stu."

⊛

Tuesday, July 1, 1986

At work I got a letter commending me for outstanding service, with a check for $50, minus withholding. Upset because I could not even share that praise with Stu. He would be sarcastic about the amount, tell me I'm being ripped off, that I don't have to work.

Tonight I asked if he would give me forty thousand dollars (less than my share of our equity in this house) *before* a divorce settlement, so I can make a down payment on the Rowen Street house. He seemed relieved. "Yes. Draft a letter outlining the agreement, and I'll edit and sign it."

Worked fairly productively on a grant proposal all day, then had an excellent session with Paul Bergeson. I told him that I wish sometimes that Stu would die (as I used to wish for Mother's death) because it would be more convenient than divorce, but I want to make an offer on the Rowen Street house. We talked about a dream I had a few days ago, in which I heard the lead song from Big Pink, "Tears of Rage." I've always misremembered the lyrics as "tears of grief, tears of rage, why must I always be a slave."

"I feel guilty about doing something big for myself," I said.

He said, "You do things for yourself. You spend five minutes in the toilet, maybe treat yourself to a glass of chocolate milk once in a while." We laughed, I cried.

I guess I am giving up because it's too difficult, too painful to be the butt of Stu's anger while he does —or doesn't—make changes.

Stu: "I've been expecting it. I think it's the best thing."

⊛

Thursday morning, July 3, 1986

Dream: I visit a house I like and think of buying it. It is unusual, elegant, modern, architect designed, with sweeping spaces, and I fall in love with it.

197

I return with a friend to get another opinion. She, too, is almost immediately impressed (particularly with the stainless steel door hinges and other hardware) and urges me to buy. Then we are at a party in the house, with lots of friends and relatives. I discover a room that I had not seen before, or perhaps had not remembered, with a fireplace and three large black kettles filled with oil for fondue on special burners in the center of the floor. Bill Lange says he really likes this room and hopes to be invited to many parties in it in the future. At one point, the owner of the house pulls a fondue pot off its flame and then snuffs the flame with a specially designed metal cap. "It's not the sort of house you'd want to live in if you had small children," I remark. But then I add that since my children are older, it's fine. Everyone agrees.

The only hesitation I have about the house is the entrance. The very dingy, run-down entryway seems to be part of an awful, run-down, dirty house that is connected to this one. At the party, we talk about this run-down house. My father expresses a fear that some bum might take up residence in the dirty house and be a threat to me. A friend suggests that I could clean the attached house and rent it to someone I liked. Then I would be safe, and I could get extra income. But the owner says that's not really possible, because there's a mold growing on the walls that can't be removed. She says that entering the good house through the bad house is expedient—convenient—but not necessary; there is another way to enter the good house. My father asks if it would be possible simply to demolish and burn the old house, and the owner says yes. In fact she'd thought of doing that, but hadn't gotten around to it. Everyone agrees, then, that the new house is perfect for me.

The new house has curved walls, stainless steel fixtures, a pool with a fountain, white walls washed in a soft yellowish light (like firelight).

⊛

In that 1986 dream, I imagined young children in danger, crawling into the flames under big fondue kettles filled with boiling oil. In my waking life, I also feared for my sons. Although now it seems bizarre to me, at the time I really thought that if I left Stu, I would destroy their lives. I felt abandoned by my own parents; I didn't want my sons to feel abandoned. Even now, ten years past the decision to leave Stu, my sons grown and in college, the thought of children, properly loved and cared for, sometimes brings me to tears.

Today, for instance, a primary election day. I vote in the Dudgeon building, a solid brick structure built as a grade school in the early 1900s. It looks like a castle, complete with turrets, and although the public school closed long ago, children still attend classes there. Eli and David went to Wingra, a small private school that shares the building with a nursery school. The kids—my kids, at least—call the building "Dungeon." David once told me that the janitor showed him the boiler room, and it really was a dungeon.

The schools hold bake sales on election days. Baggies of cookies and slices of pound cake covered the table outside the library where we vote. The light in the hall was very dim. I had to put on my reading glasses to see what was in the bags. "I guess," I started to say, and then I had to stop because tears filled my eyes and I couldn't count on a steady voice. The volunteer at the table didn't seem to notice. Or maybe she thought I hesitated because I was trying to decide. "I baked for so many election day sales, I guess I have to buy something," I said and chose the chocolate chips.

I left, munching a cookie. But the happy, high-pitched voices yelling on the playground started me crying again.

❀

Friday, the Fourth of July, 1986

We slept together last night, but I couldn't make love I woke resolute in my determination to declare independence today.

Felt terrible all morning, as Stu tried his best to make me feel we had a future. But he was still down on psychiatrists and therapy and, ultimately, full of blame for me, trashing my belief in dreams while we were preparing food for lunch and finally telling me that he might not release forty thousand dollars for the down payment. He wants to hold out hope. I guess he is heavy into denial right now, and the anger is yet to come.

We muscled the motorboat hoist into the water when Bill and the rest of the crew arrived about eleven-thirty for lunch and the Fourth of July race. Unfortunately, the wind was too high for a sailboat race, so everyone was hanging around getting ready to put the motorboat in the water when I left for Rowen Street to sign the counteroffer. I felt very shaky when I got there, but immediately calm, sitting around the table talking with the owner and his wife. I felt as though I was doing the right thing, sitting there and signing papers to buy a house on Independence Day.

When I got back home, Stu was clearly upset. "You'll always have to rationalize acting on a dream, for the rest of your life," he warned. (He meant the waking dream I had last fall when I realized that I was reacting to him as I had to Mother.) But of course, I'm not acting on a dream. There's just too much of me that I have to compromise to keep Stu from getting angry, and I can't do that anymore.

"Do you think you'll ever have it so good again?" he asked.

I said, "No. Not financially."

"Emotionally?" he asked.

I wanted to scream out, "Of course, that's why I'm doing this!" But all I said was, "Yes, better, I hope."

"With a man?" he pressed. "Do you think you'll ever fall in love and live with a man again?"

I said I hoped so, but I didn't know.

Finally he said, "I figure I have a week to think about strategy. You're an expensive woman, Judy. You always have been. If I don't let you have the forty thousand dollars, and you have to forfeit the earnest money, I'll split the loss with you, fifty-fifty."

Unfortunately, this house purchase is not something that is quite out of his control.

※

Only once in my life have I ever been more anxious than in that second week of July 1986. For a few hours in November 1981, I waited for a nurse to call with the results of a biopsy. Waves of nausea swept over me. For the first time ever, I was so anxious I couldn't eat. I tried to concentrate on my work. I was typing an application to go to a weeklong seminar in San Francisco for independent radio producers, all expenses paid. If I wrote a good enough essay, I thought, I would get to go to the seminar. If I wrote a good enough essay, if I really concentrated, the biopsy would surely be negative.

The phone rang. I jumped. My heart raced. The nausea returned. But it wasn't the nurse. It was my sister Bobbi, ecstatic. She'd just learned she was pregnant. How could I tell her I didn't want to talk, I was waiting to hear if I had cancer? I said very little. Eventually, she hung up.

In July 1986 I felt again the nausea, the hyperrational coping, the magical thinking. I couldn't eat. Anxiety ruled my days.

But my journal entries are bloodless. Stu refuses to accept my decision to leave. He tries to decide how to prove his love: should he let me buy the house or not?

❀

Monday, July 7, 1986. We have a session with Martin Shapiro. I try to get Stu to understand that I have made up my mind. He says, "You can leave whenever you want. You don't have to buy a house. You can rent a small apartment and go."

I reported in my journal:

When I protested that I could not, would not leave the kids, he said, "I am more stable than you are and, therefore, a better parent for our young sons." The things he says in anger only stiffen my resolve to leave.

Helen comes for dinner. Just before she leaves, she asks, "How are you two doing?"

"We are near the end," Stu says. He is angry and upset.

As soon as Helen left, Stu came at me, threatening. "Anger leads to violence," he said. "You'd better pack your bags tomorrow and get out." I didn't respond. A few minutes later, he pleaded, "Love me, don't destroy my world." And now he is begging me to go to bed with him.

Tuesday, July 8, 1986. I meet with Paul Bergeson. He thinks my decision to leave is very clear, very well made. It's apparent in the dream about the house with stainless steel fixtures and a fountain in front, like Stanford Hospital. It's a house where I can be healthy. He asks me about the dingy, attached house. What does it represent? My marriage, I suggest. He says he thought it might have been my child-hood. "I see your childhood and your marriage as very much the same. They're both places where you make a deal in order to be taken care of. And you do get taken care of, to a degree, but you can never say what you feel."

Paul quoted Maurice Sendak's book, *Higgledy Piggledy Pop,* in which the little dog goes off to the circus saying, "There must be more to life than this." I said I didn't think that it was an accident that all this had come together just before my oncology checkup today. The checkup was OK; I'm fine. But if I got sick again without having made some sort of change, I'd be a very unhappy person.

I told Paul that it was my naive hope that we could end this thing grace-fully. He said, "That very rarely happens. It's much more likely to be ugly."

Stu is now asking me to block out two weeks in August for a vacation.

❦

One evening, I come home to find Stu on the phone with my college friend, Rachel. He's yelling at her, blaming her for making me want to leave. He turns the phone over to me, but stays in the room while I'm talking. He grabs at the receiver, tries to sit on my lap. I tell Rachel I'll call back. Stu and I talk. He refuses to release the money I need for a down payment on the house I want to buy. He doesn't want me to move. He offers to move out "for a while" if I feel I can't live with him. And then, in a rather elliptical way, he suggested that "the hurt that turns to anger that turns to violence can also turn to violence against oneself." It wasn't an explicit suicide threat, but it was damned close. Close enough to make me think seriously about whether simply letting him move out for six months is a good idea, preferable in some way to my leaving.

❦

Sunday's *New York Times Magazine* ran a long feature on Hedda Nussbaum, who was arrested ten years ago, in 1987, along with her companion, Joel Steinberg, for the beating death of their six-year-old

adopted daughter. Steinberg was convicted of first-degree man-
slaughter in 1988. He's still in prison. The prosecutor dropped the
charges against Nussbaum, who had been beaten, burned, and tortured by Steinberg for nine years. I look at the full-page photo of
Hedda Nussbaum's scarred and savaged face, and it feels as though
what I suffered at Stu's hands was trivial. It wasn't trivial, of course. I
knew it wasn't trivial in 1986. But I wasn't concerned about my
safety. Stu had never done more than slap me, knock my glasses off.
I worried much more that Stu would kill himself than that I would
get hurt.

⊛

July 10, 1986

I tried to raise thirty or forty thousand dollars for the down payment
from family and friends. I started with AA, who immediately said she could
lend me ten thousand dollars, but who thought that renting an apartment
might be a better idea. "Stu is probably more willing to change behaviors
now than ever," she said. She urged me to talk with him about signing a
binding agreement that we would either work certain things out by a
specific date or he would release forty thousand dollars so that I could
buy the house.

So I made a short list of what I wanted and went to Stu. We talked for
an hour and a half or so, and AA was right: Stu was remarkably willing to
agree to several things that we have argued about before. He said he
would become the "registered patient" on my insurance and would continue seeing Shapiro through 1986; he agreed to continue to pay 50 percent of Bergeson's bill through 1986; he talked at some length about ne-
gotiating an equitable marital property agreement; he agreed to pay 100
percent of the earnest money I will have to forfeit on the Rowen Street
house. He also said he wanted to buy me the white station wagon and
use it in August to take a family vacation.

The conversation, which had Stu positively euphoric, fell apart when
he realized that I was talking about putting all these agreements into a

legal document that would include a clause insisting that neither of us would be violent toward the other or would threaten violence. If we did not abide by the document, he would give me forty thousand dollars so that I could buy a house. He got very upset and angry. "This is just an extended one of your '*if* you don't do this, *then* I'll leave' demands," he snarled. Then he went out to get something to eat.

I called Dad, who promised me another ten thousand dollars. When Stu came back, I told him I did not need his signature for a down payment to buy the house, but said that I would be willing to give up the house and stay with him so long as he signed the agreement we'd discussed this afternoon. I especially emphasized the importance of the "no violence or threats of violence" provision. I said I would definitely leave if I ever had reason to be afraid of him.

Stu said I should draft an agreement. He would sign it. So once again, to be cynical, he is attempting to buy my love.

⊛

We are more than a week into April. Lake Mendota opened on the first; the last gray rafts of rotten ice sank and disappeared. A day or two later, when I raked, I uncovered two patches of yellow and purple crocuses, and two robins hopped around the raked-up lawn, rooting for grubs. But this morning, snow dusts the blue plastic bag protecting the *New York Times*. We set the clocks forward a couple of days ago; this week should mark the start of the biking season. But Sunday morning, the wind howled around the house, sixty miles an hour. No cyclist could have stayed upright. And now the temperature has dropped into the twenties; if the first evening ride of the season happens, it will wheel away from the park minus me.

It could be worse: Minnesota, northern Wisconsin, North and South Dakota are digging out from a blizzard that dropped three feet of snow. It's still hard winter on the shore of Lake Superior. At least we have had crocuses.

What a familiar mantra: buck up, things could be worse. The mother is sick and pees in the living room. But the father hasn't left, as so many fathers do. The husband pours too many drinks; night after night, he climbs the stairs from the kitchen, three times, four times, five, ice cubes rattling in his glass. But he has plenty of money; it's not as though the children go hungry while he spends hundreds of dollars on Jack Daniel's and Tanqueray.

These days, at least, I am able to state clearly what I see. The cold has frozen the crocuses, which lie limp on the raked-up ground.

✦

Saturday evening, July 12, 1986

I have been up and down, upset and calm, so many times in the past two days that I can barely figure out what's happening. Stu has been at a regatta, coming home nights. Yesterday I had to tell the owner whether I could remove the contingencies on the offer to purchase the Rowen Street house. I panicked about the decision: should I, could I, buy the house? What finality. Stayed in bed until eight thirty, completely forgetting a breakfast meeting, agonizing. Panicked about Stu becoming violent or suicidal; upset by the thought of what would happen if I gave up the house and thus gave Stu more control. Talked with Helen and with Martin Shapiro. (Martin had no answer to my most pressing question: Will Stu kill himself if I leave?) Mostly I sat paralyzed, unable to do anything. Finally took Eli to the new Historical Society Museum, then came home about four-thirty. Talked with Helen again, for an hour; got Eli a quickie supper at Dairy Queen and dropped him at the Theater Guild (where at age eight, he's volunteering backstage on *Life with Father*). Came home, swam, called Evan Holmes and said that Stu would not release the money for a down payment and I could not remove the contingency. Evan still wanted me to buy the house. He assured me that I could get a sixty-five-thousand-dollar mortgage on the basis of a twenty-thousand-dollar down payment and was willing to let me move in substantially before closing—perhaps in three weeks.

This morning I woke from a dream in which Eli, at a neighborhood party on Rowen Street, learned by accident that we were moving. He was very upset. The dream made me think that perhaps I was making the wrong moves; perhaps I should try again. Went to Farmers' Market with

205

Eli, came back and called Rachel to ask for a ten-thousand-dollar loan. She is not able to do it, so I really do have only twenty thousand dollars, plus whatever of my own savings I want to sink into a down payment. But I told Rachel about the long conversation Stu and I had on Thursday, and she urged me not to get hung up on the house, but to keep trying, if Stu is willing to make changes. She emphasized the need to work toward economic equality.

When we hung up, I wrote Stu a three-page letter with ideas for starting again. His response was awful: before he saw the letter, he was loving and eager, but after he read it, he was angry and snide. Finally, as I was standing at the sink, he jabbed me in the rear and then tried to strong-arm me into a hug. I had/have been very explicit about no violence, and this was a good deal more nasty than a tease. It got me upset enough to come upstairs and work on the financial disclosure statement Carol Madsen needs to file for divorce. And to get together the bank statements the mortgage company will need.

Tore my right lens this afternoon. Not pleased to be back to glasses.

⊛

Sunday evening, July 13, 1986

Helen here for dinner. Later, Stu and I talked. He is "hurt" that I want to put everything in writing but unwilling to accept responsibility for having hurt me in the past. He doesn't trust me and wonders why I insist on economic equity. I seem to be bashing my head to a pulp on something that professes only to be loving and sympathetic. If it is so loving, why do I hurt so much?

It is not really my head that hurts but my gut.

⊛

Monday, July 14, 1986, 11 A.M.

Last night, after I'd gone to bed, Stu asked me to come to him. I couldn't; I suggested he get in bed with me. He did, and we made love, but not well. This morning he said, "I can't live with you on the basis of sanctions and formal agreements. He wanted to sign an agreement that would release twenty thousand dollars (rather than forty thousand) for me to buy the house. I cried. He held me and told me, "I love you. I don't want you to go, but I realize I can't keep you."

I feel sadness, but also tremendous relief.

⊛

Monday afternoon

I am prequalified for a forty-seven-thousand-dollar mortgage at 10¼ percent.

⊛

Monday evening

Stu said (à la Douglas Adams), "So long and thanks for all the fish," and left to spend the night at Helen's.

Jekyll and Hyde

I have been sorting through too many photographs. I unearth snap-shots from the horse-packing trip the kids and I took in Wyoming with my sister Ellen, the year after I left Stu. David is a pudgy twelve-year-old; Eli a cute, short, nine. Two years later, we visited the Thompsons, who were living in Japan. David and Eli stand under a black umbrella in the Hiroshima Peace Park, beside mounds of origami cranes. David has stretched out; he towers over Eli, who still seems very young. A ski trip with Maggie Thompson and her kids in northern Wisconsin; another, the next year, in Utah. Eli has lost his little-boy cuteness: he sights down a cue to line up a pool shot, and he looks very cool. The house changes. David and Eli stand in the backyard, beside the old, falling-down porch. Long tim-bers prop the porch roof during the construction project. David graduates: my father and Charlotte, AA, my sisters, David and Eli, eat dinner on the new, big porch. David disappears from the photos; shows up again in Bolivia. At nineteen thousand feet, David, Eli, and David's high-school girlfriend stand outside the crude stone entrance to a mine. I find Eli's concert pictures: he stands stiff, a middle-schooler in a white shirt and tie, holding his trombone; he sits in the back row of the Youth Symphony, playing at East Towne Mall; he's with the Highland Brass Trio, wearing his tux, playing a graduation concert in a university recital hall.

The pictures telescope a decade, shrink it into the few moments it has been. I send e-mail to Rachel, my friend for more than three decades: I have lost too much in the past year, the boys, Helen, my youth. She e-mails back: I think we get to deal with loss from now on, even more than before.

⊛

Tuesday night, July 15, 1986

Stu came home from Helen's about six-fifteen this morning. At seven I smelled coffee brewing. When I went downstairs after taking a shower and getting dressed, Stu asked, "Do you want breakfast?" and whipped up a couple of scrambled eggs. He was really in an extraordinarily accommodating mood.

I said I was confused. He said that he wanted to talk this evening. I went to work and began to feel the tension mount. The anxiety. What was Stu going to drop on me today?

I worked for six hours straight on a grant proposal, with time out for a long phone conversation with Helen, who said she'd read the long letter listing the conditions under which I'd agree to stay with Stu. She'd decided I didn't love him. "You might as well admit it and stop confusing him." Well, she wasn't quite as hard on me as that, but she did say I had been giving Stu two messages: a message to stay and a message that was very uncompromising and made things very difficult for him. She described my letter as "harsh."

Talking with Helen was when the anxiety started to mount. She said that she hadn't seen Stu this morning, but she was quite sure that last night he had been resigned to the fact that I was going to leave. He didn't like it, but he wasn't freaking out.

With great good fortune this occurred on a Tuesday, and so I went to see Paul Bergeson at three. He's such a fantastic guy. I talked about why I was confused and about finding evidence yesterday that David had taken a match to an ottoman in the lake room. And then I finally asked him if he would read the letter I'd written to Stu and give me his reaction.

And his reaction was that it was a very clear, very cogent document. "A very political document," he said. He used the king analogy again and said he thought the letter was an attempt to redress grievances. He found my demands for economic equality reasonable. But, "You're asking the king for equality," he pointed out.

I told him—as I had told Helen—that I think I have two kinds of responses to Stu because I am responding to two different people, or two different parts of one person. There's the Stu who is very thoughtful and gentle and kind, and then there's the brutal and hostile Stu. I cannot stand the brutal and hostile Stu, and I can't stand the unpredictability of not knowing who I'm going to be dealing with.

Paul basically affirmed the letter as a political document that made a very good statement of my position: either I get what I ask for or I leave. And so I started to talk with Stu this evening with a wonderful certainty that I was doing the right thing.

I started out by insisting, "If there's any more violence, I'll leave." And then I described my perception that there are the two kinds of Stu.

At first he got defensive, pleading, "Don't call me a schizophrenic."

"I'm not calling you a schizophrenic," I said. "I'm saying that there's the Stu I want to stay with and the Stu I want to leave, and I need to have a way to say 'enough of this' to the Stu that I want to leave, without him reacting defensively." I explained that *that* was why I talked about sanctions and why I put a three-month time limit on staying: it was a way of dealing with the unpredictability and knowing that I had an out, a way to escape from the Stu I want to leave.

I think he finally understood.

We went over my letter point by point. He accepted every condition in the letter and also accepted my explanation of wanting to live with only the Dr. Jekyll Stu and not with the Mr. Hyde, or with the uncertainty of which one he will be.

So I'll withdraw the offer on the house and settle in for a three-month stay. If Stu is able to recognize the Jekyll-Hydeness of his behavior, that is a major turning point, I think.

⊛

A couple of months ago, I sat next to a runway model on a plane back from Los Angeles. She wore a skimpy, white, cropped sweater and hip-hugging black bell-bottoms over her very long legs. She carried a stuffed black carry-on bag marked Bordeaux Models; before she stowed it, she took out a plastic two-liter bottle of water. There were two more in the bag. When she stretched to tuck the bag into the overhead compartment, I got a good view of her navel.

We didn't say a word to each other on the three-and-a-half-hour flight. She studied her ticket. She was going to Paris. She wasn't especially pretty: short, shaggy, two-toned hair, medium brown streaked with blond. Plucked eyebrows. A pouty mouth. But it was her eyes that made me stare. Green eyes, mascara thick on the lashes, eye shadow coloring the sockets from cheekbones to temples to brows, a bruised brownish-yellowish-purple feathered over both upper and lower lids. She looked as though someone had punched her, blackened both her eyes, eight or nine days earlier and the tissues had reabsorbed the most obvious blacks and blues.

⊛

Saturday, July 19, 1986

Life has definitely been less stressful since Tuesday, but I have also wondered on several occasions whether I have given up my chance to go for the gold—or sold some birthright for a mess of pottage. I have schoolgirl fantasies about finding a white knight, a man of the caliber of Paul Bergeson, if I could only leave the bastard I chose to marry.

Well, no matter. I find I cannot retain my dreams when I sleep with Stu, and I am left only with fragments of tours of ruined houses, with an eye toward reconstruction.

I have been looking at desks and sofa beds to furnish my new office on the third floor; planning to go to the Northwest the first week of September to backpack with Shelly; talking with Stu about two weeks of family vacation in August; and beginning to panic about getting three *Marriage and the Family* programs done before we leave. Especially when Shelly and Ellen will each be here, visiting, for a week (and we have two house guests right now). Still, all this busy-ness seems preferable to the disruption of separation.

The painter has finally finished all the work I planned for this spring: painting the living room and dining room, my bedroom, my study, the peeling woodwork in the little den.

I have lived in this house longer than any other place in my life; it will be ten years next month. When I cleared out the bedroom a couple of months ago, I realized I'd never dusted the baseboard behind the bed. I'm a terrible housekeeper—like my mother, even before she got sick. But until now, it never really mattered. Before my home got so deeply dirty, I moved someplace else.

In the three years after I graduated from college, I lived in five different places. Finally, I moved into Stu's house in Redwood City. I lived there for three years, until I gave up on graduate school.

Our next home was the blue Dodge van, in which we traveled the United States. Before we left on our journey, Stu taught himself carpentry. He went to the library, took out books about cabinetmaking, learned the difference between a nailed joint and a rabbet. He bought a booklet on how to customize a van. He modified the plans, bought plywood and two-by-fours, showed me designs for furniture: a benchlike couch that opened into a double bed; a cupboard with drawers and a hanging closet that fitted behind the driver's seat; a tall, skinny cabinet for dishes and books and canned goods, a small cabinet with a sliding shelf for the cooler and a pull-out silverware drawer.

Stu sat in the driveway, sawing and sanding and painting, inventing a system of turnbuckle latches to fasten the cabinets snugly in place. A little boy from down the block, too young for school, kept him company. He lived with his mother; his parents were divorced. He loved to spend time with Stu, to play with wood scraps, to watch.

My job that spring was to clean the house, get it ready for sale. Stu bought a carton of trisodium phosphate (TSP); this will do a good job, he said. I began in his study, on the sickly green painted walls. I dissolved the TSP in a bucket of water, pulled on my rubber gloves, climbed a ladder, dipped the sponge in the water and squeezed it out. I ran the sponge along the wall. It took up a layer of yellowish grime. The study wall turned blue. Stu smoked two or three packs a day. Years of his smoking, I soon discovered, had yellowed the entire house.

I didn't like washing walls, especially walls turned dingy by someone else. Why couldn't Stu wash the walls? I asked. Why couldn't I build furniture? Stu pointed out that he knew how to do carpentry; I could barely hammer a nail. And we wanted to finish the van, sell the house, get on the road as soon as possible.

❀

Tuesday, July 22, 1986

Paul Bergeson and I spent a fair amount of time struggling this afternoon, trying to figure out what to talk about next. I said I'm concerned about having "solved my problems" and therefore not having a reason to keep talking with him. I said I can't talk with other people: other people won't validate my decision to stay with Stu, although they would support my decision to leave.

"Why is that?" Paul wanted to know.

"It has to do with my feelings that I don't love Stu. Or that I define love differently than other people do." I was surprised at how upset I became when we finally got down to the question of love.

Paul said, "This is an old problem, isn't it Judy?" And I said yes, and I was very upset.

When I start free-associating about love, a lot of things become clear. I was loved—I thought, I felt—for what I did, not for who I was. I didn't love my mother—I hated her I feel guilty about that. I have loving feelings about her from when I was a little child, but not after she got sick. It makes me uncomfortable to think that Stu loves me more than I love him, and yet I don't believe that he loves me for reasons that have to do with me. He loves me for reasons that have to do with him.

❀

I look out the window at the daffodils and tulips in the yard, at the lush leaves and tender flower spikes of the lilies of the valley, and I want to think that spring is here, new beginnings; all in good time, love will flow naturally. But a cloud crosses the sun and the tightly curled leaves on the oak look like small balled fists to me.

I blame my personal history: the abusive ex-husband, the sick mother, the overwhelmed father, Nana—frail and elderly—who (having long before told me to save myself) accused me of lacking compassion. How can a person imperfectly loved become a lover herself?

But it's not just me. I think of all the friends over the past ten years who've said, "I feel as though I'm a teenager again, learning about men." These are divorced women, smart, accomplished professionals who also failed Love 101. Or did it fail us?

We were brought up to believe in fairy tales. Prince Charming would give us whatever we lacked: faith in ourselves, a structure for life, financial security. Children to make us whole.

It's just as easy to fall in love with someone rich, Nana said, as someone poor.

I'll support you through college, my father said. But if you get married, it's your husband's responsibility.

"You'd better marry a rich man," my childhood dentist said, scowling at my teeth. He was a friend of my father's, and he'd decided that braces were a luxury my father couldn't afford. I once told this story to a boyfriend.

"That explains it!" he said. "That's why you keep your lips so tight, you're almost impossible to kiss!"

How often boys told me that in one way or another, I was not loveable. "I think we should break up," my first boyfriend wrote me in junior high. "You don't wear nice enough clothes, and you don't have nice enough friends."

"You're the ugliest girl I've ever seen," a young man said, the summer I was twenty. I was in New York; I'd won a guest editorship at *Mademoiselle* magazine. I'd just gotten a free haircut at Charles of the Ritz. This guy (he was drunk) was one of the crew rounded up by young *Mademoiselle* staffers to entertain the out-of-town guests.

Boys don't make passes at girls who wear glasses.

⊛

Tom broke up with me in 1966; I met Stu in 1969. Maybe it was my new contacts. Maybe it was the times: the dawning Age of Aquarius. Plenty of boys made passes in the years between Tom and Stu. The way to catch a man was legs open, on your back. The men I met fucked to Bob Dylan and the Stones. They fucked politics. They fucked your brains out.

Once when I was twenty-three or twenty-four, I tried to count all the men I'd slept with. I stopped when I got to twelve. The number seemed enormous. But not only that: I couldn't remember all their names. There was the medical student I'd met at the laundromat. He admired my wide hips: "Ideal for bearing children." There was the Aussie I'd met on the street who had an adorable furry bum. There was the guy at Yosemite, a rock climber who disdained shoes. I had a terrible crush on him. But even then, memory failed. Did I just imagine him in bed? And how many others had slipped out of the data bank?

It was a relief when I finally met Stu. He wanted to be introduced because he admired something I'd said after a lecture on Vietnam. He liked smart women. He had good politics. He had enough money to live on. And he showed a little respect. He took so long to make a pass—so much longer than the guys I was used to—that I began to wonder if something was wrong.

"This can't be love," the song goes, "because it feels so good." Well, not so good, maybe. But not bad. Not at first.

⊛

Wednesday, July 23, 1986

I have named my new white Volvo "Gus." It just seems right. After Paul BerGESon.

Monday, July 28, 1986

I can't remember a week when I've felt so good for so long. Exhilarated tonight by Mozart's Sinfonia Concertante in E-flat (K. 364) on the radio, a grand performance by Pinchas Zuckerman and the Los Angeles Philharmonic. I played it at full volume all through the first floor. And it helps to have a grant proposal about ready to mail and the "Socialization" program for *Marriage and the Family* ready to turn in. But it's more than that: thinking about talking with Paul Bergeson about love; a week of low/no tensions with Stu; biking forty-five miles and swimming laps every day; a good party here Saturday evening with the Houcks and Dan and Jeanne.

All these details don't explain my general euphoria, though. I just feel up. Like flying. Eli reported a dream in which he and I jumped off the Sears Tower together, wearing helium-filled vests. Like that!

Thursday, July 31, 1986

Another pleasant day. I am astonished at the ability we seem to have to string good days together, all of a sudden. I wonder whether it is possible that it can go on and on. At the same time, I am sucked in, feeling more loving of Stu every day; and then puzzling over whether the love I feel for Paul B—because he is taking care of me—somehow makes me more accepting of the idea of being taken care of, loved, and hence makes me loving. I think often and fondly of Paul B, but also fondly, much more often, about Stu.

Memorial Day is past, the summer "officially" begun.

Yesterday, I decided to hike around Lake Wingra, avoiding most of the roads. I struck out into the woods behind the boat house. Purple and white violets lined the path. I passed the duck pond, followed the trail through the oak savanna—and then it petered out. I found myself in a broad expanse of downed and matted reeds, walking on a mat of rushes laid over hillocks and stubble. In the distance, a young man trained binoculars on a hawk. He heard the crackling reeds, saw me coming, moved away.

I headed into a marshy wetland. Thickets of willows, a meadow blooming with pink shooting stars. I headed for traces that changed, as I approached, into small streams and rivulets. I jumped across or walked the banks until I found a few stepping stones. I favored high ground, guessed at directions, circled back on myself. I knew I couldn't get lost: I could hear the traffic. But I felt like an explorer, making my way through a wilderness.

Soon the willow thickets grew too thick to breach. Mounds of moss and clumps of marsh marigolds formed islands on a sea of black muck. Mats of watercress clogged the flowing rivulets. I had to cross a swamp: neither water nor land. I balanced on brittle bridges of shrubs; searched for footing on rotting tree stumps, mounds of bog plants, abandoned beaver dams. When I misjudged the depth of vegetation, or could not stretch my stride far enough, the muck oozed over my boot tops, sucked me in.

Grabbing at branches for balance, I crossed another stream, pushed through some willows, and found a walk made of planks and two-by-fours. I had entered the Arboretum. A couple in tennis shoes eyed my boots, the mudstreaked cuffs of my jeans. "Taking the hard way?" they laughed.

I shook my head. "Circumnavigating Lake Wingra." But what I truly was doing was trusting the skin of the earth.

⊛

Friday, August 1, 1986

Helen was here for dinner; another interminable evening of pleasantries. I was very uptight. Finally, after she left, I realized that I am *furious* because Stu has very cavalierly decided to spend Sunday afternoon sailing, even though Ellen will be in town and that's when we planned to get together.

⊛

Later

Stu implores me to talk with him about why I am upset, but when I do, he calls me irrational. I leave; he implores me to return. We have a conversation in which he is interminably self-justifying.

The details of the conversation really are not so important as my feeling that Stu wants to put an enormous Band Aid on our relationship and say "everything's OK" without acknowledging the validity of my feelings. His suggestion that we each "have a half glass of wine and go to bed and then get up at six-thirty and go to Farmers' Market" (something I believe he has *never* done, which makes it an Enormous Concession) doesn't do anything to make it "all better." So I told him I was too upset and uptight to sleep with him. Which seems to have made him cold and angry. Tough shit.

In the bathroom, getting ready for bed, I developed an almost physical urge to send a wrecking ball through the wall of the house: to destroy and to break out.

※

This weekend, my friend Emma introduced me to a man who spent twenty years in a Buddhist monastery. He left a few years ago to go to graduate school. I asked him how he decided to stop being a monk after so many years. "It wasn't really a decision," he said. "I just listened and knew it was time."

We sat on the porch of the Trempeleau Hotel, overlooking the Mississippi, eating lunch and talking about the difference between making rational decisions—weighing the pros and cons, checking the bottom line—and listening to learn what the universe says is the right thing to do. I called this "intuition." Alex said that his Buddhist practice had taught him to correlate and connect what most people call "intuition" with rational decision making. "The important thing," he said, "is not to indulge in second-guessing."

Emma said that when she was small, she was aware of overwhelming intuitions, powerful sensations for which she had no name. "I'm having feelings," she told her mother when she was eight, and her mother responded by holding her hand, telling her it was all right, reassuring her until the feelings resolved and Emma could go on with her life.

It seemed the exact opposite of my childhood. I not only could not trust my feelings; I had to deny that they existed. My father praised the rational; he scorned his grandmother's superstitions. I don't remember him ever asking how anyone felt. He denied my mother's depression and ignored, so far as I can tell, not only her MS but his own grievous childhood. How did he feel about his father's desertion, about his mother's death from tuberculosis? I knew only his extremely controlled anger at Tante and Unk, who raised him and his little brother. They favored their own son; Morris got the best food, and of course, he got their love. "But they were good people," my father insisted. "They didn't have to take us in."

※

Wednesday evening, August 6, 1986

Saw Shapiro today, the first time in a month. Stu was very fearful, afraid of going. He wondered aloud in the session, "Why can't we just love each other? Why all these formalities? Why do we have to see you [Martin]? When we're here, we just talk about our disagreements and we attack each other."

Martin stressed the importance of keeping up with the formalities "so you don't go back to the old ways. The issues lie just under the surface," he said. And he asked Stu, "Do you think you have behaviors you need to change? Or is it just Judy who thinks you need to change?"

"I think Judy exaggerates when she describes my behavior," Stu said. "For example, my behavior in her family's presence. I do need to bite my tongue perhaps more than I do, but I would never want to suffer fools lightly."

Stu was particularly upset at my notion that he has two personalities, that sometimes he's warm and charming like Dr. Jekyll and sometimes he's a fearsome Mr. Hyde. "That's impossible," he said. "For each person, there is only one bell-shaped curve with extremes, not two bell-shaped curves."

This all took on different colors tonight when Stu—having had at least two strong drinks, and probably more, after his sailboat race—asked Shelly whether she ever felt the need to pay a "shrink" to solve her problems.

Shelly was quiet for a while. Then she said, "It's really none of your business, but since you're my sister's husband, and I think talking about it will help her and you, I'll tell you." She said that a few years ago, she'd seen a therapist and she would do it again, if necessary, "to help me deal with and bring into congruence the different parts of my identity." Stu couldn't understand what she was talking about, so she went into pretty personal detail about her life and how she sometimes felt like one kind of person and sometimes like another.

Stu attacked her for talking about "pieces of identity." "An identity is a whole, a sameness," he insisted. "If you don't accept my word for it, let's look it up in the dictionary."

Shelly, very angry, said, "You're not my husband and I don't have to fight with you about this. Millions of people use the word as I do," and left—in tears because she had tried to be level, show herself honestly, and he'd simply trashed her.

I went up to the third floor to talk with Shelly for a half hour or so and then came back down to the second floor to sleep by myself. Stu pursued me with the dictionary, slamming doors again and again. "Let's be loving," he insisted. "Let's not let someone else's wrong-headed definition of 'identity' come between us."

But I wasn't having it. "Leave me alone. I will not talk with you while you are drunk." Of course, that upset him. He kept pursuing me. Finally I had to go out and sit in the car, planning to go to a motel if he wouldn't leave me alone.

❦

Thursday morning, August 7, 1986

At 4:40 A.M., Stu barged into the bedroom and woke me up. "Come join me in bed," he urged. "Let's be friends." He wanted to make up after last night's horror show. I tried to ignore him; finally decided I'd get back to sleep faster if I simply obliged him and moved to the porch, but I did

220

stipulate "no making love." I still had trouble getting back to sleep. I was very tense and only dozed off after realizing I would have to make it clear that I *never* want another argument about whether or not I should come to bed with Stu and that I *don't like* being awakened in the middle of the night to change beds.

In the shower this morning, I tried to think of the best way to say this to Stu. I thought about his pleasure a few weeks ago when I asked him "as a favor" not to drink for an hour before bed. Suddenly I was struck by the significance of his taking pleasure when I phrased my desires as requests for favors. How much more servile can one get than relying on the favors of the king to meet one's needs?

Halcyon Days

Eli turns nineteen today, so I am beginning the last year of my decade as the mother of teenage boys. Today that seems much less momentous than where I am, physically: back at Norcroft, working in the same writing shed I inhabited last October! I arrived yesterday, on the summer solstice, for a week that is really pure gift of the gods. Or goddesses.

I wasn't sure it was going to be worth the long trip, especially when I set out in a driving rain. I had the windshield wipers going at high speed for the first couple of hours while I hydroplaned through the puddles on Interstate 90. But it did clear up—or more precisely, I drove out of the storms—and by the time I arrived, after eight and a half hours on the road, the sky was blue, the clouds white and puffy, the air clear and fragrant with cedar and pine. I walked into the lodge, looked out at Lake Superior, and started to cry.

The task now is to find a rhythm that works for such a short time. There's so much I want to do: write, of course, but also ride Eli's mountain bike, and hike the Oberg Mountain loop, and revisit the Temperance River, and maybe even find a place to swim. I am sustained by the knowledge that I have been awarded another writing residency later this year, four weeks in November at Ucross Foundation in eastern Wyoming. My life feels abundant with opportunity.

A few days before I came up here, David arrived in Madison to help Hal and Stu clear out Helen's house. They found a small packet of letters I'd written to Helen and Richard, including several from the year we lived in the van. That year had its ups and downs, but it was the best Stu and I ever had.

The van trip was my idea. I always thought I should see my own country before I ventured abroad. But the summer before I started college, I was given a scholarship to join an East-West study tour organized by the American Friends Service Committee. I spent eight weeks in Poland, Czechoslovakia, East and West Germany, and Switzerland, before I'd seen much of the United States. When our Swissair jet lifted off from Idlewild in June 1962, I had been as far west as eastern Ohio, as far south as Washington, D.C. I had gone east to see Nana and Poppy in New York City many times. When I applied to colleges, I visited Vassar; Poughkeepsie was the farthest north I'd been.

By the time I met Stu, I'd seen more of the country. I'd flown to Chicago and on to college in Portland in September, 1962. I'd traveled back and forth between Pittsburgh and Portland six or eight times by train, a couple of times by car, once by bus, once in Chuck Goldmark's father's private plane. I'd spent Thanksgivings and spring breaks with friends in California. And just after I met Stu, I'd made a quick tour with Shelly and Patrick to the rim of the Grand Canyon and other highlights of the Southwest.

But I hungered for more. In 1968, when I started graduate school, I bought an old Volkswagen beetle and a set of metric wrenches. I wanted to learn to work on the engine. Some day, I thought, I would trade up to a used camper van and then I'd take to the road.

By the fall of 1971, the antiwar movement was winding down. The body counts at Kent State and Jackson State and the University of Wisconsin's bombed Army Math Research Center had both angered and sobered Stu and me. The revolution seemed unlikely to happen soon, and we were tired of going to meetings, of arguing about tactics and strategy.

I was equally tired of graduate school. I'd spent the summer in Boston, working as an intern for the *Christian Science Monitor.* On weekends, I made forays into New York City, doing preliminary research for a Ph.D. dissertation that would study the way community organizing groups used the public access channel on the newly franchised cable television system. One day, I stepped around a comatose body on an East Village stoop and made my way up the stairs. The stairwell smelled of urine. The hallways smelled of garbage. I sat on an Indian print spread thrown over a bed and observed a meeting in someone's apartment. A group of radical filmmakers and several militant Puerto Rican Young Lords were discussing their plan to document the lives of the poor on the new medium of videotape. Their excitement was thick in the air, and contagious. Why would I want to *study* something like this, I wondered. I figured I already knew what would happen with whatever the Young Lords produced. The tape might get scheduled on the public access channel, but hardly anyone would watch. The whole point of work like this was the process, not the product. The video project would allow poor people to tell their own story, give them tools to change their world. If this sort of thing interested me, I thought, I should be a hands-on media person, not a degreed academic.

Besides, in order to write a dissertation, I'd have to live in New York for another six months or a year. I'd only been East two months and already I missed Stu.

I went back to California. I told Stu I wasn't going to write a dissertation. I would finish my last year of classes—and then what? I described my dream of touring the country. It didn't take much discussion. We loved to travel. Neither of us had a job. Stu could sell his house; we could live on his investments. We decided to buy a van.

⊛

Sunday evening, August 10, 1986
Gooseberry Falls Motel, North Shore, Lake Superior

Left home about ten-thirty yesterday morning—a false start. We'd forgotten the binoculars, and we circled back to get them and bird books. Out of practice! It has been thirteen years since we traveled in the van. We had further evidence of how out-of-practice we are when we hit Duluth at six in the midst of an enormous rainstorm, only to discover that there were no motel rooms. In fact, there were no motel rooms for over a hundred miles, and we ended up in Saint Paul. Incredible rain all the way there. Stu was relieved to stop driving, finally, at ten; the kids were relieved to find civilization. We spent the night at a Best Western across the street from the Deluxe check printing plant.

When we were living in the van, we knew better than to wait until evening to look for a place to spend the night.

Still, everyone is in remarkably good moods, except Stu briefly this morning when he somehow (in a dream?) decided I don't love him. I spent the day trying to prove I do.

When we were living in the van . . . The mantra of halcyon days. For fourteen months, we answered to no one except ourselves, traveled when and where we wished, slept until we were rested, hiked and camped and drove through some of the most spectacular scenery in the world. We pitied the people we visited, friends and relatives tied to the treadmills of jobs and families. But we also scorned the retired couples, hooked on television and refrigeration, who polluted our off-season campgrounds with the roar of RV generators.

We were the only people we knew who were doing things properly. When Stu signed on to my notion of traveling around in a van, he made it clear that he wasn't thinking of a used Volkswagen bus. In November 1971, after serious research in *Consumer Reports* and an unscientific measure of the relative heat-collecting capacity of vehicles of various colors parked in the sunny Dodge Center lot, Stu put a deposit down on a blue Dodge B-200 van.

Nadine—we named her after a woman in a Chuck Berry song— was delivered in January 1972, and I recorded the event on the first page of the typed log of our adventure. The following two or three pages, snapped into the green vinyl binder, document Nadine's outfitting: the professional roof painting and vent installation, Stu's furniture building, my epic search for fireproof curtain fabrics, our shopping expeditions to backpacking specialty stores and van customizers from Berkeley to San Jose. And then on June 30, at Atwell Mill Campground in Sequoia National Park, I note our departure, the previous day, from the San Francisco peninsula. One year, two months, and nearly two hundred single-spaced typed pages later, just after Labor Day 1973, we drove into Davis, California, to look for an apartment.

Last night, I began to reread the journal and discovered it to be a closely observed chronicle of oblivion. Painstaking descriptions of backpacking routes. (An early start took us over Franklin Pass. The climb is fairly steep at first, out of a lush meadow dotted with rocks; quickly turns into a lot of drudge, up a lot of sand and scree.) Meticulous notation of geologic features. (Headed east on Route 124, through beautiful rolling farmland of light brown loess.) Compelling descriptions of strangers, like Dan, a grower of "bush"—pronounced "boosh"—who discovered us bathing in a stream in southern Oregon's Kalmiopsis Wilderness. (A slender guy of medium height, in his twenties; very long hair, heavy-duty britches with a double crotch, boots falling apart and soles worn almost flat, carrying a rifle. He puffs on a corncob pipe, which he fills with green tobacco from the pocket of his brown work shirt; we smell faint whiffs of marijuana before the wind takes the smoke downstream.)

The only moment I've found, so far, where I begin to acknowledge my feelings about our enterprise comes early in the journal, before we set out on the road. We had planned to trade my elderly Volkswagen in on the van. At the last minute, the Dodge Center reneged on its offer of two hundred dollars, and I gave the bug to my friend Gwen. I feel its loss as a loss of some independence. I still always have a car at my disposal, but it is not *mine;* when (as I did last Wednesday) I leave the lights on and run the battery down, Stu gets pissed as he wouldn't have if it had been the VW battery. But, good radical that I was, I translated my unease into self-criticism. I think it's more part of my equation *of my own things* with *my independence*—a real private property hangup—than Stu's reaction, I wrote.

226

Wednesday, August 13, 1986
Shoreline Motor Hotel, Thunder Bay, Canada

We've been following the Lake Superior coastline, along the North Shore, through Minnesota and into Canada. Hiked and camped at Gooseberry Falls and Cascade River State Parks, wandered through Grand Marais, shopping at the trading post and visiting the Cook County Museum, spent a night at Grand Portage Lodge, a pretty nice resort. Spent yesterday at Old Fort William, a really extensive "living history" site.

Had steak and ribs for dinner at the Prospector in Thunder Bay. Somehow, I managed to flip a barbecued rib off my plate and upend it in my water glass. It was very funny. "Like something out of *Airplane*," David said, approvingly.

※

The first summer in the van, 1972, we stayed in California. We spent most of July backpacking in the southern Sierra Nevada Mountains, near Mineral King, where the Sierra Club had, for years, been fighting Disney Corporation plans to build a huge ski resort. We were interested in the politics of the place, and we wanted to see the wilderness before it disappeared. As the season advanced and the snow in the high country melted, we headed north to Yosemite for another nine days on the trail and then drove down to Los Angeles to spend a week with my college friend Rachel. In mid-August, we dropped in on the Bay Area for a few days to resupply, visit old comrades, and have routine maintenance done on the van. And then back to the mountains again, the Trinity Alps, just north of Mount Shasta.

We planned to head east after Labor Day. And although I never mentioned it in the log, I wanted to get married before we visited our families. I had been living with Stu for three years. Our parents knew. So why get married? Then again, why not?

I had two reasons for wanting to marry. First, I felt acutely uncomfortable being financially dependent on Stu. While I was in school, I had a source of income. I couldn't live on my fellowship alone, but once I moved in with Stu, I no longer had to pay rent. I had plenty of money to cover my fair share of food and utilities, my clothes, and birthday and holiday presents for my family and friends.

When we started to travel in the van, Stu covered all our expenses. This didn't bother him; in fact, just the reverse. He had plenty of money, and he was generous with his friends and family. Spending his money was only a problem for me. We argued when it came time to buy carpeting for the van. I wanted to economize with cheap nappy felted squares. Stu pointed out that we only needed enough to cover a very small area. Why not buy the heavy-duty foam-backed loop that would stand up to wear and tear? He criticized my attitude. "Stop acting so poor," he said.

I was pretty sure that once we married, arguments like this would disappear. After all, most husbands supported their wives. Somehow, wifehood would make me feel less guilty about spending Stu's money, I knew.

I told Stu that marriage might make me stop acting like the "poor little rich girl" he scorned, but I probably didn't spell out my other reason for getting married. I was almost twenty-eight. We expected to travel for at least a year. By the time we settled down, I would be twenty-nine. I wanted to have children, and I felt that I was running out of time. Unless Stu agreed to marry me, I thought, my twenty-ninth year would be better spent finding a different boyfriend than tooling around in a van.

❀

Thursday evening, August 14, 1986
Grain's Motel, Pass Lake, Ontario

The evening has a sordid feel to it. The motel room smells of stale cigarette butts, beer, and Eli's vomit, and I have the memory of an execrable supper of split-pea soup with uncooked peas and a turkey sandwich on "brown" bread, hold the condiments, at a local truck stop. Over the hill is beautiful scenery and Sibley Provincial Park, but it was foggy and rainy all day so we opted for a motel instead. Good thing too. We have spent a good part of this trip battling lice that the kids must have brought along from Madison. This evening, just after we all deloused (yet again) with lindane (no prescription required in Canada), Eli got sick. It doesn't feel so very much like a lovely vacation right now!

⊛

Late August 1972. We drove up through Lava Beds National Monument and into southern Oregon. Labor Day weekend we met Sam, a thirty-year-old woman from Detroit. Tall, too thin, Scandinavian-looking with long blond hair, which she braids and piles on top of her head, I noted in the van log. She got a master's degree in education at Berkeley a year and a half ago and has been looking for a job since. In June she said, "Fuck it, it's summer," gave away a lot of stuff, stored the rest with her cousin, and took off in her twelve-year-old Volkswagen with Georgie Girl, her dog. She's spent the time in California, Oregon, Washington, and Idaho, mostly on beaches and in free Forest Service campgrounds. Sam had dinner with us and was in seventh heaven over the food. The pot roast turned out quite well, but I think her ecstasy was more due to the sad state of her budget and stomach. Georgie Girl liked the bones.

I liked Sam, and I admired her independence and spirit. She'd been reading up on mining claims. She's settled on a very remote stream on the east edge of the wilderness—two days' walk in from a quite rough road—to look for gold and plant a garden plot.

But Sam lived on the edge. She didn't seem to care about finding a husband or having kids. I knew I wasn't like her.

⊛

Saturday evening, August 16, 1986
Gurney-by-the-Sea, east of Nipigon, Ontario

Eli revived gradually yesterday as we drove through Sibley, enjoying the woods and the views. Took a short (three-mile) nature hike, on which both kids dragged and complained; had lunch near a lookout on the Thunder Bay side of the peninsula, on flat basalt. Then back in the car and drove past Nipigon, into the land of red rock and granite, and camped right on the shore of the lake at this campground-and-cottage resort. Today, went for a walk on a lovely stony beach, with kinnikinnick ground cover, blueberries, and amazing lichens just beyond the stones. Walked along the railroad track, a very busy line, on the way back to the car. Eli was very nervous, afraid that a train would come, and also embarrassed because Stu was wearing nothing but his purple underwear!

Must record our funniest event, as we ate breakfast at a picnic area yesterday overlooking Lake Marie Louise. The local fox, with a beautiful bushy tail, came begging, and David, Eli, and Stu fed him blueberries until David caught two small crayfish in the lake. Stu put the crayfish in a bowl and set it down for the fox as a special treat. But the fox grabbed the bowl in his mouth, shook the crayfish out, and ran away. As we walked back to the car, we found the bowl just off the trail—with a little present of scat. So much for us, and for the crayfish, which we never saw again.

We spent the first part of September 1972 camping in Oregon and northern California and then met up with Stu's brother Hal at the Reno airport. Watched a very nicely put together wife in her early twenties shepherding her extremely drunk, shirt-tail-out-of-his-pants young husband across the street to the terminal with the aplomb and gentleness of one who has saved the airline tickets from the Harrah's casino cashier. (Or was it the aplomb and gentleness of one who is satisfied at having dragged her boyfriend to the Little Chapel of Wedding Bells?)

Eight days later, I married Stu. Hal had gone back to Wisconsin after spending a couple of days with us. We'd dropped him at the San Francisco airport early on a Friday morning and begun the process, as I put it, of "getting our business done." Had premarital blood drawn at the People's Medical Clinic, stopped by the Dodge Center to warn them that we would be bringing the van in on Monday morning for a checkup and body work. Hurried over the weekend to clean the van and get it ready for delivery. Rushed around Monday morning to find a nice-looking ring—finally deciding on one at the last place we knew to look, a store on California Avenue. The jewelry maker happened to have a set of rings that he'd made for a couple who'd disappeared. The woman's ring fit me, and he decided he could probably make another one by the time he found the couple again.

Dealt with the State on Tuesday: applied for absentee ballots, went off to the San Mateo County Department of Public Health to pick up our blood test results, back to the San Mateo County Clerk (who didn't recognize us from the absentee ballot applications) to get a marriage license, renewed my driver's license, and finally—at five o'clock—met our witnesses at the Redwood City apartment of a retired minister and got married. Don't remember much of the ceremony as I was concentrating on not giggling and not shaking, unsuccessfully.

Later that evening, we had a party to which we'd invited everyone we knew on the peninsula. No champagne, no wedding cake, but mulled wine and dips. We told everyone we'd just gotten married. A lot of people—including my thesis adviser, who'd just gone through a nasty divorce—wanted to know why. "We were in the courthouse anyway," we joked. "It just seemed like the thing to do."

❀

Thursday, August 21, 1986
Sault Sainte Marie, Ontario

Spent the day on the Algoma Central's Agawa Canyon sightseeing train. There is nothing like being in a smoking car to emphasize the tyranny of someone else's addiction.

But the train trip was rather funny: a tenderfoot's introduction to the great outdoors. We wound through the woods and along a canyon, where we stopped for a picnic lunch. Really, all the passengers should have been wearing white duck trousers or lawn dresses with parasols. I wolfed down lunch with Stu, David, and Eli, and then climbed up to the lookout. Below me, the train and the valley were like a model under a Christmas tree. Then I hiked to the falls, Bridal Veil and Beaver. On the trail, an elderly couple with New York accents and Miami Beach sports clothes (she in a pink jersey top with gold chains, *très élégante*) were bickering about the distance to Bridal Veil. He didn't like walking so far. They were quiet as I passed. Then—

She: (Peremptorily) Les, wait here.

He: Why?

She: See. Look at her. She leaves her husband behind and goes where she wants to go. That's what I should do.

Later, I saw an older couple from Michigan bantering with coeds from Ball State.

He: I read a story years ago. Why do girls go to college? They go to find their future husbands! (He snorts.)

She: That used to be. Nowadays, believe me . . .

The world makes progress. It's just hard to see it in one's own life. Though I've been thinking about trying to focus on creative writing, perhaps even taking a class at the university, if I can arrange satisfactory meat-potatoes-and-health-insurance work, still part-time. It feels like a good plan.

In the year after we got married, we made a giant (though somewhat erratic) circuit of the United States. We crossed through the northern tier of states to meet Helen and Richard in Door County; headed east to spend Thanksgiving with Shelly and Patrick on Long Island; dropped down to Washington, D.C., to visit Stu's high-school sailing buddy, Geoff Dorsey, and his wife Lou; stopped in Pittsburgh on the way back to Madison. We gave ourselves cross-country skis for Christmas and drove north in early January to practice our parallel strides on the Door County cottage road.

Although I continued to note our whereabouts in the log, the entries are summary and brief. I thought I understood why. It's quite difficult to keep the journal going when we are with people with whom we want to spend time and are doing things which I am not convinced are worthy of record. This was a very public log of our travels, always subject to Stu's review. A good place to note Stu's first visit to a McDonald's (in Bloomington, Indiana); to observe that it's difficult to find a place to pee in New York City; to record that on November 19, on Interstate 80 in Pennsylvania, we saw a West Virginia license plate, completing the "collection" of fifty states we'd begun five months before. Not such a good place to describe the feeling I had at Helen and Richard's of being hopelessly outclassed. The log makes no mention of the attack of nerves I had the evening Helen asked me to set the table and put butter knives at each place. Where do they go? Next to the regular knives? Or on the bread plate? Or maybe above the dinner plate? Finally, intensely embarrassed, I asked Helen. She made it clear that the proper placement of butter knives really didn't matter to her.

🕮

Friday morning, August 22, 1986

I have had some good dreams the past few days—that is, long dreams that I remember. One involved being in a dean's office at a new Black college, advising a young black woman to go to a different college than her boyfriend. Meanwhile, the boyfriend was telling me how he plays his flute, variations on the scale, like a well-known jazz musician. I think of trying this and discover that my flute has been crushed at the joint between the head piece and the body. This part of the dream has to do with Pittsburgh, my high school involvement with the American Friends Service Committee, and the first couple of years I was in California, before I met Stu. (I was taking flute lessons then.) I understand that I am comfortable with and accepted by these blacks because of the way I lived back then.

This dream makes me think that my urge to write fiction has to do with unblocking the flute and making this end of my life as meaningful and honest as the first part. Perhaps writing of a young person's aspirations toward beauty and aesthetics—and the achievement of it, an essential integrity, only at the cost of something else.

🕮

Soon after we started to live in the van, Stu said that he didn't know what I wanted to get out of our travels. He had a clear purpose: he was teaching himself botany. He'd decided to resume his career as a scientist, but he wanted to change fields. Instead of doing organic chemistry, he planned to do research on biological systems. Learning about plants was part of his plan. We visited public gardens and arboretums everywhere we went. On every hike, Stu dissected trailside plants. He sat at picnic tables, thumbing through fat taxonomies. In Florida, he had his first meeting with a professor who did biological nitrogen-fixation research. He was beginning to scout for a job.

I didn't have any real direction or any particular reason to go any particular place. What I wanted was to see the United States. It didn't matter to me exactly where we went; I'd never seen most of these places, and I was happy just to go along for the ride. But Stu complained that he was tired of making all the decisions, tired of driving me around. He pushed me to come up with a kind of a mission, my own purpose for our trip.

I thought of myself as a sometime journalist. When we first set out in the van, I re-established my old connection with an editor at the *Christian Science Monitor*. I filed a story about the Sierra Club's battle with the Disney corporation after our Mineral King backpacking trip. Months later, when we reached Miami, we heard about another story that piqued the interest of my *Monitor* editor. Art Weiner, a popular professor of marine biology at Florida Keys Community College, had gone up to Tallahassee to testify in favor of legislation that would restrict dredging and filling. The college president headed an organization of Realtors and developers intent on killing the anti-pollution regulations, and he was trying to fire Weiner.

Stu was enthusiastic about spending some time in Key West, doing a little investigative journalism. Art Weiner, it turned out, had been his aunt Martha's neighbor and once saved her from a mugger. We headed down the two-lane Intracoastal Highway and parked the van in a Key West campground where tents and recreational vehicles crowded cheek-by-jowl along the edge of a landfill peninsula. Stu did "power structure research," reading back issues of the local

234

edition of the *Miami Herald*. I used my *Monitor* credentials to interview the college president. He spent a couple of hours trying to convince me that he was no proponent of "dirty water" but a realist who
knew that to bring the Keys out of their isolation it would be essential to do a certain amount of dredging and filling.

Stu and I hung out with Art Weiner and with the undergraduates
who were mobilizing to save his job. They took us on tours of hid-
den backyard gardens full of exotic tropical plants. They advised us
on places to eat. We shared our research with them. They used my
interview notes to prepare pointed questions for the college president. He refused to answer them. "Let's just go sit in his office like
they do at the big schools," one kid said in disgust.

That week in Key West was the best of the entire trip. We weren't
just tourists; we were doing politics. And after the *Monitor* published my article, I could see that what we were doing might interest
a wider audience. I began to think of the van log as notes for a book
about American attitudes toward land. I thought about some of the
characters we'd met: retirees who followed the migrations of song-
birds in their Winnebagos, a park ranger who used his campfire program to rally the audience against a jetport in the Everglades, free
spirits like Dan the "boosh" man and Georgie Girl's owner, Sam.
Americans were just discovering environmental politics. The first
Earth Day, April 22, 1970, had received a lot of publicity. Maybe I
could tell these stories and also make some important points about
American attitudes toward the environment.

I started buying books about the history of the places we visited.
I told Stu that my travels did have a purpose. And at Cedar Key,
Florida, on March 21, 1973, I reported in the van log, I am reluctant to
sit at the typewriter because I really want to finish de Beauvoir *(The Man-
darins)*. But as we were driving here and I was staring out at the scenery, I
kept thinking through the book I'd like to write, and I know it will be difficult enough to do with scanty notes, much less with no notes at all.

235

Friday evening, August 22, 1986
Home again

Spent much of the day, as we were driving back to Madison, very upset about a weird lump on the outside knuckle joint of my right-hand index finger. Cancer of the pointer finger? Relaxed a bit when a Mozart piano concerto came on the radio, but I'm still pretty tense. What to do? See if it goes away by Monday or tell my oncologist, who left a message on the answering machine last week? Something about tests; but he did not return my call this afternoon. What is *that* about? Does he want to talk about the results of my July 8 blood tests or mammogram? And if so, why did it take him five weeks to call? All this makes me realize how close to the surface my terror is. I was beginning to think I was just coping with my own anxieties by projecting an illness, alcoholism, on Stu. But then we got home, and before dinner, he downed half a quart bottle of Old Crow and I had to think again.

✿

I sat at picnic tables across Florida, along the Gulf coast, and into Texas, typing up my notes. In April 1973, in Big Bend National Park, I started a handwritten entry: The night noises are too nice to cover up with the sound of typing. From the evidence—a penciled exclamation mark in the margin, initialed SK—Stu obviously agreed. In fact, my typing became a recurring issue. Once again, nearly a month without typing journal entries, I wrote, months later. I have become so used to taking notes by hand that I don't break out the typewriter, especially as Stu has complained about the noise.

Still, we reveled in a spectacular spring, hiking through national parks and monuments, visiting Indian ruins, and photographing blooming cactus in Texas, Arizona, and New Mexico. By late May, we were back in California, visiting friends. We planned to spend much of the summer backpacking, but we wanted to get out of the Sierra Nevada and explore mountains we'd never seen. In July, we met Stu's old friend Geoff and his wife Lou and spent a week in Utah's Uinta Mountains. A scene from that week is etched in my memory:

It's a layover day; we'll spend two nights at the same campsite. Lou and Geoff have gone on a day hike to look for a waterfall. Stu and I sit in the hot sun on separate rocks on the edge of a clear mountain lake. We are fighting. He asked me to mend his hiking pants. I refused. "Why should I sew on your buttons and patches? Do it yourself!"

Stu says, "You know how to do it. I don't."

"I hate sewing," I tell him. "Besides, I'm not very good at it." Women's liberation is on my mind. I've been reading Simone de Beauvoir. But this is no intellectual exercise.

"They didn't teach sewing at Harvard," Stu says.

"Do you think they teach it at Reed?" I scream. "Do you think my parents paid for me to go to college so I'd learn to mend your pants?"

⊛

Monday morning, August 25, 1986

The first day of school for David and Eli. The sky is appropriately overcast, but it is still bizarre to start school in August, before Labor Day.

My finger bump is disappearing, I sometimes think. Or is it? I have minimized panic, but not eliminated it entirely. It is a knife blade—less than that—from me at all times. Disconcerting to learn, or relearn.

⊛

The second summer in the van continued its rocky course. After Geoff and Lou went home, Shelly accepted our invitation to join us. She planned to fly out from New York and meet us in Great Falls, Montana. Less than a week before her flight, we were in Glacier National Park. Stu very upset about prospect of dealing with two Strasser sisters; said he was thinking of taking to the road before Shelly arrives and we could meet somewhere at the end of the summer.

Our visit to Glacier was tense because I was afraid of grizzly bears. A backcountry grizzly had recently mauled and killed a woman. Rangers suspected the bear had been attracted by the odor of menstrual blood. Stu wanted to backpack in Glacier, but I expected my period. I didn't want to camp in grizzly territory. My fear annoyed Stu; he thought it was irrational, and he criticized me for being "unliberated." But I prevailed. Instead of backpacking, we stuck our toothbrushes in our pockets and hiked up a long trail to a rustic room at Sperry Chalet, where we joined a ranger-led glacier tour and spent the night in a comfortable bed.

We compromised, too, on the rest of the summer. After we met Shelly, we returned to Glacier for a couple of days of sightseeing. Then we all drove to North Cascades National Park, where we spent about two weeks backpacking. Stu and I agreed that after a year in close quarters, we needed some time apart, so I took Shelly to Seattle to catch her plane to New York. For the next eight or nine days, Stu backpacked by himself while I car camped and typed to my heart's content. I caught up on months of journal notes and began to work on a first draft of the book. Already August half gone. I sometimes feel as though I have wrecked this summer. On the other hand, I have worked hard this past week, writing forty-seven pages. None of it is good, but at least it is there.

The summer, and the van trip, ended just after Labor Day. I met Stu at a trailhead in the North Cascades, and we did a little more hiking together before we returned to Seattle for a day or two, made a quick circuit of the Olympic Peninsula, and then drove down the Oregon coast and into northern California. Labor Day weekend, we retreated from traffic in a national forest campground. And on September 4, 1973, we drove into Davis, where Stu had decided to begin a serious search for a job. I find myself with a lot of nervous energy, I wrote two weeks later. I think it is due to an unconscious—and finally, tonight, conscious—reluctant realization that we are here and have made a decision to settle in. The prospect is upsetting in a way. There are so many travel-type things I still want to do, that it seems preposterous to have wanted to stop. I don't want to be preoccupied with a "time is too short" attitude.

Monday evening, August 25, 1986

Finger lump still present and not disappearing. The oncologist called this afternoon to report that the mammogram on July 8 showed a small lump, about one-quarter inch, no cause for alarm ("If we thought it was cancer," he reassured me, "we'd have you come in for a biopsy immediately") but I should have another mammogram in early October for comparison.

"Which breast?" I asked, and he was obviously disconcerted.

"Ah, actually, both." And then proceeded to tell me that mammograms are wrong 10 percent of the time. Wrong about what?

Cause and Effect

A day or two after we arrived in Davis, Stu and I signed a month-by-month rental agreement for a furnished one-bedroom apartment in a brand-new building near the University of California campus. Stu soon found a part-time job with a professor who agreed to sponsor a proposal Stu was submitting to the National Science Foundation. He wanted to study the nitrogen-fixing abilities of a tiny fern that the Vietnamese grew in their rice paddies. He thought that California rice farmers might be able to use *Azolla* instead of expensive, petroleum-based inorganic fertilizers, to supply their crops' nitrogen needs.

I continued to work on my book about American attitudes toward land. Mostly, this involved research. I developed an enormous bibliography, hunted down the books at the library, and spent much of the fall sitting in an armchair in our tiny living room, reading and taking notes. We set up Stu's battered Smith-Corona portable on a little desk in the bedroom, but the apartment seemed too small. If Stu was home, his presence intruded on my writing. I knew the closed bedroom door didn't muffle the typewriter clatter. I waited until Stu went out to return to my draft of chapter 1.

⊛

Wednesday, August 27, 1986

I am sitting in my third-floor retreat, in my new chair, delivered this afternoon along with my new desk. The room can't really be said to be taking shape—it's all boxes, white walls, and glaring overhead light—but it is progress.

But a room of my own isn't enough. I spent the day in the doldrums until we saw Martin Shapiro at three. No grand fight this time, but tense discussion of differing goals. Stu was clear that he wanted to resolve our sexual differences. He said, "You don't take enough initiative."

"Do you want Judy to be more aggressive?" Martin asked. Stu quickly said, "No."

Martin suggested that, for our next session, we each come up with a list of goals so we can agree on a "contract" that spells out what we want to accomplish with him.

This evening, Stu sailed; Eli and I made dinner for ourselves and David. After dinner, I called my old friend Beth and talked for an hour. The sailors returned, exultant that they had sewed up another series, and settled down to eat leftover clam spaghetti—and I drove off to a laundromat to wash our sleeping bags. On the way, I smelled someone's wood fire. And found myself suddenly happy. Why? Because Beth reminded me that I was very strong through my sickness? Because Paul Bergeson helped me understand enough about myself that I could tell Stu and Martin that my greatest fear about having breast cancer is that I would lose power in the relationship, and Stu would be cruel again? Or because it is fall and that is, truly, my time of year?

⊛

Sometimes an image shakes me out of my rational head and allows me to enter the heart of poetry. The most fruitful images carry tension, contradiction. Plenty cheek by jowl with poverty. Abundant life face-to-face with death. Somewhere in my slide collection, there's a picture of a palm tree dusted with snow. I don't need to see the slide to remember the image. The tree—a palm with long, full, graceful fronds—stands in front of the Davis Amtrak station. Stu and I saw it in the early morning of January 4, 1974, as we waited for the 6:00 A.M. eastbound train. I'm sure the snow melted by noon; Davis, warm enough for palm trees, never stayed really cold.

I wasn't writing poetry; I hadn't written a poem since "First

Storm," fifteen years before. My head was full of words, but fully rational. We were headed to Saint Louis, where Stu was going to interview for a job, and then to Madison. I wrote to Helen and Richard, "Stu is planning to see several people at the university who are doing nitrogen-related research, and I am hoping to use Hal's electric typewriter to do a final copy of chapter 1."

No matter that I lived in my head; that snowy palm tree took root in my heart. It remains, the strongest image of the trip.

Of the train ride east, I remember mostly my swollen, weeping, arms. I had a bad case of poison oak. I slathered the rash with cortisone cream and swaddled the goo in gauze.

Of the time in Saint Louis, I remember a woman walking down her snowy driveway on a street of mansions surrounded by slums.

Of Madison, I remember only leaving town: Richard, suffering from some unspoken illness, stoic but admitting to feeling "bum," piloted his big green Ford wagon twenty miles through the bleak winter-bare countryside to Columbus, Wisconsin, where Stu and I caught the westbound Empire Builder. A blizzard stopped us somewhere in the Plains. We arrived a day late into Seattle and changed to the West Coast Limited, which took us south to Davis.

Soon after we unlocked our apartment, the manager knocked on the door.

"Call your mother," she told Stu. "She's been trying to reach you."

The night we left, Helen told Stu, Richard died.

⊕

Thursday, August 28, 1986

Last night, Stu seemed to want me to take the initiative for sex. I did, but he fell asleep. I didn't really mind; for me, soothing him to sleep is pleasant, like soothing a baby to sleep in my arms. I'm sure he wouldn't have the same reaction to me falling asleep—and probably wouldn't appreciate my point of view about last night.

Now he is depressed, retreating, having fits about our session with Martin yesterday. He is angry with Martin for pressing him to say how he feels, angry with me for being "brutal." He says, "I'm a private guy who takes his time responding; if you want a fast talker, try to find one." And, "I'm thinking of breaking my promise" to continue seeing Martin. He's clearly thinking through the consequences of refusing any more therapy. He holds himself like one of the walking wounded and is retreating and moping at the same time. We are to go to the theater this evening, and I hope it's good; otherwise it will be a miserable evening.

☙

Later

Made it through the evening moderately well. After the play, I asked Stu what elements of love he thinks are most important: passion, intimacy, or commitment. He said, "Passion is essential; the other two flow out of that."

☙

Richard's death helped convince us that it was time to settle down. We understood, a little better than before, that we wouldn't live forever. But it wasn't just a brush with mortality that prompted Stu and me, at thirty-five and twenty-nine, to begin to act grown-up. American troops had left Vietnam. Nixon was on his way out. In the van, we'd heard it coming. One day we sought a place to park on high ground where the radio reception was good. We spent hours cleaning out the van and listening, with wonder and no small amount of glee, to the Watergate hearings. We hated Richard Nixon. Whatever brought him down made us feel victorious. It's obvious now that Vietnam and Watergate heightened Americans' mistrust of government and set the stage for a new conservative era. In 1973 and 1974, we didn't worry about the future. We were proud that we'd ended the war and gotten rid of Tricky Dick.

In Davis Stu and I met activists who opposed the giant agribusiness companies that dominated California agriculture. We supported Cesar Chavez in his efforts to bring a living wage and decent working conditions to California's fields. We bought most of our produce through a local co-op. But mostly, we wanted to express our politics in the work we chose to do. For Stu, this meant doing research that might ultimately free farmers from expensive and environmentally destructive chemical fertilizers. For me, it meant writing my book about American attitudes toward land.

By the spring of 1974, I knew how I wanted the book to unfold. It would begin with history, tracing the white man's conquest of the continent, the sense of Manifest Destiny that cleared the land of trees, buffalo, and indigenous humans and made it safe for white settlement from sea to shining sea. It would continue with a discussion of how different peoples related to the land: the reverence of Native American tribes; the powerful concept of private ownership; the macho ethic of resource exploitation that regarded the earth as a woman ripe for rape and exploitation. I would rely heavily on research other people had done. My book would synthesize recent scholarly work on environmental, historical, and land-tenure issues and illustrate these issues with stories from our travels in the van.

I worked steadily on the book. In June, I took it with me to Pullman, Washington, where Stu attended an international conference on biological nitrogen fixation. I typed in our dorm room while Stu went to meetings. He was still waiting to hear about his *Azolla* proposal. But the real excitement at the conference had nothing to do with nitrogen-fixing ferns or rice or conventional breeding techniques. The controversial techniques of recombinant genetics— gene splicing—were in their infancy. I wrote to Helen from our dorm room, "Virtually all of the younger scientists are geneticists trying to identify the nitrogen-fixing genes (called nifs) in various bacterial strains so that they can transfer those genes to other, related strains that do not fix nitrogen. The goal is to discover a system that will permit nitrogen-fixing bacteria to grow on crops like wheat or corn. No one knows whether such a system can ever be found, but the race is on for the big prize."

Cause and Effect

Saturday morning, August 30, 1986
En route to Seattle

Stu is completely wigged out: by our session with Martin Shapiro Wednesday, by my backpacking trip with Shelly, by my interview yesterday for a state telecommunications job. And perhaps more—it's hard to tell.

Last night, as we were making dinner (and Stu was drinking steadily), he went on and on, complaining about "women becoming like men." This was because I'd worn a suit for my job interview and because this past week, when I stayed home from work, I "ran around like a chicken with its head cut off," going to Children's Museum meetings at seven-thirty in the morning instead of "having fun with the family."

I did argue—I think in a relatively intellectual and dispassionate way—about his generalizations, and I suggested that it was pretty elitist of him to put men or women down for trying to make it economically by dressing appropriately. I did get sarcastic: "I gather you'll be wearing your jeans and flannel shirt when you testify as an expert witness." But on the whole, the discussion wasn't too heated. Fortunately, I don't want the state job, because I think Stu would take it as an enormous threat if I went to work in some high-paid administrative position that required sixty hours a week and lots of travel.

I think Stu wanted a romantic evening, but I was packing, and then someone came to pick up fundraising letters for the Children's Museum, and finally Stu gave up and went to bed on the porch. I joined him about a half hour later, and he really was despondent. I caressed him, but he didn't respond.

Suddenly, out of the blue, he asked, "Do you know where Shapiro went to school?" I said I didn't, but that didn't stop him from trashing Martin. "He doesn't appear to know the meaning of the word 'diffident,'" Stu complained. "And he can't tell the difference between being 'aggressive' and being 'loving.'" Then he said, "If the next session is as bad as the last, I'm not going to see that asshole any more. You can leave and take the kids, or I'll leave, or you can just go without the kids." He raged on and on, virtually incoherent—and then he got out of bed to have a cigarette in his study.

I followed him. "I don't have to sleep on the porch tonight," I offered. "But I love you and I do want to make love with you." He came back to bed. We groped and fell asleep.

We both woke up about five. "At least you aren't going to see AA," he said. "I know you're going to come back fucked up. It happens every time you see anyone in your family." Then he corrected himself. "Whenever you see a member of your family it fucks *us* up."

⊛

Spring, 1974. We have moved out of the furnished apartment in Davis into half of a duplex across the street from the community pool. A Mormon couple with a four-year-old son lives in the other half. We have a new interest in young children. We want to have a baby. Our little next-door neighbor likes to open our screen door and wander in for visits. We have a few toys, mostly trinkets that Helen has sent us, wrapped as Christmas presents "for the cats." We also have a lot of empty cartons, because we've just unpacked our books. We put the toys in one of the boxes in the corner of the living room and tell Billy that he can come to play with them any time. One day, his mother stops by to fetch him home for lunch. She is appalled to find him happily rooting around in a Tanqueray box. He never wanders through our door again.

I miss Billy, but value the uninterrupted time. Every morning, I work on the book. At noon, the lifeguards kick all the kids out of the pool across the street. I swim laps for an hour and then eat lunch and continue writing. I never consciously think about the book between noon and one—I'm too busy counting laps—but somehow, knotty problems of structure and wording resolve themselves while I'm swimming back and forth. I discover another advantage to strenuous exercise. I can eat anything and still lose weight. In August, when I get pregnant, Stu and I are elated. And I'm in terrific shape. I'm strong, I'm tan, and I weigh less than I have since high school—and certainly less than I have ever since.

⊛

Cause and Effect

Wednesday evening, September 3, 1986
Soleduck Campground, Olympic National Park

I am writing by flashlight after making a walking tour of the campground: some campfires; a couple reading in their car; a wee girl walking around her site while her father, through clenched teeth, said to her mother, "I *told* you not to touch the camp stove." Mother: "I didn't, I just . . ." The child starts crying. Mother: "Now don't worry, we're not fighting . . ." I walk on.

I thought today on the trail, coming down, down, down for seven or more miles, of things I can do for Stu: grow my hair long, agree that the first topic to deal with in Martin Shapiro's office is sex, get a boudoir portrait taken to give to Stu for Christmas.

I called home after Shelly and I had soaked in the hot springs pools for a couple of hours. It was dinner time, and everyone seemed quite calm and happy to hear from me. Stu said, "Bring back pretty rocks and leave your psychology books behind."

It won't be hard to find pretty rocks. We are going to the beach tomorrow for two nights. And we sure are seeing pretty scenery. I was overjoyed to be in the high country again for the past two days. The hike today: first up sharply to a ridge, then along the ridge, with a glimpse of Mount Olympus—and lots of blueberries—and down, down, down to the Douglas firs and the waterfalls. I prefer the forest when it is wetter and more lush, but the blueberries come later, in the dry season.

Maybe that's a metaphor for life.

⬡

And are black flies metaphors too? The black flies have come to Norcroft. One has bitten me on the back of my neck. I can feel a big welt and an annoying itch. The bugs aren't as bad as I expected though. Or maybe I'm spending too much time with my nose to the computer screen.

I did take a bike ride a couple of days ago, part way up the long hill to the Oberg Mountain trailhead. Marian—one of the other residents—met me as I was struggling to the top, and we went the rest of the way up in her van and then hiked the loop trail.

The hike was like much of the week: nice, but not nearly as exciting or satisfying as the time I spent here last fall. The Keep Children in Hand signs near the overlooks, so heavily symbolic in October, seemed barely worth reading. The vistas, sweeping expanses of green trees and sun-struck water, seemed less interesting than last fall, when the trees were bare, portents of winter coming on. Everything was lovely, but not magical, as I remembered it.

I suppose there are plenty of reasons for the lessened intensity. I hiked Oberg Mountain alone last fall and this time I was talking with Marian; I came to Norcroft this time with certain expectations; I don't have time, in a week, to develop a satisfying rhythm of work and play. And a disturbing possibility: memory plays games with the truth.

Maybe my visit in October was also less than completely wonderful. Maybe I just don't remember missing my children or wishing for better biking weather or feeling frustrated with my work. Every morning, those three weeks, I went down to the gazebo by the shore and wrote in my journal. If I reread those entries, would I discover the Norcroft I remember or something quite different?

There are so many ways to tell a story.

Marian describes her marriage. She and her husband both work part-time jobs for sustenance so they both have time for art, the work they really love. He cooks all the meals for their family. He cares for their young children while she spends a month at an artists' colony. To me, it sounds idyllic. And yet she's very unhappy; she's thinking of divorce. What has she failed to tell me? What would I know if I saw them together? What does her husband think? What does her journal say?

※

Tuesday, September 9, 1986

Haven't written anything since I got home two days ago. Things seem to be different here. Stu has moved things around in the bedroom so that we can have a headboard made for the captain's bed. And he's been

248

wonderful since I got home, in many different ways. On Sunday afternoon, we went walking along a pretty-much-abandoned railroad track. David and Eli dug up old tie nails and other kinds of junk; Stu and I looked for *tradescantia,* a lovely deep blue wildflower that he saw two summers ago when we took a steam locomotive ride along this route. We didn't find the *tradescantia,* but we had a good time. Helen came for dinner and we had the salmon that I brought home from Seattle.

Both yesterday and today, Stu made school lunches for David and Eli. He seems very relaxed and easy about doing this. He seems intent on turning over a new leaf.

۞

My last afternoon at Norcroft; my last afternoon to write. But also my last chance (this visit) to play on the North Shore. The memoir will have to wait. I don't want to waste this beautiful day, shut up in a writing shed. I'm going to get some poems (some of the winter's rejects) ready to send out again. And then I'm going to close up shop and go take a long bike ride or hike. Writing might be my life, but life is way too short to spend it all inside!

۞

Saturday morning, September 13, 1986

Late yesterday afternoon, after being cooped up inside for two days at a conference, I decided to take a bike ride. When I got to the Dorseys', I stopped in to say hello. Lou invited me to a private showing of some handmade sweaters in the early evening. Eli had a friend sleeping over, and I had some qualms about going out since I'd been away from home for two full days, but Stu encouraged me to go. "When you get back, we can watch a video together."

But by the time Lou came to pick me up, Stu had been drinking a fair amount. He had a hard time understanding where we were going. When I got home an hour or two later, the kids were watching *Revenge of the Nerds* and Stu was passed out on the couch. He woke up enough to ask if I'd bought a sweater and then went back to sleep. I sent the kids to bed when their movie was over, but I decided not to wake Stu; I figured I'd wait until he got up and then we could watch our video. But he stayed asleep, so about eleven I decided to go to bed.

A little later, Stu woke up and came upstairs to find me. He wanted to make love. He smelled of alcohol, and I was turned off. He got terribly upset—pushy and grabby and wanting to talk. He kept saying, "Don't run away from me. Don't go away from me."

I said, "I wasn't running away from you."

He disagreed. "That's what you've been doing for the past two days."

"I was at a conference related to my work," I said. But there is some validity to his complaint. I did want to be away from the house when I went for the bike ride. And I definitely didn't want to make love. I felt that I was being swallowed up by Stu's sexual demands.

But he said something I'll have to think about: "Ever since Wednesday, when we had a pretty good time in bed, you've been running away." He insisted that I was running away from him because I was scared of sex.

❀

It's nearly six weeks since I returned from Norcroft; six weeks since I've worked on this memoir. It's not that I've stopped writing. I've written several poems about my new relationship, with a man named Carl. At work, I've written a long proposal to the National Endowment for the Humanities, requesting funding for a series of programs about the American land. The proposal takes some of its themes from the never-finished book I started in the van. My life swoops back on itself in circles, and I have been writing detailed audio treatments, about wilderness, private property, nature—subjects I first approached twenty-five or thirty years ago.

The relationship—it's too soon to call it a "love affair"—also shares themes with the past. Carl travels constantly for work. Every other weekend or so, he commutes to another time zone, flying home to his wife. She won't move to Madison. He doesn't like the commuting, but he's been married forever, and he wants to stay married, he says. Clearly, I'm risking abandonment. I congratulate myself on learning, at long last, to make myself vulnerable, to tolerate this risk.

And then, one evening, Carl is tired and goes back to his apartment instead of spending the night with me. Red alert!! I don't know what to do. I, who have lived happily without a man for ten years and more than seven months, don't know how to fill the few hours before it is time to go to bed. I wander nervously through the house, open all the kitchen cupboards, search the fridge. I need food. Consolation. Something to shield me from this sense of abandonment.

⊕

Monday morning, September 15, 1986

It is taking extraordinary effort to find time to write. I suspect that "relationship-building time" (being together, making love, etc.) is intruding on writing time. All I've done in the week since I got home from the backpacking trip is record things on my little handheld recorder.

Yesterday I moved the contents of my closet up to my third-floor room, a project that took more than four hours.

⊕

How easy it is for writing to drop to the bottom of my list when I'm not someplace, like Norcroft, where I'm *expected* to write! Almost anything is easier to attend to than the blank computer screen and the serpentine mess of hurt and memory. On a late-summer day like today—fresh air, blue sky—I would much rather be outside. Eli is home for two weeks before his sophomore year begins. I tried to get him to go canoeing; he was set on riding his bike and didn't invite me along. But I still managed to figure out how to spare myself long hours at the computer. I invited our old housemate, Sara, for dinner. It's her birthday, and what's more, she's moving, to live with her lover in Illinois. I spent a long time this morning cooking, and soon I must leave the study to finish the elaborate meal.

There's been plenty to occupy my mind these weeks when I haven't been writing. We buried Helen's ashes, emptied and sold her house; it feels like we've put a large part of the past to rest. I did very little of the work. Stu, David, Hal, and Julie got the house ready to sell; they refused my offers of help. But I've been a beneficiary: of an antique maple table and a set of hand-painted Chinese dishes; of a substantial monetary inheritance; of an apparent mellowing in Stu's attitude. After we buried Helen's ashes, we hugged. With David hovering nearby, smiling encouragement, we had a reasonably comfortable conversation. Stu suggested that Hal and Julie invite me to dinner. It has taken more than a decade to accomplish this. It is no surprise, I guess, that I am reluctant to return to a project likely to torpedo these scraps of familial civility.

I want to make nice. I was raised to make nice. There's nothing nice about what I'm writing. It's time to turn off the computer and make the Thai spring rolls that will take me the rest of the afternoon.

⊛

Tuesday afternoon, September 16, 1986

Found it very difficult to think of things to say to Paul Bergeson this afternoon, very difficult to know how to relate to him. He said I was about as jumpy as anyone he'd ever seen go through the transition from having and discussing problems to ending therapy—and asked me over and over, "Why are you so jumpy with this transition period? Why are you uncomfortable with being strong, successful, powerful?" We talked a good bit about power: about whether I was fearful of being a powerhouse, and whether I *ought* to be a powerhouse. "Do you think that I can't handle you being a powerhouse?" he asked. "Maybe the reason you're having so much trouble with this is because you're attracted to me."

"Maybe," I said. "But actually I've been feeling *more* distance from you, less attracted, as my relationship with Stu gets stronger." I feel as though I'm in a waiting pattern. I feel able to deal well with Stu, and that I'm really just waiting for another problem to emerge: that is, for me to have breast cancer or whatever the hell I'm going to find out in late October or whenever I do find it out. And I don't feel I have that much to say to Paul between now and then.

⊛

Cause and Effect

Tuesday evening

Walked through the park in the late afternoon, thinking hard about questions of power and strength. It really seems to me that what is habitual about my behavior this afternoon with Paul is my unsureness in ambiguous social situations. If a relationship is clear-cut, as in doctor-patient, or friend-friend, I know how to behave: what to say, how to act to please (or at least not displease) the other person. I am good at giving back to people what they want, in situations when they let me know what they want. But I had no problems to present to Paul today, and could not figure out how to behave as an equal—a powerful, strong person—with him.

So what do I want from Paul Bergeson? Certainly, in some sense, something I don't want to ask for because I know it's not possible: a close friendship; even at times, a sexual relationship. In another sense, I just want to know he'll be there if I need to come back to him for support and help. And today I didn't want anything other than to be told I was fine and done with seeing him. But that is what he called my "jumpiness"—which makes this very circular:

More grant writing at work today. I have a very strong urge to quit in January if I can clear up the mammogram problem. I wonder if full-time students can get health insurance? And if I could be a student in creative writing for a while? Something to investigate, anyway.

✿

Peter Kramer's new book, *Should You Leave?* arrived at work a few days ago. With a title like that, I figure it will sell about two billion copies. I interviewed Kramer after *Listening to Prozac* came out; he's articulate, provocative, a good interview. I rushed across the hall to suggest we get Kramer again. "I've scheduled him already," my colleague said. And then, *sotto voce,* "You know, I have a personal interest in that question."

Don't we all. I took the book home and read it over the weekend. I told myself I was checking it out. Was it good enough to recommend to Carl, the new—and unhappily married—man in my life? I thought I could have used a book like this in 1986. Straight talk

253

from a psychiatrist. But as the subtitle hints, *Should You Leave?* is not exactly a self-help book. *A Psychiatrist Explores Intimacy and Autonomy—and the Nature of Advice.* A lot of the book explains why Kramer—and most good psychotherapists—resist giving straightforward answers to their patients' straightforward questions about their lives.

In chapter after chapter, Kramer describes fictional relationships. A woman learns her lover is sleeping with someone else. A man is captivated by an immature, needy blond. A couple squabbles endlessly about soda bottles left uncapped and theater tickets misplaced. None of the situations have much to do with Carl and his wife. More to the point, I realize, Kramer's not telling me what I really want to know. The question for me is not, should I leave? It's—still, nearly eleven years later—was I right to have left?

Eventually—on page 222—I come to the chapter that speaks to me. It's called "Simple Gifts." In it Kramer describes men and women who are "enslaved," trapped in abusive, often violent, relationships. Everyone but the man or woman—Nora, in the case Kramer presents—knows it is time to leave. The relationship's destructiveness, Kramer writes, "falls well into the range of the obvious." Nora is married to a man who got her pregnant and agreed to marry her only if she aborted. Years later, he decides he wants children. But by then—maybe because of the abortion—Nora cannot conceive. Her husband trashes her in public, calls her "a dried-up prune." But Nora still isn't sure she should leave. She feels unattractive, petty, unworthy of this man who can also be very charming.

Kramer is in a bind. He knows Nora should leave, and she's asking for his advice. But, he says, she wouldn't be able to hear it. She has filled her life with "authoritative others," her husband included, who tell her what to do. He does not want, as he says, "to validate that model. One must not accede to the sacrifice of self."

Those sentences yank me back into Paul Bergeson's office. I see him sitting in his chair, waiting for me to tell him what I want. I see myself chattering, telling him dreams, telling him stories, filling the silence. I want to tell him what he wants to hear. I try to figure out what that might be. I can't. I want him to tell me what to do. He won't.

⊛

Sunday, September 21, 1986

Officially fall, but it is warm and humid, enervating. I want a high pressure front to come through and blow us some cool, dry air. On the other hand, my hair looks great today.

Spent the day emptying boxes and filling desk drawers. Also fitted blue carpet remnant in my freshly painted closet and moved chests in. I have not moved my clothes yet. I was going to do it after we folded the laundry this evening, but I was too tired. Things are still quite a mess up here—so much junk to sort through and put away. It horrifies me to think that I was going to move an entire household.

⊛

Monday September 22, 1986, 6:15 A.M.

Can't get back to sleep. Big thunderstorm an hour ago. Stu got up to check windows. When he came back to bed he said, "Don't be scared." I thought he was talking about the storm, but soon he said, "I don't want to go," in a very agitated voice, and I realized he was talking about Martin Shapiro.

He got out of bed and went into the study. I thought about it, then followed him. "Do you want to talk about it now or in a few hours?"

"What Is there to talk about?"

"I'm not clear whether you're refusing to see Martin or you just don't *want* to see him."

"I can't see that I have a choice," he said. "If I refuse, I'll be breaking a promise I made to you, and you'll be very hurt." A little later, back on the porch, he asked (a little bitterly, I thought), "What have you ever promised me?"

"Not buying the house on Rowen was a promise," I said. "It was my promise to stay, to try to make the marriage work, to love you to the best of my ability."

He wouldn't accept that as an answer. "That wasn't a real *commitment*," he said. "You can buy a house whenever you want to."

I started to gather my things to go up to the third floor. He panicked. "Don't go." So I stayed. But he tossed and turned and finally got up and went back into the study, and then downstairs to the kitchen. And I could not get back to sleep, so I came up to my room and realized how close to morning it is—and decided to write.

⊛

Monday, 4:30 P.M.

Interesting session with Shapiro: possibly our last, though I am going to leave it up to Stu to decide, I think. Stu was in one of his vile moods all morning and afternoon, as I came in and out, trying to be cheery, first after a conference call at work, then after an excruciatingly long session of waiting for the pediatrician to see Eli, who seems to have a viral infection, but may develop pneumonia.

We went to Martin's office separately. I got there first; then Stu arrived, stonily silent and incredibly angry.

"How are things going?" Martin asked.

"Fine," I said, "until last night—"

Stu interrupted me to announce to Martin, "You keep asking me what I want to get out of these sessions. I want only three things from you: a bibliography of clinical literature on therapy for sexually inhibited women; a bibliography of nonsexist pornographic literature; and a catalog of non-sexist, nonexploitive porn videos."

I was incredulous.

Martin patiently explained that he didn't have any bibliographies of pornographic literature or videos. "I'm not a librarian, and I can't provide any of these things for you."

The rest of the session revolved (and it *was* circular) around a

256

conversation between Martin and Stu about what could come of therapy. "Nothing," Stu insisted. "I'm only here because Judy wants me to be."

"We won't get anywhere useful if you start from that premise," Martin agreed.

"But Judy will leave me if I don't come to therapy."

"Is that true?" Martin asked me.

"No. I won't leave so long as our marriage continues to improve. I think it has improved in the past few months, and I think the therapy is helping."

"You can't prove that scientifically," Stu said. "We have no control. How do you know that it's the therapy that's improving things?" We all agreed that one can never be sure about cause and effect when dealing with emotions.

At one point, Stu tried to explain what he meant by "our differences in sexuality." He told Martin, "I don't want you to get the idea that it's only a mechanical problem, a matter of inches."

"Maybe the difference can be described by two stories from this week," I said. "I got turned on when you volunteered to drive the kids to school. You got turned on when I invited you up to the third floor at two-thirty in the afternoon."

He dismissed my invitation as "ceremonial" and "only once." Then he said, "Getting turned on because I drive the kids to school is perverted. That's a good example of what's wrong with your sexuality." And he went on to argue that we should be having this sort of discussion in private. "We don't need Martin to listen to this."

I disagreed. "It's useful for me to talk about sex with Martin around, because I'm not scared to tell you how I really feel when someone else is listening who isn't ridiculing or demeaning my feelings. And what I said about how I respond physically is true. In fact, my response to you is sometimes dictated by things having nothing to do with you: worrying about Eli's asthma, or about my equivocal mammogram, which I think of every time we make love."

Stu was incredulous. "I can't imagine thinking I had testicular cancer every time you touched my balls, even if I had an equivocal 'testiculagram.'"

And then he quoted one of his favorite movies, Kurasawa's *Ran:* "We are born, we grow old, and then we die." He said he thought that was more elegant than what's on a lot of T-shirts: "Life's a bitch and then you die."

"They're both pretty fatalistic," Martin said.

Stu was startled, then agreed.

I am *not* fatalistic, and I despise that attitude. Maybe that's our problem.

Trouble on Its Way

A poem in the new issue of *Prairie Schooner* begins "My sister asks if / I have fed the house." The poet, Faulkner Fox, hears this as metaphor. But the best metaphors describe how the world really works.

I do not feed my house. That is one of the true pleasures of living alone. I spent part of Labor Day weekend attacking piles of paper that have accumulated—on the dining room table and buffet, on the stairs, on the floor around my desk, on my desktop—over the past two or three months. (I haven't balanced a bank account all summer.) But I canoed all day Monday and visited friends much of Sunday, and a good deal of Saturday I simply relaxed. There are still piles of paper in the bedroom and all over my desk. I never got to the ironing; I have not gotten to the ironing since March or April. I didn't vacuum the carpets, which, if you care to look (I don't), reveal a not-so-fine layer of cat hair. I will wait to scrub the kitchen floor until the soles of my shoes stick to the linoleum. I didn't mow the lawn. I didn't even pull out the window box weed that towers above the impatiens.

A couple of weeks ago, I said to Carl, "I'm not much of a housekeeper."

"I noticed," he said, dryly.

So far, this does not come between us. We barely have a relationship. Or—to be more optimistic—we have a relationship that's barely begun. Things that could, in a marriage, be grounds for major argument go on the record as funny incidents. A week ago, we left his apartment to go to a concert. "Let's take your car," he said. "Do you have your keys?"

I said I did. He dumped his key ring on a bookcase. "It's so nice to be unburdened."

When we got back, he expected me to unlock the door. "You have the keys," he said.

"No, I don't."

"But I asked . . ."

I laughed. "You did. And I do have my keys. My car keys."

He laughed, too, and went to find the extra set of house keys he keeps in his car.

How long would we have to be together before a little miscommunication became a cause celebre? Before my tolerance for cat hair morphed into major malfeasance? Before I must feed, not only a house, but a hypersensitive ego? This is hardly a fair description of Carl; not, in fact, a description of him at all, but of my own trepidation. With thoughts like this, it's hardly surprising that it's been so long since I've allowed myself to fall in love.

❦

Tuesday, September 23, 1986

Met with Bergeson today and babbled on for about a half hour. I reported that Stu has revealed himself to me much more this week. He clipped an A. R. Price cartoon from the *New Yorker* and put it on my desk: a slob of a man with a beer belly and several days' growth of beard is passed out in an armchair; several empty beer cans are scattered around. His wife, in another armchair, is reading a book titled *Smart Women, Foolish Choices*. And the cartoon was not all: the scene in Martin's office was also incredibly revealing.

I told Paul what I'd been thinking about power and about helping a friend at work with her marital problems. But then, suddenly, I had nothing else to say.

"Well, here we are where we were last week," Paul commented. And there was this dead silence. So I tried to get him to tell me something about myself—about my character. "I'm not going to respond," he said. "The main thing I see about your character right now is your determination to get me to take the initiative and say something. But I want to see what you need from me before I say anything."

"I think I need your assurance that I've made progress. That even though we might not see Martin again, things aren't going to revert back to the way they were before."

"I have confidence in you as an individual," he said. In fact, he said that several times.

"Yes, but what about having confidence in the marriage?" I asked. "I'm not sure that Stu can do what he needs to do for things to really get better."

Paul agreed that we're in a mixed situation: in some ways things are improving, but in other ways things aren't. "What progress do you think you've made?" he asked me.

I talked about that for a while. To put it briefly: I can look back a year and say that my anger has been defused; I've come to realize how much my desire for a "normal" family is keeping me in this marriage; I understand some of the things that provoke Stu's anger and therefore can keep my cool more easily. "I've even gotten a room of my own," I said. I described the unnerving "single parent" dream I had last night. I had lost David and Eli in a city that was a cross between Pittsburgh and Madison. At the end of the dream, David and I were looking at our house, trying to find Eli. David said, "See the rooms on the third floor, with the lights on; he's looking for the Valium there."

Finally Paul said, "What more?"

"I want you to assure me that I'll be able to handle things without you, even if they get worse. Will I?"

"I don't have extreme confidence that you'd be able to handle absolutely anything that came your way," he said. "After all, you have both the waking nightmare of breast cancer to deal with and also the sort of mixed dream you had last night. That says that you're unsure—and I'm unsure too. But one way of finding out how strong you really are is to set a termination date for our sessions."

"I've been thinking about that," I said. "It would be fine with me to terminate on October 25, after I see the oncologist again. That is, assuming that I have a good mammogram and he gives me a good report."

He said, "Well, think about the date." And then he said—and this

261

almost sounds like magic—that with a planned termination, "things happen that give us an indication of how strong you are or aren't."

❦

This morning, at 7:30, the dental hygienist greeted me with that cheery, distanced "we" that health professionals like to use. "We're going to do a couple of new things," she chirped. "We're going to probe around each one of your teeth to see if the gums are healthy. And we're going to do a cancer check."

We got tense, my inner self and I. Of course, it's wonderful to have a dental hygienist concerned about our health. It's a good idea to check for oral cancer every time our teeth are cleaned. But the *c* word makes us queasy. And it crops up, in my life, more often than you might think. Just last night, in a dream, my mother appeared to take me to a doctor. She was convinced I had breast cancer.

It was a long night. I went to bed at 8:30, completely exhausted from a day of sun and strenuous canoeing. I slept deeply, but surfaced frequently, coming awake enough to remember bits of dreams obviously based on things I've recently read. The breast cancer came from a review in the *New York Times*. The reviewer said the novel (or was it a memoir?) begins as the heroine discovers a small, sharp lump. I didn't finish the review. I thought it was a book I probably didn't have time to read.

At any rate, the dental hygienist gave me two new toothbrushes, one regular and one very tiny, and a relatively clean bill of oral health. "You really need to work on that plaque," she said.

I'm not too worried. My mother—dead twenty-nine years this month—often appears in dreams to shepherd me through to health.

❦

Wednesday, September 24, 1986

As we were preparing dinner, Stu mentioned Hal's recent letter from Grenada. I said, "They don't seem to be doing much except standing in line for the telephone." And I added that I was struck by Hal's comment that they like Grenada because the natives are not hostile to people in big boats.

Stu immediately became angry and argumentative. "Hal's boat is not big." (It's thirty-eight feet.)

"Maybe not in relation to the bigger yachts," I said. "But certainly it is in relation to the local fishing boats."

Eli was in the kitchen, listening to us.

"Don't tell my children what to think," Stu spat at me. "You're just as bad as Shelly!"

I was outraged and walked out of the kitchen—then back in, to have dinner and speak calmly of trivia: books Eli is reading; how wet David must be getting playing soccer in the rain. David came home at seven, and Stu and I left to see a play. We had an argument in the lobby when I said I didn't mind debating Stu, but I didn't like his *ad hominem* attacks.

"I'll tell whatever truths I know," he replied. "You have a one-dimensional mind, or at best two-dimensional. You see things only in terms of black and white and make everybody into stick figures, interpreting everything according to your sexist perspective."

I decided I didn't want to hear any more and went up to my seat. I wasn't sure Stu would follow, and indeed, when he arrived a few minutes later he hissed, "You're lucky I didn't take the car and leave."

I understand too well where Stu's anger came from: he feels awful about being a rich white male and at the same time feels he should be loved for what he is. But what's depressing is knowing that I can't say what I think about a whole complex group of important categories without touching off that anger. I was probably being unreasonably and unnecessarily provocative talking about Hal's letter. On the other hand, there really is a huge range of subjects on which I have opinions that are restricted as topics of conversation with Stu, because his head is so fucked up.

And I wonder if this is the "magic" Paul Bergeson talked about: I make things worse, subconsciously, to see how I will deal with the situation.

But I fantasize about resolving my problems by finding some wonderful person with whom I *can* talk and falling in love with him—or staying put until David and Eli are grown and then leaving. No, that's not possible: it's too long to live less-than-well.

The question really is whether I can be content to keep my mouth shut on sensitive issues. We can get along reasonably well so long as we restrict our conversation to soccer, burritos, and an occasional cultural event. But money is now taboo—and so is a lot more about which I have strong feelings. How far will compassion take me?

❦

This weekend I went up to Door County to ride my bike in the Door County Century, a fundraiser for the Artist-in-Education program at Sevastopol School. Nine or ten years ago, I was one of the artists funded by the program. Mostly, I worked with middle-schoolers who produced a short audio documentary about the area's history. But over a three-week period, I also spent at least an hour in every classroom in the school. With the little kids, I played listening games.

Close your eyes. What do you hear? Lockers slamming. Kids on the playground. The teacher across the hall.

Now. Close your eyes. Imagine walking into your bedroom, sitting down on your bed. What do you hear? The squeaky springs. The TV. My baby brother crying. Cows. My dad yelling at my mom.

❦

Friday morning, September 26, 1986

Woke in the middle of the night when Stu got up to piss. I went up to the third floor bathroom to relieve *my* bladder. When I came back, Stu caressed me. I responded sleepily. Stu left, obviously upset, and went into his study for a while.

I woke about six and started caressing Stu. "Did you leave last night because you'd had a bad dream?"

"No," he said, "a good dream." Apparently an erotic dream: a dance of some sort. "I was upset because you didn't reciprocate the way the woman did in the dream." So he went off and masturbated. "And I decided that life is passing me by. I think if I moved into a condo I could find a woman who would give me the kind of loving I'd like to have." He

264

trashed me for being a person who only thinks sex is "appropriate" between eleven-thirty P.M. and midnight.

I do think life is passing Stu by, but I don't think it has much to do with me. If he were involved in the outside world to *any* small extent, he would have a place to expend some of his energies and sex would be less freighted with life-affirming significance. Also, and not incidentally, he would find that he, too, was busy in the afternoons and tired in the wee hours of the morning. But rather than look at *himself* for ways of grabbing on to life and living ecstatically, he makes me the cause of his discontent.

⚾

Friday evening

Stu depressed and distant most of the day. This did not get to my inner core, which sparked with happiness and self-satisfaction, especially after I explained to him that I am no longer willing to be told I am inhibited and sexually inadequate. That is a completely inaccurate and inadequate analysis of what's going on. (I chuckled later when Stu insisted that there were no mosquitoes outside because they weren't biting *him*. It is the same egomania.)

⚾

Sometime during the Door County ride last weekend, I thought of Carl saying, "You work harder at relaxing than anyone I know." I wouldn't call a bike ride relaxing. Enjoyable, almost always. Sometimes even an endorphin high. But not relaxing. In fact, it's very difficult for me to relax. I remember my mother sitting in the green armchair, leafing through a magazine. Not even reading the articles. Spacing out, my kids would call it. The memory makes it nearly impossible for me to sit still. To sit at all, unless I'm doing something else. Working at my desk. Or reading and eating, simultaneously. I wash dishes while I'm talking on the phone. I almost never watch television. Just sitting, doing nothing: that would make me crazy.

265

Although I'm sure a lot of people think it's much crazier to bike one hundred miles.

My mother, in her illness, lost the ability to process thought rationally. She screamed hysterically at us whenever we did something she didn't like. Once my parents went to New York, taking Ellen and Bobbi. I was a high school senior; Shelly was in ninth grade. That Saturday—with our parents' permission—Discussion Group met at our house.

When Mother and Daddy came back from New York, they asked how Discussion Group went. Great, I said, all enthusiasm. A lot of people came. Even the kitchen was crowded. People sat on the stove! on the counters! there was even someone on the fridge! Only one problem—a couple of kids were on the piano bench and broke one of the spindly legs. Mother ranted for days about how irresponsible we were, how it was just like us to be so rotten, how we didn't take care of our things. She was furious about the piano bench, which was easily repaired. But what made her really crazy was my report that our friends had used the kitchen appliances as chairs. She shrieked, she threatened us with her favorite lines. "You kids don't know how good you have it. You'll be sorry when I'm gone."

This morning, Carl looked at the snapshots of my mother on my dresser top. "You look like her," he said. I cringed.

Today is September 9. My mother died almost exactly twenty-nine years ago. I don't remember the date. It seems like something I should know, so I try to look it up. I scrabble through some dusty boxes, looking for the stash of condolence notes. I think there's a newspaper obituary with those notes, in whatever box they're in.

I'm distracted by a studio photo of a bunch of little kids sitting solemnly in front of a stone fireplace. A couple of stockings hang from the mantel. On the back, in my mother's neat pre-illness script, it says Falk School Junior Nursery, December 1948. I'm in the picture, wearing a plaid skirt with suspenders and pigtails.

I seem to remember the fireplace, in the same vague way I seem to remember a mother who was kind and attentive. It's much easier to remember my mother in her indolence and in her hysteria. I try hard not to be like her. Maybe that's why I'm not very good at relaxing. Or at shifting over to right-brain work, writing poems, writing memoir, leaving my rational mind.

⊛

Sunday, September 28, 1986

Helen came for an early lunch yesterday, to pick David and Eli up for the weekend. Stu and I were on the road about half past eleven, headed to a motel on Lake Michigan to celebrate my forty-second birthday. I didn't feel too peppy and drowsed in the car. By the time we got to a motel, a rather dismal place, I had a headache. Stu massaged it away, we made love, and dressed for dinner at a fancy restaurant nearby. I ate part of my salad and my share of the escargot appetizer before my headache, which had returned, made me so nauseated I literally could not eat. Sat and stared at my walleye, trying not to barf, while Stu ate dinner. The waitress was very upset that I had not touched my meal.

Back to our room, where I crashed about ten and slept until eight-thirty or nine. Made love, ate breakfast at a greasy spoon, drove slowly back, taking the scenic route through the Kettle Moraine. It was very pretty with fall colors, though the sun was not out most of the time. Good talks with Stu about money, vacations (I have to see if we can go to Hawaii with the free tickets from last spring), and even therapy. Stu seems willing to continue to see Martin Shapiro if we have an agenda. We talked some about possible agenda items, including unequal sexual response. All very constructive and certainly civil.

I'm afraid I may have ended the conversation when I suggested that Stu and I want different things out of our marriage. "Our relationship seems to be the only really important thing in your life," I said. "But for me, it is a solid background to many other experiences." Stu got much quieter after that—but maybe only because we were getting back on the interstate.

I also told Stu that I am thinking of quitting my grant-writing job so I have time to write. He was mildly surprised, I think. And he wanted to know what *market* I'd be writing for. But I just want to *write*. Not for a market.

I now seem able to take this risk.

⊛

An old postcard from Philadelphia's Franklin Institute hangs on my bulletin board. It shows a jet, a Boeing 727, attached to the rear of the science museum. The jet's gone now, but you used to be able to walk through it, right down the center aisle. On one side, you passed upholstered seats, overhead compartments, tray tables neatly stowed. It looked like any old plane, waiting for boarding passengers. On the other side, a cutaway revealed the airplane's guts. Tangles of cable, life preservers, galley innards, the belly of the plane where all the cargo is stowed.

I bought the card to remind me of the powerful dream that arrived a few days before my forty-second birthday. In the dream, I was driving down a street with David and Eli in the car. Suddenly, an airplane pulled out in front of me. I recognized it as the jet from the Franklin Institute. We went into the museum to see what was happening. The building, a classic nineteenth-century structure, had marble halls, tall columns, vast empty spaces.

A big piece of plywood covered the hole in the wall where you used to enter the plane. Other familiar exhibits were also gone, including a model of the earth that used to be suspended from the high ceiling. I asked a museum guard what was going on, and he shrugged. "They're changing the exhibits." It wasn't clear what would replace them, but it was exciting to see the change. I told the kids, "We'll have to come back in the spring to see the new exhibits."

⊛

Tuesday afternoon, September 30, 1986, my birthday

Back from a session with Paul Bergeson. I set November 25 as my termination date. How sad. But rather than be sad, I babbled on about how wonderful I am at risk taking, solving difficulties with Stu, deciding to write,

268

not getting unduly upset about Eli's medical problems. (He has had pneu-monia so often, the pediatrician wants him to be tested for cystic fibrosis.)

Paul sat silently through it all. Finally he said, "You aren't asking me to do anything but admire you, so I'm admiring you."

I told him my dream about the Franklin Institute airplane and devel-oped it as a metaphor: even my solid (stolid?) personality is able to change. The building (which reminds me of Carnegie Museum in Pitts-burgh, where Shelly and I used to spend every Saturday morning), is like my childhood home, but it is not the kind of "home" I would want for my children. It is too impersonal, grand, monumental. But how will it change? What will the new exhibits be? The dream doesn't say, but I can now read poetry, which I haven't been able to do since high school, and I want to write. I am not sure what will replace reason and logic as coping mecha-nisms because they have been so useful to me in the past—and even now, for example, in coping with Eli's illness. And Stu certainly likes me to be logical and rational. How do you solve problems with a poem? Hard to say.

❀

After Paul Bergeson suggested that I was in a transition period, headed toward the end of therapy, I decided to find a crystal ball to give him at our final session. I told Helen, "When I ask him whether something's likely to happen, he always refuses to say. Maybe a crys tal ball will help."

She offered me her Finnish crystal paperweight, a cast sphere with bubbles inside. I thanked her but turned her down.

On my birthday, we went to her house for dinner: steak and po-tatoes, not exactly my kind of meal. She gave me a check and two gifts I'd requested: a wallet and ivory candles for my brass candle-sticks. Also the Finnish crystal ball. I didn't understand why it should come to me.

As David said, "If you tried to tell the future in it, all you'd come up with is bubbles."

❀

This year, for my birthday, I asked Carl to go with me to L'Etoile, a very good, very expensive restaurant. The last time I was there, probably five years ago, I was so appalled by the price of entrees that I ordered only an appetizer, a salad, and dessert. But I want to celebrate. I'm fifty-three, or will be, and there's a man in my life! And it's also an exercise in knowing what I want and asking a man for it. Of course, that should be second nature by the time a woman is fifty-three. I didn't ask Carl to pay for my dinner; in fact, I offered to pay for his. All I want is an escort, a dinner companion. And I know he likes to spend time with me. But it still feels like a Big Deal.

❀

Wednesday morning, October 1, 1986

It's sunny today, crisp and clear, just like October ought to be. I woke this morning very tense. All I could think about as I was showering and getting dressed was that I want Paul B to tell me what he feels—*feels,* not thinks—about me. I have a sense that I made a fool of myself yesterday, asking him to tell me how wonderful I am. That's not what I want. I want to know what his emotions are about me. I want, before we break up, so to speak, to have something of him and his emotions to hang on. I feel very bad about leaving. I want to feel bittersweet.

I love Paul because he takes care of me. After I leave, who's going to take care of me?

I would like to finish the story I began last fall, to give to Paul before I leave him—or rather, the day I leave him. He has made it possible, I think, for me to *feel* enough to write.

❀

Thursday evening, October 2, 1986
Door County

Stu picked the kids up after school; we were packed and ready to leave for Helen's cottage by four. Had dinner on the way up. I spent the whole car ride in a kind of trance, imagining conversations with Paul Bergeson—opening gambits for my next session:

"We have eight weeks to get me out of love with you. Help me."

"I'm going to start by asking something I should have asked months ago. What would you like to be called: Paul, Dr. Bergeson, Gus?"

"I'm furious that you made me feel like a fool who just asks to be patted on the head."

"Will you be sad that I am gone?"

And so forth. To all of which, in my imagination, he just sat and looked at me, expressionless. I find I cannot see him, in my mind's eye, except in three-quarter profile. I realized a week or two ago that I can't even remember whether he has a moustache. I *think* so. But I can't remember the shape of his mouth or the space between nose and mouth. Mostly it is his eyes and his general cragginess—and his long legs—that I remember. But this is a man I have looked at for an hour almost every week since last December—and to whom I have a strange kind of attraction. And I can't recall whether he has a moustache?

It was glorious driving in the dark with classical music on the radio, thinking—feeling—about this "problem." A luxurious, sensuous feeling. And a place in my mind to which I can escape almost at will.

Helen and I once spoke about God. She said that as a child, she decided to be a devout Episcopalian. Her parents were appalled. But her devotion lasted only a week or two. As an adult, she never went to church. She marked Christmas with beef tenderloin, a small tree, mounds of presents, and a mantel full of tiny, hand carved angels arranged around a nativity scene. On Easter she hid jelly beans on the living-room couch, balanced on chair rungs, on the back of a soapstone frog. She had a flair for jelly bean camouflage. Helen hated Ronald Reagan's politics, but she admired his taste in jelly beans. Jelly Bellies, Reagan's favorites, came in subtle colors that made them ideal for jelly bean hunts. We could never find them all.

Helen never went to church. But she told me that she believed there must be "something greater than ourselves." She would never speak of this to Richard, she said, or to her sons. Men, she'd decided—at least those men—were unlikely to understand. She thought this was a pity. "A little humility," she said with a sly grin, "might do them a world of good."

She asked if I was religious. "Not really," I said.

"But you think of yourself as a Jew."

I explained that I was about as Jewish as she was Christian. A secular Jew who believed in some kind of power greater than human beings.

She seemed relieved that we saw things eye-to-eye. She would have had a problem with a devout daughter-in-law: a pious Catholic, a churchgoing Lutheran, an observant Jew.

Still, I am a lot more Jewish than I ever admitted to Helen. I have never been moved to join the pacifist Quakers or the politically liberal Unitarians. You can't convince me that a Christmas tree is either a pagan symbol or a "Chanukah bush." I admire the spiritual practice of some of my Buddhist friends, but they inhabit a foreign shore. I don't respond, emotionally, to the autumnal equinox. What I look forward to are Chanukah, Passover, and coming up, Rosh Hashonah and Yom Kippur, the High Holy Days of the Jewish year.

⊛

Monday morning, October 6, 1986

Last night, just before going to sleep, Stu asked, "What are your plans for tomorrow?"

"I don't have any plans," I told him, "unless we have an appointment with Martin Shapiro." I was scared to say anything about Shapiro. Stu wanted to talk about the appointment and my fear (I'm very anxious, having breathing problems), but I said I didn't want to talk about it last night, so we didn't.

This morning I said, "If you're going to cancel our appointment, you should do it as soon as possible."

A few minutes later, Stu came upstairs. "Do you have an agenda for a meeting with Shapiro?" he asked.

I said (not for the first time), "I have plenty of things to talk about with him. Some of them are relatively trivial, like why did you ignore me when I said, quite clearly, that what I really wanted for my birthday was cut flowers and that I did not want houseplants? Some of them are not so trivial, like why did you insist on masturbating in front of me on Saturday night? And some of them are global, like sexual incompatibility. I think it would be useful to continue our conversation about our differing kinds of sensual reactions. But I don't think that we should go to see Martin just because *I* want to go or because *I* have an agenda. If you don't have an agenda, too, we won't accomplish anything."

Stu kept saying, "I don't see why we have to go. I don't see why we can't solve our problems together without a shrink. We just have to share more." He said he doesn't get angry with me anymore, just disappointed. "I'm consciously trying to suppress my anger."

When I said I was disappointed about the flowers, he tried to tell me I had "demanded" flowers, and he would never cave in to my demands.

He couldn't think of anything he wanted to put on the agenda with Martin, and whined, "Martin said that we don't have to come every week." I pointed out that we *haven't* been going every week—it's been two weeks since we were there.

I said, "If you don't think we have anything to talk about, usefully, with Martin, I don't see any point in going." But I let him know that I'm extremely hurt and extremely upset. (And I'm crying as I write this.) It's clear that I don't have any power other than the power to leave.

"We could talk with Martin about how you feel toward my working," I said, "especially since I'm planning to stop."

"We can just set an appointment for a time that we could talk about that," Stu suggested. "Just the two of us."

"That's fine, we can do that. But that's what we did all last spring—and I don't think it helped very much."

"Well," he said, "things have changed between us since last spring."

Frankly, I don't think they've changed that much. I think that the reason things have changed to the extent they have is because of the people he denigrates as "shrinks." I don't know—I don't know how long I'll be around.

⊛

Monday evening

We canceled the appointment. I am still angry, upset, sad. My impulse this morning was to get the fuck out of here. My impulse now is to stay away from Stu until he apologizes, makes it clear that he knows he has upset me and is *sorry* about it. Takes some responsibility.

I spent the day finishing the script for "Marital Quality." The ironies are endless. Took Eli to soccer, bringing the drinks to a field far away. It was a brilliant day, and I enjoyed talking with parents and watching the game. Eli was really happy to be playing at last after being sick.

⊛

My birthday today, and it seems like an odd coincidence to have it fall on a Tuesday, a writing day. It's overcast, chilly, windy. The oak tree outside my window is beginning to turn; most of the leaves are green, but small reddish brown clumps are scattered through the crown. Yesterday, when I biked to work, it was glorious fall, one of those brilliant days someone described as "blue October" (although it is still September, at least until midnight tonight). A day like the day I searched for PICADA, eleven years ago. Blue sky, puffy white clouds, warm sun, gusts of wind sending the first fallen leaves scuttling across the street. Locust trees lining the sidewalks, turning gold as I watched.

By late afternoon, though, the weather had changed for the worse. I biked home as fast as I could, to escape scattered drops of rain.

This evening, Carl and I are going to L'Etoile. I am a little anxious: will this evening, which I engineered (Stu would have said "demanded")—will this evening be a success?

I am full of anxiety about Carl; lovesickness, I think. When he is out of town, I miss him terribly. I can't concentrate on anything. I walk out of the house to bike to work and have to return three times for my helmet, my backpack, my keys. But then, after I've worked myself into a frenzy, the bottom drops out. I decide I am only in love with the idea of love. If Carl never calls, why should I care? And the next moment, I know I am building defenses. If he never calls, I will be depressed. I will be devastated. Some part of me will die.

I don't recall such an emotional yo-yo in my first months with Stu. I wanted to be with him because he seemed interested in me. When he said Tuesdays were the best nights for him, I dropped out of my pottery class. I had only gone to one or two sessions. We'd just learned to wedge clay and do a little hand building. I worked at a big wood-plank table, folding and pounding the cold gray stuff until my arms ached and my fingers were stiff. I dropped out before we got to the part I really wanted to learn, how to throw pots on the wheel.

Stu pursued the courtship at a steady enough pace. Maybe I had no reason for anxiety. Maybe I wasn't in love. I wasn't looking for passion. I wanted someone reliable, someone interesting and smart, someone who offered security, good father material. Stu doted on his two black cats, Stokely and Simone. He said, "I'm a good cat father. I think I'd be good with kids."

⊛

Tuesday, October 7, 1986

Had an emotional session with Paul. I finally brought myself to ask him what his friends call him. He said, "Paul." So I call him Paul. He said, "This is a wonderful way not to define a relationship! For nine months, you don't call somebody by their name!"

We talked pretty thoroughly about two dreams I had this morning. In one, Rachel told me that she was pregnant, and I said, "I hope your baby is a girl." In the other dream, which was mostly about a therapy session, Rachel was sitting in Paul's waiting room with a little baby on her lap—the baby she'd told me about in the phone call dream.

It was very upsetting to realize how much I wanted a little girl: "a companion," Paul said, and I almost broke down crying. It wasn't clear whether the little girl who would be my emotional companion would be me or whether I was talking about somebody or something else. When I told Paul the dream in which he met Rachel (who is also a psychiatrist), Paul suggested that maybe the baby was me, a child of Paul and Rachel—or that part of me which is emotional, open, not rational.

I looked at Paul closely today, and of course he has a moustache!

I was very pleased at the end of the session when Paul asked permission to use my Franklin Institute airplane dream in a lecture that he's going to give. He connected what we did today with that dream. "Now we're into the transition," he said, "and we're beginning to see what the new exhibits are going to be about." He reminded me that last week I suggested what they might be when we talked about writing fiction and reading poetry. "We see it now even more."

Paul noted that I used the rational side of myself to deal with problems that have to do with children, illness, and love. "Marriage," he said; I said, "lovers."

I said, "I've been wondering whether writing fiction would be an adequate substitute for seeing you." He said, "Yes, we have to see whether it's enough to nurture this baby that's been born."

❀

I think I have a clear picture of Paul Bergeson's office, although I haven't been there for many years. I sit on a couch, my back to the wall; above me hangs a Brueghel print. Or maybe it's Bosch; I can't see it, after all. Many small figures, at any rate. Paul sits across from me in a modern, wood-and-nubby-cloth armchair, balancing a lined yellow tablet on his knee. There's a floor lamp near his chair. On the wall to my right, a small bookcase under a large window that doesn't open. I spend a lot of time staring out the window or over his shoulder, avoiding his gaze. Eye contact makes me uncomfortable.

To the right of Paul's chair, a long table piled with papers and set with an old manual typewriter. To the left of my couch, file cabinets. Bookshelves and a door on the wall that faces the window. There's a coffee table in front of the couch and a box of Kleenex on the table. I don't generally need the Kleenex. I am much too self-controlled.

But there's a lot I can't remember. I know that somewhere—perhaps over Paul's chair—hung a photograph of some place he'd hiked. Was it a mountain? Someplace in Europe? I know we discussed it. It never sank in. I have a general impression of light wood and neutral colors, the couch, the chair, the coffee table. The walls were beige, I think, but maybe off-white or tan.

Memory is so selective. Once, Carl and I went to a bar to hear a band we liked and ended up on the dance floor. Later he told me he'd found a place where we could take dancing lessons, but he was afraid he'd miss too many classes, because he's out of town so much. I was surprised that he knew I wanted to learn to dance. "Why?" he said. "You talked about taking lessons." I couldn't remember that I'd mentioned it at all.

Things I remember: The sound of ice cubes tinkling in a glass as Stu carries it up the stairs. The dull edge of the painted wood-frame study doorway pressing into my upper back. The reflection of his desk lamp on the thick glass protecting his dark oak library table. The lush emerald green carpet he chose for the study floor.

⊛

Wednesday afternoon, October 8, 1986

About eleven last night I went to Stu's study and asked him the question I'd been thinking about all evening: "When you refused to see Martin on Monday, were you saying that we would never go back or that you just didn't want to go back then?"

"I'd be perfectly willing to go back when we have a program. Come up with an agenda, something to talk about with him," he said.

This started a conversation that lasted for the next two hours. I said, "It doesn't matter what we talk about. But the point isn't that I 'come up with something.' Do *you* think we have problems Martin could help us with?"

"Like what?"

"One goal he can help us with is to be more intimate with each other," I suggested. "For example, we could learn to communicate our hopes and our fears, things we like and don't like. We could learn to share things that are very important with each other."

"The problem is that you don't tell me the things that are important to you," he said. "That's why I don't share the things that are important to me."

"That's what I mean. It makes me sad that I can't talk with you about the most important things that have happened to me in the past year because you have no respect for therapy. I can't even talk about dreams because you don't like dreams. You don't think they're important, and you make fun of them when I talk about them."

"I don't have any problem with dreams. Dreams are fine so long as you don't live your life by them."

"I don't."

"You do. Last fall you had a dream in which you equated me with your mother—and you've used that to guide your life for a year. That's why we're at the impasse we're at today."

"No, you don't understand. That dream reflected something that I was feeling—that you were an alcoholic. I don't equate you with my mother, except in the sense that after I went to PICADA, I realized you were sick, and I was reacting the same way that I reacted to my mother when she was sick."

"Do you still think I'm an alcoholic?" he asked. He'd been drinking vodka all this time.

I said, "Yes."

"How do I act when I'm drunk?" he asked.

I told him, feeling calm and certain. "You get belligerent, you won't listen, you say and do ugly things. And you get hypersensitive."

"What does that mean? Define hypersensitive."

I tried, but I didn't get very far because he really didn't believe in hypersensitivity. He didn't want to understand: "What do you mean? That I listen better when I'm drunk?"

As an example, I described how rude he'd been when we were standing in line at Headliners and he got the mistaken idea that someone was trying to get in front of us.

"Do I suffer fools gladly when I'm not drunk?" he wanted to know.

"It's not a question of suffering fools gladly," I said. "It's a question of being considerate."

Then I said I wanted to come back to the question of seeing Martin.

He reiterated: "I think you should come up with a program that I can look at, like the three-page program you outlined last summer, when you were going to leave." The conversation started to get very circular because he insisted that *I* should come up with a program, and I think *he* needs to decide whether we can accomplish anything further through counseling.

About one in the morning I got really tired of the argument. I said, "I just want to know whether you'll go back because I'd like to tell Martin the real reason we canceled. He thinks one of us was sick. So let me know. I have to wake up early tomorrow, so I'm going to bed. Good night."

I went up to bed in my new room, and as far as I know, Stu slept on the couch. Or perhaps he didn't sleep at all.

This morning he told me he'd decided I didn't love him "because all you can do is hurt me." He is really beside himself with anger. He said, "You don't know what love is," and began to hurl epithets at me: "You're self-centered and self-indulgent. And separatist."

What a laugh. And (imitating me, he thinks), he minces around and says, "I'm tired of it." Good—he can leave. I do love him, but I sure don't like him when he's like this!

❀

Wednesday, 10:00 P.M.

Stu is still very angry. I am having trouble breathing. I try to be as nice as possible—If anything, this makes him angrier. But it seems better than getting angry back. Eli is super-solicitous. "Why is Stu angry?"

"I'm not sure. I think because he doesn't want to go to the marriage counselor, and I think it's a good idea."

"Why doesn't he want to go?"

"Stu doesn't like to let his feelings out, and that's what you have to do when you go to a marriage counselor."

"I hope I'm not like that," Eli says.

After supper, I suggest to Stu that we read a pop psychology book I picked up today, *Why Can't Men Open Up?*

"Did you tell Eli that I have no emotions?" he wants to know.

"No," I say. "You *have* emotions. You just don't like to *feel* them."

"You once told me that you thought you were too logical and rational for your own good," Stu says. This idea appalls him. Or maybe terrifies him. He suggests that we go out tomorrow night for dinner and then to a bar and talk about splitting.

I do not want to leave, but if that is what he wants to do, I will not stop him. But this time, I do not intend to move out. He can get an apartment, and I will figure out how to manage in this house, with the kids, until I'm good and ready to move. But I don't really believe he wants to split. He put on too convincing a show last July, when I was going to leave. I think he needs me—is dependent on me—and hates that dependency, and me for it.

What is he scared of finding if he opens up? Hatred for his father? Or for his mother? Or what?

What was I scared of finding? I still don't think I know.

❀

What was I scared of finding? That I had been cruel to my mother: that I had ignored her, disdained her, hated her, run away from her need. That I had abandoned my youngest sister. That I married for security and for children, that I used Stu to achieve my selfish goals, that I did not really love him. That I was not a nice girl after all.

However true all this may be, it seems insufficient cause to close myself down so thoroughly. I come back to the strongest image from my year of therapy. I sit on the couch, staring out Paul's office window into the gathering dusk. It is winter. The sun has already set. Paul asks what I am looking at. I see myself, very small, flying through the dark. "I see a little me," I tell him. "Little me, all alone, hurtling through space."

❀

280

Thursday morning, October 9, 1986

I don't remember any dreams, but I woke up with the refrain to a rock song (Creedence Clearwater?) in my head: "I see a red? (full?) (bad?) moon rising / I see trouble on its way."

⊛

Friday, October 10, 1986

Last night, Stu wanted to go to a bar and talk. We went to a place called Old Friends. He asked what I mean by the phrase "opening up emotionally."

"I can't give you a definition," I said, "but here's an example. I was amazed to discover in therapy—from a dream—how sad I am that I don't have a daughter. The feeling must have been there all along—but I wasn't in touch with it. At Stanford, the doctors told me I might not be able to have any more kids, and I said I didn't care because I already had two sons."

"We could adopt a daughter," Stu said.

I told him that wasn't the point. But during the whole conversation I really felt that Stu was listening, curious, not critical. I told him how happy that made me. "I've been afraid that I couldn't talk with you about these things because you'll be upset and say that I'm not 'rational,' not thinking well."

A couple of hours into the conversation, Stu asked why I feel that my sons and husband are "alien" and why I think a daughter might not be. I tried to explain the concept of the "other," and suggested that if he read *Intimate Strangers* by Lillian Rubin, he would get a better idea of what I meant.

"What is Lillian Rubin's field?" he asked.

"Clinical psychology."

Suddenly he got furious. He attacked me, and clinical psychology, and psychology in general. "I know all about psychology," he insisted. "It's all about the 'average,' the normal and the abnormal—what's on the curve and what's not on the curve. I'm not going to read books about that. What interests me is what is extraordinary and individual. Maybe if a cultural anthropologist who did cross-cultural comparisons wrote a book

281

about the 'other,' it would interest me." He told me that I was too impressionable; that since I'd started working on *Marriage and the Family*, I'd allowed myself to start thinking like psychologists, instead of being properly rational and critical of the field.

I got *very* defensive and very upset and very angry. I felt that he was attacking me and my way of thinking. I said, "You don't know anything about psychology. You never took psych, did you?"

"A lot of my friends at Harvard took courses in psychology. I spent enough time listening to them bullshitting to know what the field's about."

I said he was wrong. And the lovely conversation we'd been having ended with me so defensive that I was hissing at Stu. I stormed out of the bar, trying to escape from his attack on my very being.

We continued arguing on the way home—at one point I got out of the car and said I'd walk. But Stu convinced me to get back in. When we got home, we talked about it some more.

I explained, "I felt as though you were attacking me for bad thinking. And that's exactly what I had just told you I was afraid of."

He said, "I was afraid that your thinking *was* irrational. I was trying to give a rational response to your fear that your children are becoming alien."

I saw the pattern suddenly and said, "What are you afraid of, when you think I'm being irrational?"

"I'm afraid we won't have an extraordinary family because of your belief in psychology. You always want to look at what's normal. I don't want us to be a normal family."

I tried to point out to him that what had just happened was a common pattern. "I revealed an emotion—fear—and talked about sadness. That made you afraid. So you started attacking me and my way of thinking in order to rationalize away your fear." I'm not sure he understood. But I think we resolved the argument.

&

Mid-October and the weather is suddenly cold. This morning I turned on the furnace. When I look over the computer, out the window, I see the sun, strong on the neighbor's leaf-scattered lawn, and the storm pane, framed in aluminum, hovering at half-mast. I should slide it into place. But this requires moving the desk and the computer. Closing the storm window is a nuisance, a two-minute job that takes a half hour to do. Besides, it brings back the first fall we lived in Wisconsin.

It got cold in mid-September. We had to close all the windows, seal the house against drafts, turn the furnace on. I hadn't wanted to move to Madison, and the prospect of seven months trapped in the house with my own bad air made me like the place even less.

Stu introduced me to the seasonal rite of screens and storms. (Somehow, although I grew up in storm-window country, my family never made a big deal of this. But then, clear vision was not high on our list of priorities.) First we washed all the windows, dozens of leaded casement windows, each with sixteen tiny panes. We washed the heavy, old-fashioned storm windows too. We perched on the edge of the sills, leaned back, hooked the storms onto the window frames and pulled them snugly closed. Stu worked hard at these jobs on the crisp autumn weekends. He carried the Wisconsin Badgers or the Green Bay Packers with him from room to room. I worked much less eagerly. I hate radio football, the frenetic, high-pitched din. I'd rather be outside; I seized every chance I got to rake. Besides, I didn't much care whether or not I had a crystal clear view of our ragged backyard, or anything else.

⊛

Sunday, October 12, 1986

Stu is drunk tonight and in his drunkenness complains because I took Lou Dorsey to see my new third-floor studio when she dropped by this afternoon, and because later, when Julie was here for dinner, she asked to see the studio and I took her up. I think he's upset because I haven't invited him up there to bed. He's argumentative and slurring his words, and I find it disgusting.

⊛

Monday, October 13, 1986, Yom Kippur

I didn't wake Stu up this morning, so he was just getting out of bed when the cleaning lady arrived. It seemed a useful way to let him suffer the consequences of his drinking.

When he did get up, I told him I'd be willing to discuss the things that upset him last night. He had a lot of complaints. He doesn't like me "bragging" about having my own space. "What do you tell your friends that makes them want to see your room?" he wanted to know. He was also upset that on Friday evening, I rode with Bill and Linda to the yacht club banquet and then spent the time before dinner talking with Linda and another woman friend. "I didn't feel like a couple," he said. And he didn't like the fact that I entertained Julie in the kitchen before dinner last night. "I'm sorry I didn't make the salad so you could join us right away for the cocktail hour," he said. But he was also angry because, after he ordered us out of the kitchen, we went upstairs to see the studio, at Julie's request.

Now it's time to say good night to Stu and go to bed. Perhaps I'll invite him to sleep up here because it's so cold on the porch.

I wonder if I am just playing some kind of perverse intellectual game with him.

✿

What a way to spend Yom Kippur, the day of atonement!

This year I went to services at Shaarei Shamayim, a small Reconstructionist congregation that shares a Unitarian meeting house. Prairie Unitarian's building is not much to speak of: a big, blank, '50s-ish space with tan linoleum on the floors and plain glass windows set in blond wood frames. The congregants sit in curved rows of metal folding chairs. The Torah lies on a folding table covered by a white linen tablecloth.

But services at Shaarei Shamayim make up in their inclusive spirit and spiritual intensity what they lack in physical splendor. The congregation shares copies of a photocopied and spiral-bound *machzor,* or prayer book, compiled several years ago by the Ritual

Committee. Led by a part-time rabbi and a female volunteer cantor, the community prays and sings in Hebrew and English, always careful to refer to God in both the masculine and feminine and to invoke the biblical foremothers—Sarah, Rebekah, Leah, and Rachel—as well as Abraham, Isaac, and Jacob.

I return to Shaarei Shamayim every year for Rosh Hashonah and Yom Kippur, although I still feel uneasy about religious observance and uncomfortable in a community of Jews who are much more observant than I. The rest of the year, my involvement is pretty much limited to meetings of the Social Action Committee, which decides how to distribute *tzedakah*—the congregation's charitable donations—and organizes members into occasional do-good activities.

Yesterday morning I drove out to the Second Harvest Food Bank warehouse with a car full groceries, 432 pounds of peanut butter and pasta and tuna fish in bags that the Social Action Committee passed out to people who came to Rosh Hashonah services and collected on Yom Kippur.

The manager offered me a tour and walked me past pallets of food donated by companies: cartons of sugared cereals and artificial-strawberry-flavored ice cream syrup, bags and bags of spiral-shaped pasta, flats of fruit cocktail and canned peaches. "Maybe a forklift spears a carton and destroys some of the contents," he said. "The company gives us the carton. We throw out the damaged stuff and donate the rest to homeless shelters or group homes. Sometimes we get stuff that's unlabeled." He pulled a bag of chocolate chip cookies out of an unmarked carton and set it on top, as a display.

I began to see why we were asked to collect protein-rich food. A lot of the corporate contributions are food frills. A carton of tortilla chips. A pallet of salsa. The manager gestured toward some long folding tables set up in the middle of the warehouse. "These things," he pointed at jars of peanut butter in assorted sizes, round boxes of oatmeal, a few cans of chicken soup, "come from church groups and individuals."

Beggars can't be choosers, as my mother always said.

I thought of my own *tzedakah* shopping. Before services on Yom Kippur, I had pushed my basket up and down the Super Saver aisles. I chose a family-size can of tuna fish. A big jar of chunky peanut butter. A two-pound bag of pasta. Unsweetened applesauce. A bag of dried black-eyed peas, and a bag of mixed dry beans for soup. I imagined I was shopping for a single mother and two small boys. I tossed in a tin of sardines for the mother, Tastee-O's for the kids.

⊛

Tuesday morning, October 14, 1986

Two dreams or dream fragments.

In the first, I'm in an airplane. The seat belt is very strange and I can't figure out how to buckle it. I realize that I'm carrying the music-box pillow that David used to have in his crib and that the kids (who are with me) are too old for it. It's fairly heavy, and I'm going on a fairly long trip. But I tell myself I really don't mind carrying it—in fact it will come in handy.

In the second fragment I'm in a small, modern apartment. A couple lives in the apartment. The wife looks like a Hispanic woman I knew when we lived in California, Maria Ramirez, but in the dream I think of her as Razma, the Pakistani woman who took care of David when he was a baby. While I'm at the apartment, Eli's first baby-sitter, Mary Dunlop, calls Razma to ask about child care for her daughter. Razma and her husband talk with each other, too, but they ignore me. They are drinking wine, but when I want some, I have to pour it myself.

Then they get ready to take me someplace in their car. We drive through a place that looks familiar. I realize that it's Door County and think perhaps we're headed to Helen's cottage. But I'm seeing the scene from a different perspective. I'm really excited, and I try to explain that the car is so low that I'm seeing things differently than I had seen them before.

⊛

Tuesday afternoon

Paul and I spent most of the hour going through the dreams I had last night, finding all sorts of caretakers in them: David's child-care person, Razma; Mary, who used to take care of Eli; and my old friend Gwen, who gave me the music-box pillow, which I identified as my security blanket, when David was born. We found some caretakers who forgot me (Razma), some whose friendship was recoverable (Mary, who disappeared from my life for a year or two when I was sick), some whom I had grown away from (Gwen, whom I haven't seen for years). And we found that when people (like Razma and her husband) treated me like a child, I didn't like it, so I withdrew and found myself a way to feel good. I poured my own wine and took my security blanket along on risky trips (the buckle I couldn't fasten was like a test pilot's shoulder harness). And when I was traveling out toward Helen's cottage, on a trip I really didn't want to take, I amused myself by seeing things as I did when I was a small child, lying on the backseat of Daddy's Buick and looking out the window at a small slice of the world going by.

Paul suggested that the dreams were a message to him: "Look, Bergeson, I'm going off on this dangerous trip, and I don't know how to buckle my seat belt. I need to be comforted and taken care of." Maybe—but it's also instructive to me to know that I need comfort, I crave being taken care of. And to know that one of my coping mechanisms, especially with regard to Stu's anger, is looking at a slice of reality instead of its totality. Paul agreed that this is important, but he thought we should also talk about what I do that triggers Stu's fear and makes him react with anger. He suggested that we talk about this next time—this cycle Stu and I have.

Of course next time will be just a few hours after I've seen the oncologist, and who knows where my head will be at that point.

Who *is* going to take care of me on my trip—my journey through the next, experimental year with Stu?

⊛

Tuesday evening

I have had breathing problems all day. Dreaming of Maria/Razma, I realize, was dreaming about breast cancer. Maria was the first woman I ever knew who had a biopsy. I don't know whether the breathlessness has to do with fear of cancer, fear of losing Paul, too much thyroid medication, or some other physiological cause. Or perhaps I am allergic to October; I seem to remember breathing problems last fall too.

Enormous Rage

Early November 1997. I am at Ucross, a writing retreat in northeastern Wyoming. I will be here a month; by the time I leave, I hope to have finished the first draft of this memoir.

From my studio window, I see a small grove of leafless trees, the brown tufts of dried grasses, a gray sky. Snow flurries. Winter descended on the High Plains a couple of days ago, as I drove through the Black Hills of South Dakota. Yesterday, the day I arrived here, the temperature was in the single digits. But the sky was a brilliant blue; the first full day of sun I've seen in weeks. (Madison has suffered a fall of such unremitting gray that despite the cold, I feel as though I've left Wisconsin for better climes, the way people head to Florida or Saint Bart in January.) In the Big Horns—about an hour's drive away—snow glistens on the peaks. I brought my cross-country skis with me. The whole prospect seems highly promising.

❦

5:00 A.M. Wednesday, October 15, 1986

Just woke up from a genuine nightmare. It started out fairly benign. Maggie Thompson and I were out in the country somewhere, on some open land where a lot of Boy Scouts were tenting. For some reason, I was holding one of Helen's antique Chinese plates. I threw it like a Frisbee; it landed on the roof of one of the tents, and one of the Boy Scouts helped me get it down. The plate didn't break, which pleased me. I paid the boy fifty cents for his help. Then Maggie and I were in a house that was out on

289

the same land, at a big party. A lot of people I knew were there, including many who've had problems with their marriages. Stu and the kids were there, and I think Shelly too. Somehow the party faded into the background, and I was with a woman who was a psychiatrist. She was trying to help Stu and me resolve an argument about shopping. The woman was clearly on my side and kept asking Stu how he saw things and how he felt about things that had more to do with division of household tasks than about emotions or anything like that. Eventually Stu left, I think to go shopping. Then I had a conversation with some women about making quilts. All the women, including the psychiatrist, were helping me decide what kinds of fabrics to use. I was going to build the quilts from the kids' sleeping bags and baby blankets.

While we were discussing the quilts, Stu came back in, through sliding glass doors, with a gun. He said, "I'm not going to tolerate any more of this crap." He forced me down and stuck the gun in my mouth. Or maybe he pointed it at me, and I was so afraid he was going to shoot one of the kids that I helped him or encouraged him to put the gun in my mouth, to protect the kids. I woke up when he stuck the gun in my mouth.

☙

I've come to Ucross to focus on this memoir, but I've spent most of the past three days revising (yet again) my poetry manuscript, *Some Poems Want to Be Stories,* for a contest with a looming deadline. I've been writing poetry for eleven years, getting it published in little magazines for six. For the past three years, I've been working on *Some Poems,* sending it out in its various versions to compete in the cold, cruel world. Very occasionally, it reaps encouraging comments from one of the contest judges. On good days, these make me think that someday it might be published. On bad days, they make me think I'm throwing good money after bad. Every contest entry sets me back between twenty-five and forty dollars for printing, postage, and reading fees.

Why do I do it? It's the poetry biz. It's the only way I know, other than self-publishing, to see a book into print. The odds against winning are huge. The big contests—the ones that offer, in addition to publication, cash prizes of five hundred to five thousand dollars—attract as many as two thousand manuscripts. Even in regional contests, several hundred entrants vie for a single award. Who am I kidding? No one, really. When I take my manuscript to the post office tomorrow, I will think of myself as buying a high-stakes ticket for a long-shot lottery.

Still, some days the chances of winning publication for *Some Poems Want to Be Stories* seem much greater than the prospect of this memoir seeing print. A woman dreams that her husband has stuck a gun down her throat. It could be a dream about kinky sex. (That, at least, would sell.) But it isn't. It's as clear a warning as a wife could get. Still, she doesn't leave, doesn't even admit she feels threatened. What kind of story is this?

Thursday night, October 16, 1986

It seems like such a long time since I wrote yesterday's entry. It has been a long and emotionally arduous day—and it ends with me sitting alone in my hide-a-bed writing, because Stu is very upset with me. He didn't want to talk to me when I volunteered to help with storm windows at three-thirty or four o'clock. He sat rigid through dinner and through *Peggy Sue Got Married*, which we saw with Bill and Linda. He calls me "hostile" and "rancorous."

So here's the play-by-play.

I'll start with the easy things first. I went for my mammogram today and felt considerably relieved because the technician told me she would just take a mammogram of the left breast and then show it to the radiologist, and if the radiologist wanted a picture of the right breast, the radiologist would tell her. The radiologist did not want a picture of the right breast. My interpretation of this is that if the lump had not stayed the same size or gotten smaller, she would have wanted a picture of the right breast. So I felt much better—much relieved.

291

However, the whole thing triggered another episode with Stu. Before my doctor's appointment, I went for a haircut. When I came home Stu wanted to do an errand, returning a borrowed car.

"No," I said. "We can do that later, after my mammogram." And then I changed my mind. I realized that I was feeling bad that Stu wasn't coming with me for my doctor's appointment. I really needed him. I really wanted him. But instead of directly asking him to come with me, I blurted out, "OK, let's return the car and if we don't have enough time to go home before I have to go to the clinic, it won't hurt you to sit while I have my mammogram." Of course that was not a good way to put it.

Stu did come with me while I had the mammogram. Afterward, he wanted to check out a health club, but neither of us had had lunch, so I suggested that first we get a bite to eat.

We went someplace for hamburgers and had an extremely intense conversation. Stu said he knew I'd been anxious and upset, at least for the last couple of days. "You were bummed out and grumpy, so I've been trying to be nice and caring."

But the fact is that in the last couple of days all I've seen is Stu being nasty to Eli at dinner, Stu getting drunk on Sunday night. I haven't seen him being solicitous or kind to me. I said, "Why didn't you just tell me, 'Judy, I know that you're anxious about this, scared, upset'?"

"I didn't want to do anything to increase your anxiety." (This seems even more absurd and patronizing now than when he said it.)

I told him that for the two months that I've been anxious, including the week in August when I was terrified, I've felt I had to hide my fear. "Otherwise you'd tell me not to worry."

"You should try me," he said.

So I said, "OK, I will say to you that next Tuesday I would really like it— I need you to come with me to the oncology clinic when I go to hear the mammogram results." His reaction—I could read it on his face—was terror and anger. I asked, "Why are you looking like that?"

"Why did you have to say it that way?"

"What way?"

He said, "You made it a demand."

I was furious.

I'd been thinking when we left the hospital that I didn't need to *look* at a health club—I needed to go out and *do* some exercise. And Mary Ellen and I had talked about walking this afternoon. So I said, "Look, I just want to go home. I don't want to check out the club." And in the car I said, "Please don't think I'm running away from you if I call Mary Ellen and go for a walk with her when we get home."

But of course he does think that I ran away from him and his complaint. He says, "You don't need me for the good times—you only need me for the bad times—we can't have fun together—you run away from me two or three times a week to show that you don't need me."

As I thought, walking with Mary Ellen was the best thing I could have done. I insisted that we go to the Ice Cream Shoppe because I do feel that I need to indulge myself, nurture myself, take care of myself. After a walk and an ice cream cone I felt much calmer. But of course Stu is walking around looking like a wounded bird. I went up to him when he was taking the storms off the windows to wash them and said, "You know I love you, I really do." He just looked at me like I had hurt him terribly.

But the point is, I don't need him all the time. But I do need him at important times. And at those times, he doesn't seem to be there. Sometime this morning it occurred to me that in my dream, Stu wasn't killing me physically or making me sick; he was murdering my soul.

⊛

The care of the soul. It has brought me to Wyoming, to these vast sagebrush spaces where the pronghorn antelope graze, where the cars on the highway are few and very far between, where I am housed and fed and cleaned-up-after so that for four weeks I can do nothing but sit here and write.

The pronghorn are tan and white. When I first saw them, several dozen grazing in fields along the highway, they had their heads down, their necks stretched to crop the grass the same way cattle do. I was tickled to see them, because antelope appeared as a kind of writing totem in a dream I had the week before I left Madison.

In the dream, two antelope were in my bedroom on the second floor at home. Two other people were in the dream: Tony, our former housemate, who now manages a public radio station, and Joyce, a poet friend. Joyce and Tony watched me herd the antelope down the stairs, through the living room, onto a porch, and out to the front yard. The antelope waited patiently as I opened two sets of French doors and proceeded through them without any fuss. Tony was particularly impressed that both the antelope and I understood that they couldn't stay inside. Joyce wondered why not. What would be wrong with giving antelope the run of the house?

At first, this dream had me terribly confused. Why would I dream about antelope? Ah! I was about to leave for a month at Ucross, in Wyoming, where the deer and the antelope play. And Tony, of course, represented work, where I was struggling to finish a grant proposal and produce one last program before I left. Not a good time for antelope. But Joyce, a writer by profession, would give the antelope free range.

I think about the antelope when I read journal entries from the fall of 1986. I was thinking about writing fiction; planning to quit my job. I wanted (as I now see it) to adopt the antelope. I was beginning to care for my soul.

❁

Monday, October 20, 1986

We had another night of being together but quite separate. Had a dream just before waking up that involved moving into some sort of communal house—showing it to Helen, to Dad and Charlotte. The kids were also around. It was an unsettling dream, discomfiting, even though I liked the new house. I woke up as tense and unrelaxed as when I went to sleep.

Spent eleven hours today meeting with members of the *Marriage and the Family* faculty team who were in town, cooking dinner for them, eating in a rush so they could make their planes.

Exhausted, spent the evening playing Life with David and Eli and reading my high school yearbook, answering twenty-fifth reunion questions.

Had trouble breathing after pesto dinner. Allergic to Parmesan—or terrified of tomorrow's appointment with the oncologist?

⊛

In my last year with Stu, I often felt quite separate, even when we were together. With Carl, I sometimes feel quite close, even when we're apart. Though maybe I should put that in the past tense too. Exactly four weeks ago the two of us drove north from Madison to see the geese at Horicon Marsh. It was mid-October, time for the great migration. But the fall had been warm; we had not yet had a frost. The geese were a little behind schedule. A ranger said they expected 350,000 by the end of the month. "Right now there are only 100,000 in the area."

One hundred thousand geese is still quite a lot. In the late afternoon, we saw hundreds and hundreds flying, winging in to the wetlands from the surrounding fields of corn. Higher—so high we needed binoculars to really make them out—long strings of geese darkened the sky, in advance of the oncoming dusk.

We'd had a wonderful day, driving the perimeter of the marsh, stopping to take short walks, identifying migrating hawks and a half-dozen species of ducks. We'd laughed about the Illinois tourist who asked, "Did you see the pelicans?" Pelicans in Wisconsin? Not likely! We'd held hands, stopped to kiss on the nature trails, eaten a picnic lunch and lain, side by side, in the tall grass, our bodies touching from shoulders to feet. We thought about making love, but there was a chill in the air and the parking lot was too close.

The night before, we'd stayed up talking until two in the morning. Carl needed to figure out what he wanted; he needed to find out whether he could make things better with his wife. I needed to love someone I didn't have to share. We agreed that we should stop seeing each other. But we couldn't bring ourselves to break apart right away. We couldn't bear to abandon our plans to go to Horicon. ("What's thirty hours more or less?")

The looming break gave Horicon a special poignancy. "Whatever happens," Carl said, "we will always have this day."

I was sure I'd hear from him before I left for Wyoming. But the days went by, and he didn't call. I began to understand that this might really be the end.

I wrote a poem about our day at Horicon. "'Whatever happens / we will always have this day,'" I quoted Carl and added, "Not to mention whatever it is / that makes pelicans of geese." It was, my poetry group agreed, an ending with just the right touch of irony.

And then a friend told me that she'd seen white pelicans in Wisconsin. My Golden field guide, *Birds of North America,* shows them migrating, spring and fall, along the Mississippi flyway. The guide says, "Migrates in long lines in V-formation and often soars at great heights."

I want to tell Carl we were mistaken, but he still hasn't written or called.

❀

Tuesday evening, October 21, 1986

Quite a day. Went to work; at ten, met Stu at the oncology clinic. We sat in the waiting room for nearly an hour, my blood pressure rising by the minute. Finally, the oncologist told me the mammogram had not changed. He described the problem in greater detail: a shadowy area, but no sign of calcification. This had led the radiologist last summer to recommend a follow-up in three months and the breast surgeon to recommend ignoring it. The oncologist chose the conservative route and succeeded in terrifying me because he didn't do a very good job of communicating when I talked to him in late August. I asked if there was a cyst. "No," he said, "the shadow is probably breast tissue that has atrophied due to age." ("Did you hit him?" Paul Bergeson asked me later.)

I was surprised that I was still anxious after my appointment. In fact, I'm *still* having some breathing problems, even after lunch with Stu, a walk near the lake, my session with Paul B, dinner, and a fantastic concert by Itzhak Perlman.

Paul and I spent the hour going over the gun-in-the-mouth nightmare I had last Wednesday morning. I was able, fairly easily, to interpret the fairly

296

straightforward, logical business about throwing away material security (the Chinese plate) that comes from the Kingsley family; being relieved when it doesn't break and is rescued by my therapist the Boy Scout; going to a party with a lot of other couples who have marital problems; and then building (quilting) security for my kids out of pieces of childhood.

Paul said that the nightmare was a clear warning: my unconscious was saying that Stu, who barged in on the scene through the glass doors in the living room where we first met (arguing about commas), is dangerous and threatening to my project of building security.

"Is it a warning that I will be unsuccessful, or that he will indeed kill my soul, or is it just a warning that this is risky business and I should be careful?" I asked.

Paul said, "Well, of course we don't know what the future will bring, but it's clearly a warning from the unconscious. And I think it's more than just 'risky business.'"

I said that I thought the dream referred to my ability to teach Stu how to get along emotionally in the world; Paul and I have talked about that as part of my "security building" project. "I can do that as long as I don't need emotional support myself. But I can't teach him about emotional life when something like the mammogram shows up. It's just too hard for me to sort out what's going on."

"Of course not," Paul agreed. "It's not reasonable, when you're afraid of dying, to be expected to be tutoring emotional babies." He pointed out that mine was not an uncommon problem; women tend to be the ones who are able to deal with life on an emotional level. "What are you going to do about it?" he asked. "What do all of these other women do about it?"

"They have their female friends, and they have psychiatrists."

"Yes, but you're leaving me. What are you going to do instead?"

I said, "I'm going to try to write and see whether that is a way of expressing myself emotionally that works."

"Well," he said, "that's the best reason for writing."

⊕

Fall 1986. The *New Yorker* arrives in the mail. I leaf through it, looking at the cartoons. Suddenly, I realize I am reading a poem. It's about a hiker, resting in the mountains, leaning back against rocks that have been silent for eons. The hiker-poet gives voice to the rocks.

A few weeks later, lines of poetry appear in my head. I am taking a walk, maybe just for the exercise, maybe trying to calm myself after another fight with Stu. The maples along the street have turned; they glow in the sun like big lollipops spun from gold. I stand directly under them. They embrace me in their wealth. I feel warm, expansive, glowing. Then the words arrive. They startle me. They come from nowhere, sounding loud and insistent over the general din of conversation with myself.

I have no paper or pencil, no way to hold onto these words that string themselves together without any apparent help from me. I remember that, when I was in high school, lines of dialogue, lines of poetry, metaphors, similes, the building blocks of writing used to come to me this way. I never wrote them down.

All I have is this memory: I am several blocks from my home, on my way to high school. It's spring, and hyacinths bloom in a border along the walk up to someone's house. I love tulips and daffodils, but hyacinths, clusters of rigid lavender florets, strike me as prissy, artificial, unnaturally stiff. The woman who planted them probably teases her hair and lacquers it into place. I continue along Beechwood Boulevard. Two characters materialize in my head. They discuss the stuck-up, stupid kids who live in the neighborhood. The ones who wear knife-pleated kilts with giant gilt safety pins. Who comb their hair into perfect flips. Who think it's dumb to be too smart. Who decide who gets to be popular. Whose mothers plant hyacinths.

Now after twenty-four years, metaphors, images, fragments of poems, flood back into my head. Mostly they come while I'm walking, thinking of something else. Something has come unblocked. I am open to the gift of poetry.

I know that I can't trust memory to preserve the words. I start to carry my little recorder whenever I go on walks. I don't want the images, the feelings, the language to disappear.

I went into therapy trying to decide whether to leave my marriage.

I might just as well have said, "Help me, I have writer's block." I decide, as a "thank you" to Paul Bergeson, to write a farewell poem.

❀

Wednesday evening, October 22, 1986

Rather peculiar day, as I began to come down from the anxiety of the past
two months. Spent the morning organizing Children's Museum files. Had
lunch at home with Stu, then spent a couple of hours at the station,
choosing music for four *Marriage and the Family* programs and talking
about writing and producing three units (on Hemingway, Frost, and Ann
Tyler's *Dinner at the Homesick Restaurant*) for an English literature course.
This would be from January to May, and I am quite tempted, although it
would interfere with the writing I want to do.

I find myself wondering whether Paul was suggesting yesterday that
one solution to my emotional needs is a lover—and I know I am exploring that idea, wondering, for example, about the professor I'd work with
on the literature tapes. Stu has often told me that I should take a lover.
(This, of course, would give him permission to do the same.) In fact, I have
many fantasies about finding someone whom I can really love. Sometimes
I imagine that writing will lead me into situations (conferences, or summer
workshops, whatever) where I find a soul mate.

I've always said that if I took a lover, it would mean our marriage was
in serious trouble. But of course it is.

I just discovered that the poetry that came to me during my walk to
the grocery store yesterday is gone. I accidentally recorded over it. I've re-
constructed a bit, but it really is ephemeral. Still, I know there will be more.

❀

Monday evening, October 27, 1986

Hectic day, anxious, breathing problems. Maybe they have to do with my
plan to tell my boss tomorrow to take my grant-writing job and shove it.
Walking home, my head filled with all sorts of crap. Worried about Stu

being angry that I wasn't helping him rake and bag leaves. No room for poetry, for sure.

⊛

When we first met, Stu edited whatever I wrote: my diary, grad school papers, political leaflets, a long article about the future of cable television. I was annoyed when he read my journal, but in general I valued his sharp eye for grammar, for lapses in logic; the distanced perspective that could tell whether my meaning was clear.

Heart pounding, I brought first drafts to his study. For short pieces, I hung around, looking over his shoulder, trying to guess what he thought. With longer manuscripts, I went away, took a walk, made dinner, worked furiously at something else. I waited for his verdict, hungered for his praise, hoped he wouldn't find too much fault.

He was an excellent editor. He admired my writing, but he always found things to improve.

⊛

Tuesday, October 28, 1986

This afternoon, I told Paul that I'm afraid Stu will want me to share my stories with him, and I don't want to do it. And then we talked about how Stu gets upset at what he takes to be my "going away" (for example when I go up to my room to write). It triggers his fears that I really am leaving; it makes him feel left out. He doesn't like me to be independent, yet at the same time he wants me to play power lady in bed. He wants me to take control.

I saw this as a contradiction but Paul said it wasn't. "Look at popular culture. They really do go together. You can take control and you should take the initiative, but only according to Stu's dictates and directives."

Now Stu has stopped taking the initiative, and we play this game about who's going to initiate sex. But when I do, it's never enough. I stroke his face or offer a back rub, and he trashes me for being "too predictable." He wants me to play games. But this particular game just drives me farther away from him (especially sexually).

I said, "I don't like to play games."

"You figure you'll just go on being true to yourself and maybe he'll get disgusted and leave," Paul said. That made me laugh. I thought it was really funny. The biggest game of all.

⊛

In a folder I find two articles I clipped from the *New York Times.* In one, cultural critic Edward Rothstein reflects on the 1960s. "In that dream-time," he writes, "reason itself was altered. What was once strange became common; what was once crazy, logical.

"One entered at risk and departed scarred. . . . Nothing was untouched, the experience could be all-consuming. . . . Consider the absolutist epigrams: If you are not part of the solution, you are part of the problem; if you are not with us, you are against us; the personal is political."

The other clipping reports on a study of murdered women. "More women in New York City are killed by their husbands or boyfriends," the researchers found, "than during robberies, sexual assaults, drug violence, or random attacks. One-third of the murdered wives had been living apart from their husbands, leading the researchers to conclude that "when they were killed . . . the women appeared to be trying to end the relationships."

Unlike men, who are most often killed by guns, women "are very likely to be punched and hit and burned and thrown out of windows. We were surprised by the degree to which some of these murders just spoke of enormous rage."

⊛

Stu and I are children of the Cold War; we came of age during the war in Vietnam. We shared, for a while, the kind of frustration, desperation—fury—that leads to insensate rage.

I don't like to remember my own anger and paranoia. I try not to feel the emotion that compelled me to shriek "murderer" at a well-heeled stranger waiting for a train. I think, now, that I must have been crazed, completely irrational, that day in 1970. I didn't know whether that man really worked for a company that sent napalm to

Vietnam. I still don't know, any more than I know whether he beat his wife.

I do know the '60s transformed me. The sticker on my Volvo's bumper urges Question Authority. Of course, I have mellowed a little over the past thirty years. I am no longer an absolutist. I drive a luxury sedan, even if it's ten years old. I rarely quiver with indignation. I know that although I may be part of the solution, I'm part of the problem as well. I know that those who are not with us, may just be otherwise occupied. But I still believe, with my whole heart, that the personal is political.

Stu never agreed with me about that old feminist slogan. But we chanted the others together. We despised the Establishment. We closed down Stanford labs that were doing defense research. Our affinity group ran with the protestors who swarmed the campus at night. Stu stayed at the edge of the crowd, keeping the SWAT team in sight. The thrum of a chopper's blades echoed off Hoover Tower. A light bright as day suddenly washed White Plaza. We were pinned like bugs, frozen, trapped and clearly visible in our political defiance. We stood for all that was right: jobs for the poor, power for the people, peace in Vietnam. It didn't matter. They could squash us whenever they chose.

That feeling is hard to forget. The paranoia, the old rage, resonates in the soul.

⊛

Wednesday evening, October 29, 1986

I'm too tired to write very much, but I do want to record yesterday's big event: writing my resignation letter. I was really happy about it. I know it's the right thing to be doing.

Stu's in a really weird, distant mood. He wants to see *Blue Velvet* tomorrow night. I've just read the reviews; I have no desire to see it. I have no particular desire to have a big fight about it either.

I got Stu angry when I told him, a short while ago, that if he smoked in the redecorated bedroom—which is just beginning to get its wallpaper scraped off—it would force me upstairs to my room. "I really don't want to have to deal with smoke if I'm reading and enjoying a book."

He said rather bitterly as he was walking out the door, "Yeah, and I know you're in touch with your feelings."

What can I say? I'm in touch with my feelings: I really hate cigarette smoke; I really don't want to see movies about sadomasochism.

❀

Writing makes me hungry. I wait for the floorboard creak that signals the arrival of the Ucross cook with lunch in its insulated bag. It's already half past twelve; she's usually here by noon.

The hunger disappears when I'm writing something very difficult. Instead of getting hungry, I get drowsy. I close my eyes, lean back in my desk chair. Sometimes, I fall asleep.

The first time this happened, I was writing a short story. I was a "special student" at the university, one of two in a class full of undergraduates young enough to be my children. I was ten years older than the professor. I had two sons at home. I'd recently left their father. We weren't yet divorced.

I was a radio producer who had written award-winning scripts. I was a professional journalist. I knew how to write about facts, about ideas, about other people's lives. I wanted to learn how to write the things I felt. I'd taken a poetry class. Now I was trying fiction. The stories I wrote for class were thinly veiled autobiography. One character had MS. She sat in a green upholstered armchair in the living room. The armchair smelled of piss. I willed myself into that space to watch her push herself to her feet. I wrote a sentence describing how she did it. She made her halting way to the downstairs powder room. It looked just like the one my father built after my mother got sick. I wrote another sentence. I closed my eyes to see what happened next. It was too painful. I disappeared into sleep.

❀

Friday, October 31, 1986

Slept separately last night after a major brouhaha. Stu insisted that I don't love him. "Helen is right. We should get a divorce as soon as I have sufficient liquidity to buy you out. I made a big mistake last July when I agreed to continue seeing a marriage counselor and working on making things better."

I tried again to tell him that I do love him; that I want to be taken care of and want to be cared for by him. He said, "I don't want to take care of you. I want an adult and mutually caring relationship."

This morning I tried to explain that the thing that upset me the most was that Stu didn't want to take care of me.

He said, "We have to get rid of your fatherlike relationship to me." (Some time ago I told him that I was initially attracted to him by his resemblance to Dad.)

Then he said, "You try to control me by withholding sex." This "Lysistrata-ish complex," he insisted, was what made me say that I wouldn't be in the bedroom if he was smoking there.

"I can't relax when my environment is polluted by cigarette smoke. In fact, I don't want to relax in a polluted environment," I said. "But it doesn't have anything to do with punishing you for bad behavior. All I'm asking is that you go across the hall to your study if you want to smoke. I don't think it's unreasonable to ask that two rooms—my room on the third floor and the bedroom—be smoke-free environments. This is an enormous house, and you're the only one of the four of us who smokes."

I reminded him that last summer I felt I had only one way to get him to understand the seriousness of whatever I had to say and that was by leaving. "I suggested then that we had to talk about other kinds of sanctions, but you got very upset about it and refused.

"In point of fact," I told him, "I'm not going to force you to change. But I'm growing and changing, and you're going to have to change, too, or our relationship is going to split."

And he said, "Fine, let's split."

I said, "OK."

The curious thing is that I am regaining sexual desire. Not necessarily for Stu, but I'm getting turned on more and wanting sex more. And as I'm wanting it more, Stu seems to be wanting it less.

⊛

Ucross. Northeastern Wyoming. I am here to write, but the scenery depresses me, and I wish I were someplace else. Endless acres of sagebrush and grasses, a bleak washed-out landscape, tan with a greenish tint. Brown rocks, brown tracks for four-wheel-drive pickups winding over brown hills. The few trees lost their leaves long ago; their thick bare branches, a dark gray-brown, reach into a dirty gray sky. I crave color. I know it's November; the land is resting. But I don't want dormancy. I want to see signs of life.

My state of mind is bleaker than the gray-brown scenery. This manuscript is huge, unwieldy, repetitive, impossible to shape. Maybe it's important, but I'm overwhelmed by how much rewriting it needs. All night, I dreamed of friends who were deeply committed to politics. Free trade with Cuba. No more capital punishment. Peace in the Middle East. Noble goals, goals I support. But these friends communicated so poorly, their messages were so redundant, even I was bored.

I try to break my depression with activity. In midafternoon, I turn the computer off and head out for a walk.

This country is so vast that there's no sense of scale. The snow-capped Big Horns on the horizon appear a short stroll away, but I know it's seventy miles just to reach the foothills. I decide to take a long walk across the valley to the next ridge, and it takes just fifteen minutes before I'm at the top.

I hike up a dirt road into the hills. I begin to break through the brown, to see the subtleties. Cattails in a frozen marsh. White husks on stalks of grain, barley perhaps, that's long since dropped its seed. A swath of leafless stems that turns the hillside reddish brown.

I see that some of the hills are rounded; others look like mini-volcanoes, perfect cone-shaped peaks. Snow dusts the north-facing slopes like confectioner's sugar. As the sun drops, dramatic lighting transforms the scene. A rock outcrop on the horizon assumes the hulking delicacy of a castle on the Rhine. A cluster of spiky yucca growing around sandstone boulders becomes a rock garden of Brob-dingnagian proportion.

I leave the road to explore this giant's garden. Somehow, it gives shape to the countryside. The monochrome resolves into a palette of delicate color. The brown alluvial layers of crumbling rock, cracked and dried like mud, are mottled with lichens of gray, white, purple, rust. A tiny plant shelters in a crevice. Its leaves are green and leathery.

If I attend to the details, the story will emerge.

I walk back to the road on a clear path defined by cattle and antelope.

⊛

Tuesday, November 4, 1986

I was extremely anxious going in to see Paul Bergeson—so anxious that I didn't even remember where I parked the car. I couldn't breathe; in fact I started having breathing trouble yesterday. And now, after the session, I feel wiped out. And yet all we did was consider why I have such difficulty—such bad judgment—with regard to openness and secrecy. We talked about how Mother had learned about her MS from reading my diary; how I'd found out from Tom's checkbook that he was two-timing me. I described how I used to confuse people by telling outrageous tall tales, how I always begged friends and lovers to tell me what they thought.

We talked about the "hurt my heel" game I used to play with Shelly. Paul pointed out that I enjoyed being in power then. But now, when I'm in the power position—holding the secrets, he said—I try to subvert myself.

Paul suggested that it scares me to think how far I might go in playing the game of secrecy—how cruel I might become if I hold back secrets. I don't know if that's true. I'm not even sure what my secrets are.

⊛

Wednesday, November 5, 1986

This morning it occurred to me that I've come full circle in my relationship with Stu. I used to hate him so much that I wanted him to either die or leave me. I knew I would be happier functioning alone. Now I don't hate him—I don't want him to die—but because I *know* I can function alone, I think I can say to him what I want. Even though he might not like it, and it might make him leave.

⊛

One of the Ucross artists brings me her copy of *Medicine Cards*. The book, vaguely Native American in style, goes with a set of fortune-telling cards; each of the cards features an animal. Crystal wants me to read about the antelope.

I'm not a New Age enthusiast. I'm suspicious of profiteering spiritualism based on the appropriation of other people's religious practices. I bristle at the words on the copyright page: "'Medicine Cards' is a trademark registered to David Carson and Jamie Sams."

And yet.

I read in the book that Antelope teaches the lesson of action. "Antelope signifies knowledgeable action. . . . Looking at Antelope, you become aware of your mortality and the short time span you have on this planet. With this in mind, you must act accordingly. . . . Knowing of death, Antelope can truly live. Action is the key and essence of living."

⊛

Thursday, November 6, 1986

I dream about being in some sort of conference center that is run by a religious order. There is a huge swimming pool, like a hot springs. The water is rather murky. I am around people who seem very different from me, who don't want to have much to do with me. I am in the wrong place at the wrong time.

The dream gave me a really strong sensation of being left out, a sense of wandering by myself, being on my own. Of desolation. I began to think about that feeling-state and what else makes me feel that way. I realized that the prospect of leaving Paul makes me feel that way, and then I flashed on leaving home, on Daddy insisting that once we graduated from college or got married, we were on our own. And the old meaning of being taken care of by a man, and my inability to distinguish between economic and emotional care, came back to me very strongly.

Yesterday, Daddy called to say he was going to come to Madison for Thanksgiving. That made me feel as though he really does care. In fact, he's given me his support this whole year. In July, he even offered me the money so I could buy the Rowen Street house. It was the first time since college that I'd asked him to help me out financially. The first time in twenty years. But his coming for Thanksgiving is more important. It makes me feel as though he really cares.

✿

Saturday, November 8, 1986

Stu has been moping around, thoroughly bummed out, victim, he says, of the "battered husband syndrome." Last night we went to Casa de Lara to eat and then to hear Philip Glass. He seemed moody and I asked what was wrong. He snapped, "Maybe I'm just drunk and hypersensitive." And he spent much of the evening trying to provoke me with barbs and jibes. On the way home, when I buckled my seat belt, he asked snidely, "Does it make you feel more free to have a seat belt on?"

This afternoon, we put the captain's bed back together. It stands grand in the newly papered bedroom. But when I suggested to Stu that we "re-inaugurate" it, he looked pained. "I don't want to rape you," I said. "But it would be nice to make love."

"You don't act very loving." He just wanted to go to sleep.

✿

In my early twenties, after Tom dumped me to marry Sandy, before I started living with Stu, I had a fantasy. I would find a man I could keep in the coat closet, like a vacuum cleaner. When I needed a man—for sex or just to go to a movie—I would take him out.

Why couldn't I accept Stu's suggestion that we stay married, but live in different houses? Partly, of course, because he proposed this to

308

solve his problems with the marriage, not mine. In a separate house, he could have sex with all the women he wanted; in his fantasy, they would all love him unconditionally. Even I would warm to him, perhaps out of jealousy.

Partly, though, my resistance to separate houses came from my parents' example. My father slept with my mother, in the same bed, long after she got sick. Their double-bed mattress stank of piss. I understood that married people always sleep together.

Another lesson from my parents' marriage: One spouse does not abandon another. A loyal husband or wife will put up with anything.

Separate beds would never have solved the problems Stu and I had. But now, I don't think there's so much wrong at least in theory—with loving a man who lives close by but in a different house. I want to love and be loved. I want the solace of intimacy; I want the deep pleasure of sex. But my life is pretty full: with a job, an exercise schedule, commitments in the community. I value time with my women friends; I need solitude to write. A separate house sounds pretty good. Or separate beds. Or my coat-closet fantasy.

〄

Tuesday, November 11, 1986

Bumper sticker on a car in front of me on Willy Street: Since I Gave Up Hope I Feel Much Better.

Had a flu shot after seeing Paul. It seems significant that I allowed myself to get a flu shot for the first time in the five years that they've been urging me to do it. I want to take good care of myself. Wearing a seat belt has the same meaning.

I spent the hour with Paul being about as emotional as I've ever gotten with him. Rather than going through the details of the swimming pool dream, I told him how it made me feel: lonely, desolate. I said I found it hard to be angry with Daddy; that I see Stu/Paul/Daddy all as male would-be caretakers who disappoint me. I said I was feeling closer to women; that I wished I had a daughter, because she would be like me. And I said I even felt there were two of me: the emotional me, who has the feelings I had in Paul's office, and the other me, who just goes ripping though life, numb. (Writing about this I have an incredible ache in my throat.)

I said I didn't know whether I could sustain the me that has these feelings outside his office. Paul asked me to describe the feelings, to be very clear about them. They are so complex: there's pain and loneliness and a feeling of me hurtling out through space—and there's also a great joy in being able to connect with my women friends. And a joy in being able to feel the pain. I feel great sadness and distress because Paul, who assures me that it's all right to want a man to take care of me, is leaving me.

❦

Piney Creek flows under the highway a few hundreds yards from the Ucross driveway. It's a shallow stream, ten or twelve feet wide. Last week we had several days of frigid weather, down to zero and even below. The creek froze over. It's warmer now, but on the upstream side of the highway bridge, a layer of ice still covers the water. Swirls of trapped air bubbles look like frozen currents. The ice seems thick enough to skate on and stretches from bank to bank.

I wonder whether, in winter, ice so jams the creek bed that it stops the water flow. I am amazed by the force of the stream and its power to break the ice. At a gravel "sandbar" just downstream of the bridge, the ice has begun to disappear. Water flows out on either side of the bar. On one side it ripples as it goes over a patch of stones. The ripples have washed against the clear ice, melted small holes, and turned it to lace. You can look through the ice and watch the water as it laps the lacy underside.

I walk toward the Ucross office, feeling self-conscious and "writerly," aware of trying to force the whole world into metaphor. It's late afternoon, nearly dusk. Outside the office, I stop to listen for great horned owls. I hear water gurgling at the junction of Clear and Piney Creeks, the lowing cattle, each car as it passes on the road. And then—coo-cuh-coo, hooo, hooo. One owl, fairly close, calls to another, much farther away. I raise my binoculars, find the owl in a leafless tree. It's unmistakable: enormous, with prominent ear tufts.

I keep the glasses trained on it and try my version of its call. Coo-cuh-coo, hooo, hooo. It turns its head, looks straight at me, hoots. I return the call. We converse in this way for five minutes. Each time I call, it turns its head to seek me out. Finally, it sees something more interesting and soars off toward the fields, where the sheep and cattle graze.

⊛

Thursday, November 13, 1986

I dreamed that Stu wanted to read my journal. I didn't like the idea, but I was resigned. I said OK. He said he had been curious all year. I said I supposed he had been, but it wasn't written for him, and I didn't think he was going to like it. And he said well, he'd take that chance.

I've been thinking about Stu's paranoia. He told Helen that I am deliberately trying to hurt him. Today, Helen told me that she believes him. But I honestly don't think I'm that cruel. I may say things in a rough way, and I may lash out verbally in self-defense, but it's not a deliberate attempt to hurt.

I wonder whether something I do—asserting myself, for instance—scares Stu and makes him paranoid. The more I refuse to sacrifice myself for him, the more paranoid he becomes.

Meanwhile, we have chosen blinds and drapery material for the bedroom, and Stu is prepared to hang a mirror on the wall and wants to go look at lamps and get a wall system made. I feel alienated from this bedroom—but at least it is warm there, and I am sniffling quite a lot, so I think I'll go on down.

⊛

This morning I shared the locker room of the Buffalo, Wyoming, Y with two elderly women from the senior swim class. They'd been high stepping across the shallow end of the pool while I was doing laps.

"I see they're having quite a time in Denver," one woman said, pulling up her underpants. "There's another one of those skinheads holed up with a rifle near a school."

311

"I heard they have thirty policemen surrounding the apartment," her friend replied. "I'm afraid someone's going to get hurt."

"It makes me wish we had those flower children back."

Even the very old miss the '60s. But when I remember the anger and paranoia, my own nostalgia evaporates.

⊛

Saturday, November 15, 1986

Yesterday morning at 7:50 I asked Stu out to breakfast or lunch. He declined—said he'd make me breakfast. While he was cooking eggs, he said, "Why did you ask me out?"

"It doesn't feel like a date when we eat at home. You want to read the paper or listen to the radio. And I wanted to make up for not being able to go to the Y with you on Friday when I was feeling uptight about work."

Stu quickly turned the conversation into a "you don't love me, you only try to hurt me" argument.

Finally I said, "I think you need to get some help. You're getting paranoid. You interpret everything that doesn't go your way as a deliberate hurtful attack. And when I try to be loving—for example, when I invite you to go out to eat—you refuse to see it as an attempt to show love. So then you can say, again, that I don't love you."

Bill and Linda came for dinner and dominoes. After they left, I suggested we go up and fuck. Stu gave me a great deal of pleasure with his fingers and his tongue, but when I turned to him, he was upset that I had touched myself. He was in his "you don't love me, I'm no good, I can't do anything for you" mode and made it clear that he didn't want me to do anything for him. I quickly gave up, after a bit of resigned stroking that seemed to go nowhere good.

This morning he gave me shit for fifteen minutes on the theme: "You have to touch yourself but you won't let me touch myself, and that's a reflection of our relationship out of bed."

"I wanted to have intercourse," I said, "but you seemed to be taking pleasure in my pleasure, however it transpired. And you contributed a great deal to my pleasure." But I felt depressed and, in a way, tortured by his tortuous attempts to prove I'm not a loving person. I came upstairs to write and to be away from his pushing me to appreciate his loving nature. (He loves me at my expense, I think.) He followed me up, with orange juice, wanting to make up, to touch, to be close. "Don't run away," he pleaded. Etc. Etc. He wanted to talk.

I think talking is the last thing I should do, so long as he is out to describe how "bad" I am (unloving, deliberately hurtful). I've heard all I need and plan to hear of that. He can start seeing what I *do* that is open and loving and recognize that love doesn't only happen in bed.

Monday, November 17, 1986

David's teacher called this evening to say that his irrational and terrible anger is returning. He is very explicit about adults being unfair to kids. All I can guess is that my upset and Stu's paranoia and our problems in general are getting to him.

The Gift

Last night I dreamed about Carl. I had been away on a long trip. We had made tentative plans to go to a concert, to a movie, out to dinner, when I came home. He said that while I was away he would find out performance times, make reservations, and so forth. But he was also going to see if he could make his marriage work. When I came home, I found that Carl had posted in my kitchen elaborate schedules of places to go and lists of things to do. But when I asked him whether we would be doing these things together, he said no. He'd decided to stay with his wife.

I was very angry with him; much angrier than I have allowed myself to be in my waking life. I woke up thinking how little I have changed, how I continue to stuff my emotions, refuse to acknowledge them until—the conscious mind defenseless—the unconscious serves them up.

But Eli and David were also in the dream, as young boys, eight and eleven years old, the ages they were in 1986. I was annoyed when they snuck into the kitchen, trying to hear the conversation I was having with Carl. They were upset when they heard that he was going to leave. And as I scrounged in the freezer for something to feed them, something to make them feel better, I suddenly felt myself very much a single mother of two sons. Clearly, the man in the dream was Stu as much as Carl.

Am I writing out of anger? Of course. But Stu was not the only one responsible. I feel compassion as well as anger. Sadness too. How high his defenses were. How afraid he was to understand himself. How little he was able to share. I lived with him for seventeen years and I never knew the source of his pain. It was hard enough for me to uncover the roots of my own misery.

What would our lives have been like if we'd both been able to grow?

✺

Tuesday afternoon, November 18, 1986

I'm in tears after leaving Paul Bergeson. As I was walking out the door to go to my appointment, Stu hurled another jibe at me. "Maybe you can get Paul Bergeson to help you take the garbage out and do the dishes." I was really upset, and Paul pointed out that Stu was starting the cycle again.

We talked about how strong the family system is and how slow it is to change, if it changes at all. "What do you think Stu's drift has been over the past year?" Paul asked. "Do you think he has improved?" And I guess that he has in the sense that he's not drinking as much, and not sleeping as much. But instead he occupies his time cataloging all our books on his computer. And although I've changed my reaction to the cycles of trashing, anger, and retreat, he still initiates them.

"It seems like we've come full circle," I said. "I'm back between the horns of a dilemma. I have to abandon my children if I want to save myself. Now I can see the horns, and I know how I got here. But there doesn't seem to be any help, or any hope."

"That's where I don't agree with you," Paul said. "You can share the pain."

I said, "That's why I'm so upset about leaving therapy. I can share the pain with you. Who will I share it with when you're gone? Certainly not Stu." Then I thought of one or two people. And I thought I could also share it with the world through writing.

"Are you angry with me?" Paul asked.

"Obviously, I see you as a threat. I try not to cry in front of you. You threaten to open up my emotions and open me up to all that pain. But on the other hand, that's really something wonderful that you've done for me. On the whole I'd rather feel things, however painful they may be—I can feel the joy at the same time."

We came down to the very elemental. I said, "I don't know whether I can share the pain without being cruel. If I save myself and leave Stu to find someone with whom I can share the pain, I would be abandoning my children."

"How would leaving Stu be abandoning your children?" he asked. "Because they'd have to deal with two families?"

"Yes. But more, they'd have to deal with the pain of us splitting up. I think that's a kind of abandonment. But the only alternative is to try to roll back generations and generations, so that my father's grandfather didn't abandon his son, and my father's father didn't abandon him, and my father didn't abandon my mother, and my mother didn't abandon me." I said, "The time has come to stop it somewhere—but at very great cost to me. It's very clear to me that if I didn't have children, I'd leave."

It's so hard that I'm crying as I write this. It hurts so much.

❀

"Are there any families that have not suffered such damage?" I asked Paul Bergeson.

He wouldn't answer. "Wouldn't that make it harder, if I told you that there were?"

❀

Wednesday, November 19, 1986

Slept hard last night, isolated on the bed, with my teeth clenched tight. I woke up with a lump in my throat, but realized when I was exercising that this hurt about feeling abandoned as a child explains why I got so upset years ago, when Stu pulled the pillow over his head and abandoned both me and David. And also why it triggers me so when Stu retreats from my hurt. I'm so deeply in pain right now that I can't even reach out and ask Stu for help. I have to tell him that my relationship with Bergeson is coming to an end and that it's hard for me. But I don't know how to do that without having him gloat.

In the shower I realized that my problems with feeling abandoned also explain why I've always had such a difficult time agreeing to take vacations without the kids. I was afraid they would be hurt; that they would feel I was abandoning them. And the story I started writing last fall is a story of abandonment. A little girl who is in pain because her friend Barry has died reaches out to a little boy. But the boy is incapable of dealing with his own grief, and he abandons her to her pain.

⊛

It has taken me a year to realize that the dates in 1996 and 1997—the dates on which I have been working on this memoir—fall on the same days of the week that they did in 1985 and 1986. Today is Thursday, November 20, 1997. I am about to edit my journal entry from Thursday, November 20, 1986.

Why should this make a difference? And why has it taken me so long to figure it out?

⊛

Thursday, November 20, 1986

While exercising this morning I realized I am cruel enough to leave. I am cruel. And recognizing that will make it possible, I think, for me to save myself. I am cruel, I can be cruel, I have been cruel.

I think the part of me that *wants* to be different—that wants to be alone, hurtling out in space, that wants to join spirit with others who are hurtling out in space—is the part that would inspire me to be cruel to those who are close to me. And cruelty is so two-faced, such a relative thing. I can be cruel to David and Eli, I think, by keeping them in an un-healthy family system, where David becomes the scapegoat and Eli, the goody-goody. I don't know whether leaving would free them of those roles; I suppose it might, eventually. And while it might be cruel to stop ac-commodating Stu, isn't it also cruel to keep accommodating him? That

317

keeps him in the system and in a sickness. It's cruel in the same way that enabling an alcoholic is cruel.

I feel as though I'm finally allowing my emotions to drive my intellect. Recognizing what I feel opens new possibilities that I can analyze in a rational way. I wonder whether I've been hiding my cruelty, in the same way that Daddy hid his cruelty to Mother behind the guise of a saintly, self-sacrificing sufferer. That guise doesn't sit so well with me. It makes me sick.

⊛

Several years ago, I interviewed a neurologist, Antonio Damasio. He had written a book he called *Descartes' Error,* challenging the idea that body and intellect are separate entities. Reading *Descartes' Error* made such a big impression on me that I wrote a poem about it. I began with an epigraph, a short quote from Damasio: "I see feelings as having a truly privileged status. . . . [F]eelings have a say on how the rest of the brain and cognition go about their business. Their influence is immense."

The mind/body connection fascinates and mystifies me. It's not just the question of feelings (like cruelty, say, or pain) and rational thoughts (like "now it's possible to leave"). Somehow memory, too, fits in the mix.

Can we trust the body to remember? I think of the masseuse who once asked if I'd ever been physically abused. "Yes," I said, surprised that she would ask.

"Are you still with the person who did it?"

"Not any more."

She told me to talk to my shoulders. "Tell them they can relax," she said. "It's time they let down their guard."

⊛

Saturday, November 22, 1986

Watching the sun set, molten, behind the bare trees in Burrows Park.

While I made breakfast, Stu and I had an intense discussion about why, when I reached for him in bed this morning, he immediately snapped at me, "I can be Lysistrata-ish too," and got out of bed. He said he'd suddenly flashed on how thoroughly I had trashed him yesterday. (I told him I wasn't going to help catalog books; that I didn't think much of the project as a way to occupy time.)

"You have to be nice to me," he said. "We all should be nice to each other."

"If that means being accommodating," I replied, "I'm not going to be doing that anymore."

While we were talking, Eli came in to interrupt us. Then David came in, and Eli immediately provoked him. David provoked Eli back, and they got into an enormous squabble. Stu started yelling at them, "Be nice. Shut up and be nice."

I tried to break in. I wanted to tell the kids that I knew they were upset that we were arguing. But Stu wouldn't let me talk. He got very angry and then went upstairs and refused to eat with us.

Instead of getting upset, I simply told David and Eli, "I know you don't like it when Stu and I argue, but sometimes we have to talk about our disagreements. It doesn't necessarily mean that we're going to get divorced, and it doesn't help when you try to distract us by getting in trouble yourselves."

They immediately caught on. They were playing in the living room when Stu came downstairs to have some breakfast and help me tidy up. He began to accuse me, in an angry voice, of "butting in" and not letting him shut the kids up. On cue, David and Eli came running in to the kitchen, yelling, "Shut up! Shut up!" as if they were in a funny play. It was *wonderful!* I think it relaxed Stu too.

🌀

In a few days, it will be Thanksgiving. I plan to take time off from writing and drive to the Big Horns to ski. Someone told me about a place with groomed cross-country trails.

I'm not very good at skiing, cross-country or downhill. But I like both of them. In January, my old friend Beth and I are going to Lake Tahoe for a long weekend. We were there two years ago, over Christmas; that time, we brought our kids. Eli, who was a high school senior, brought his trombone along to practice for an audition. We met David in San Francisco. He'd come straight from college. He got off the plane wearing unlaced Sorel snow boots and a tailored wool dress coat. The sides and back of his head were closely shaved; the long hair on the top, dyed and moussed, a shiny, wavy purple.

We got into a rented van with Beth and her daughter, drove to the Sierra Nevadas across the Central Valley. We stopped in Davis to look at the house Stu and I moved to a few months before David was born. It had been remodeled, a second story added. But the lot was much the same: a country acre, surrounded by farmland. The tall pampas grass at the end of the driveway rustled in the breeze. It looked idyllic.

Eli asked, "Why did you ever leave?"

⊛

Tuesday, November 25, 1986

I have spent four hours cooking—two pies, cranberry relish, a Finnish smelt dish for tomorrow's dinner—and I am sore of foot and back and still aching inside.

My last session with Paul felt a bit anticlimactic. I gave him a crystal ball (a clear marble in a velvet-lined box) so he can predict the future when his patients ask him to. And a poem, "Metaphor," a kind of record-in-verse of the last year, which clearly pleased him.

And then we walked through a dream I had several nights ago about a last therapy session. In the dream, Stu sat watching television, ignoring a circle of friends who were trying to tell him that my individual therapy had gone as far as it could and that it was time for family therapy. Paul described the dream as a wish. And I was hurt, angry, disappointed, when Stu ignored my wish.

I told Paul about the Saturday morning "shut up" incident with the kids and Stu. He laughed and said, "You've done impressively well in 'individual' family therapy." He also told me that he'd been reading the family therapy literature recently. "It doesn't seem to work very well when one person

320

is highly resistant." He came close to saying he'd made a mistake when he sent us for marriage counseling. I'm not sure; we learned something, seeing Martin.

Paul had a cold and told me he wasn't going to shake hands with me because he didn't want to spread viruses around. "If you want to come back and consult with me on how you're conducting family therapy, I'll always be available," he said. "Or if you want to talk about whether you deserve something better than what you have."

"I think that's something I have to deal with myself," I said. "I'm angry with you because you haven't solved all my problems. But if that's what I wanted, I guess I should have hired a fairy godmother, not a psychiatrist."

And that was that. Still, the pain is almost unbearable. All I can do is put on Beethoven string quartets, drink sherry, and cry.

My Madison house has a great deal of what Realtors call "curb appeal." Its cedar shakes are stained a dark charcoal gray, almost black. The trim is white, with big white window boxes under the windows in the front. There's a bright red mailbox and a front yard full of lily of the valley shaded by big oaks. I used to admire the house years ago, when we still lived in the big house on the lake. I passed it every time I drove the kids' car pool to school.

After I left Stu, I rented a house around the corner from the one I live in now. One Sunday, walking around the block, I noticed that an Open House sign had sprouted under the oaks. I called Maggie Thompson, who lived just down the street. We showed up the moment the open house started. I walked into the front hall. The Realtor was standing in the dining room, to my right. It was March; the oaks were still bare, and sunlight flooded the first floor. "How big is this house?" I asked.

She told me. The second floor had room for my study and bedroom. A previous owner had remodeled the attic with built-in beds and storage to suit her two young boys.

"I think I'll be making an offer," I said. "But I guess I'd better look around."

The Gift

My street dead-ends at an abandoned railroad track. After I moved in I realized that Paul Bergeson lived a few houses away, on the other side of the tracks.

⊛

Thanksgiving night, November 27, 1986

I'm terribly sad. I'm sad because Paul is gone. I'm sad because I had no one with whom to share the preparation of Thanksgiving dinner. I suppose I could have asked Stu to help, but I didn't. I wanted a woman to share it. I'm sad because my best friends, Beth and Rachel, are so far away. I'm sad because I'm going to go to bed with Stu, and there's no way that he's going to share my pain. He'd just take it personally.

Dad arrived yesterday afternoon; we picked him up in Milwaukee. I was incredibly tense on the way to the airport, but once we got home, Stu was lovely—present, polite, though drinking a fair amount. Dad was difficult to talk to, but not excessively difficult, and also very pleasant. I managed to relax.

Today Dad and I took a long walk up to a bluff that overlooks the lake. At first he was uncomfortable every time I tried to say something personal. He kept changing the subject, going on and on about racism in the Pittsburgh schools. Eventually he shut up and let me talk. I told him about my therapy and about beginning to write again. He had the good grace to keep his mouth shut, although I don't know that he understood what I had to say.

I left a copy of the poem I wrote for Paul on Dad's bed. I'm sad because I can't give the poem to Stu to read—because I don't have a companion—because I want so badly to be with someone who knows me and understands who I am.

For dinner I made a squash casserole, cranberry relish, turkey with two kinds of stuffing, two kinds of pie, green beans with almonds. We finished eating in twenty minutes. It could have been any night. David said, "Thank you all," and I said, "Thank *you*, David."

It seems such a puny Thanksgiving.

I called Rachel because she's the person I'm most thankful for this year.
That bastard Paul.
I miss my mother. I wish I could talk with her.

⊛

Thanksgiving 1955. Mother, eight months pregnant, is in the hospital "for tests." I am eleven; Shelly is eight. No one has told us what they're testing for. All we know is that she fell down some cellar stairs a week or two ago, and for days, Daddy has been going to work, running to the hospital, coming home to make supper for Shelly and me and Ellen, who's only two.

Thanksgiving morning, I go down to the kitchen. Corned beef simmers in the pressure cooker, under a scummy gray film. "What's that for?" I wrinkle my nose.

"Supper," Daddy says.

"But it's Thanksgiving," I whine. "Why aren't we having turkey? I want turkey!" What I really want is a normal Thanksgiving, my mother in the kitchen asking me to open cans of cranberry sauce and candied sweet potatoes.

"I don't feel like making turkey," Daddy says. "And I like corned beef and cabbage."

⊛

This year, Eli is going to Shelly's for Thanksgiving. My father and Charlotte will be there too. David will show up sometime during the weekend. I told Shelly I would call on Thursday, probably between four and five o'clock when they'll be having drinks and appetizers.

She said, "I really need you to call after they've all left."

Last fall, I went east for Thanksgiving to be with David and Eli. We gathered in the Poconos, at the home of my second cousin Larry. AA, my aunt, was there, and my cousins Alan and Lynn. At the table, Larry's children, Lynn's son, and my kids sat next to each other at Thanksgiving dinner: five members of a third generation of Weinsteins, fit into a span of three years between David, the oldest (by a week) at twenty-one, and Eli, the youngest (also by a week), eighteen. This was the first time they had all been in the same room at once. I sat across from these five and saw that they have the same beautiful, thick eyebrows. This is some of what family means.

I'm sorry not to be cooking Thanksgiving dinner this year. I'm sorry that I will be eating turkey two thousand miles away from my sons. I feel the distance, but I also feel connected, by something strong that feels like elasticized thread. A similar thread connects me with other people too. My father, of course, and Shelly. My younger sisters. AA and my cousins. Nana and Poppy (may their souls rest in peace). My mother, across the chasm of years since she died.

The thread reaches farther than eyebrow genes. It ties me to my former in-laws. It keeps Stu in my orbit, and me in his, whether we like it or not.

Sometimes the thread stretches tight. It thins until it doesn't have any give. People sicken; they get depressed. Tempers fray. People forget themselves in fury; people remember too much. A father boils corned beef and cabbage, and his daughters smell the rank greens-and-clove every Thanksgiving for the rest of their lives. A husband freezes into a terror that alcohol can't thaw. A wife finds herself in a spill of secrecy.

But the thread, I think, never breaks. Loose or tight, thick or thin, love or hate, it catches us in our solitude; spins us, thankful or not, into the web of family.

⊛

Saturday morning, November 29, 1986

Dream: A thin, dark-skinned girl of about eleven, an American Indian or African waif, hugs me, hard. I think she's my adopted child, from whom I've been aloof. I've been waiting for her to come close, show affection. While we are hugging, I am crying. My face is squinched up, and Eli (who is jealous) asks why I look like that. "Sometimes," I say, "that's what hugging does."

Then the girl takes me by the hand to an old photograph on the wall of native people dressed in native garb. She points to one of them, an old and wizened woman with a babushka tied tight around her head, and says "Mama." I ask if she means my mother? (This puzzles me in the dream, because it is clearly not my mother.) No, she says, *her* mother. I am honored and touched that she has shared this with me —opened up to me.

The girl came to me in a long, white hall—whitewashed adobe, like a mission, or a hospital, or Rachel's house. She clearly represented the spiritual, emotional, side of me—my soul with whom I have now been united, and whom I must now nurture and give voice.

❦

The Saturday after Thanksgiving in 1986, I took Dad and the kids to the Children's Museum. It was jammed with parents and children making gingerbread houses. I found my friend Maggie and her boys. "Maggie Thompson," I introduced her, "this is my father, Stu Kingsley." I was much less embarrassed by my mistake than I would have expected. Certainly less embarrassed than I was in 1969 when—not long after I met him—I called Stu "Daddy."

I was surprised, though. I'd been thinking about the differences between my father and Stu. But as I wrote in my journal, they share, without doubt, discomfort at knowing who I am and how I feel; Stu, now, more than Dad, but I suspect only because Dad knows that tomorrow morning he can fly away. They would both reject and fear the dark waif of the dream.

❦

Saturday night, November 29, 1986

After lunch, took Dad and the kids to the Y. Got home at 5:00, with company due for dinner at 6:00, and as I got into the throw-leftovers-together-make-a-salad-set-the-table-fast routine, Stu announced that he was going up to take a shower. At 5:50, with Dad setting the table, I went up to ask the kids to please help—and found Stu playing computer games with them. I lost my cool.

Stu reacted with fury and with very threatening moves toward me, which he (fortunately) stopped before he hit me.

The meal (leftover turkey and fixings, with the Langes and Claire and Tony) still felt more like a Thanksgiving than Thursday's puny dinner. Guests left at a quarter to eleven. Stu was fine while they were around, but positively surly afterward. I am angry that I have to deal with his depression, that he didn't help with dinner preparations, that after he suggested I invite people over for our last evening with Dad, he tried to convince everyone to eat fast so he could leave at seven to go to a basketball game. He didn't go—but I think only because he couldn't get Tony or Bill to join him.

And yet I feel alive and in fine spirits. I worry about not being nice enough, or accommodating enough, but tonight I don't worry about my soul.

⬧

Work on the manuscript is moving right along, but it depresses me. Reading the old journal entries is bad enough. But I am also living through the anniversary weeks of the events I'm reading about. I'm usually aware, toward the end of November, that I'm approaching the date that my marriage ended. This year, I'm thinking every day about how it ended, and why. And the coincidence of days and dates makes me feel as though I'm reliving 1986. My life has radically changed in the past eleven years. My marriage is long over; my children have left home; I have a satisfying job; my poems have appeared in respected literary journals. Still, when I revisit those weeks, I feel the anger and sadness again. Or I refuse to feel anger or sadness, and depression hovers over my laptop's back-lit screen.

Last night, I really needed to lighten up. I organized a trip to Sheridan to see *The Full Monty,* a film about unemployed steelworkers in Sheffield, England, who—desperate for money—turn themselves into male strippers and put on a hilarious show. About quarter past eight, four of us stepped out into the very cold night to leave for the twenty-seven-mile drive to the movie theater. Brilliant stars overhead. A broad arch of light low across the sky. The moon, I thought, rising through a bank of clouds. But the moon is a week past full and shouldn't be rising so early. And stars pierced the "cloud," a band of whitish light. Then the band pulsed and launched slow light-green rockets high into the sky. I was seeing the northern lights.

We watched the light show for about fifteen minutes and then piled into the car. When we got back from the movie, three and a half hours later, the aurora still shimmered across the northern sky.

⊛

Sunday, November 30, 1986

We all got up early to take Dad to the Milwaukee airport. Played Twenty Questions on the way and stopped afterward at a cafe for breakfast. *Très familial.* And yet hollow, because Stu and I really aren't on speaking terms and haven't been for days. We are cordial, in public, but distant—careful not to touch, careful not to talk unless absolutely essential. Obviously, I don't like it, and yet I preserve the shell of civility, the appearance that we are all getting along.

This evening, Stu was in the kitchen, helping while I was making dinner and at the same time making very caustic "jokes" about my cooking, suggesting, for example, that there might be carcinogens in brown rice. I was irritated but ignored him. The next time he starts in on that theme, I might point out that I don't make jokes about his health, and I'd appreciate it if he didn't make jokes about mine.

During dinner, we had the radio on, listening to a folk music show. The announcer started talking about a singer who has the same name as one of the guys I was seeing just before I met Stu. Stu asked me, rather pointedly, "Do you still know where to find Bob Schwartz?"

"I've known two guys with that name," I said.

"Oh, did you go to bed with the other one too?"

I was furious and ignored him. After David and Eli left the table, I said, "I don't want you ever to say anything like that about me again, especially in front of the kids."

"If you're going to get upset about my behavior," he snapped, "I'll get upset about yours."

⊛

327

Monday, December 1, 1986

Found my tire flat this morning. It shouldn't have been a surprise, since it was low yesterday, but I'd forgotten. And Stu made love to me at 6:30 A.M., and I found I could only detach, not quite thinking of his comments at dinner yesterday, but unable to lose myself at all, or to give myself to him. And the furies built at work, where I had nothing, really, to do—until I decided fuck it, and wrote another poem, "Interior Decoration."

Incredible and immediate relief from emotional tension. I don't think I was entirely aware of how much relief until late this evening, when I realized how relaxed I was, despite a reprise by Stu of the "slut" theme at dinner tonight. Again I complained vehemently and said, "Don't do that again." Then I asked, "Are you jealous of Bob Schwartz and the other men I slept with before we met?"

Stu said, "Yes, after twenty years! I'm jealous that you had so many lovers and I started kind of slow. I've been thinking I need to catch up."

I said, "If you think an affair will cure that problem, good luck. Go ahead." I was thinking that I would just as soon find someone of my own— that I would welcome an opportunity to end this marriage—that *I don't care.* But I think I really do. I just don't so fear being abandoned any more.

This evening I got "Metaphor" ready to send to an old friend who's a calligrapher. (I want to make copies for Paul and a few good friends as a kind of end-of-the-year letter.) I decided to show the poem to Stu. What the hell.

His comments: "Why call it 'Metaphor'? Isn't all poetry metaphor?" And "I think the part about July needs some work."

Tuesday evening, December 2, 1986

Sometime during the afternoon, I was amazed to think that it had been a week since I saw Paul; that I was not going to see him today; and that I was feeling fine. This morning, in fact, driving to work in the fog and drizzle/snow, I felt exultant. Writing "Interior Decoration" had resolved/dissolved my anger, life was great, I was triumphant.

Now I am not so sanguine. In fact, I have been anxious, fearful, angry, and upset since late afternoon.

It's hard to tell why the change. Mostly, I think, the strain of living an almost completely noncommunicative existence with Stu for the past week. Tonight, after he came back from curling, I suggested talking. "I know you're angry, but I don't like having it come out in ice-pick jabs. I want to hear, in a straightforward way, what you're angry about."

"I want to eat dinner," he said. So I left the kitchen. After he finished eating, he went upstairs.

Later I went into the study to weigh a letter. "I guess you don't want to talk," I said.

"I don't want to fight," he said. "Now, at least, I'm not in pain."

"But I am. And I can feel your anger in the jabs you take at me."

"Get specific."

I told him about my reaction to his jibes about my "carcinogenic" food preferences.

"What else?" he asked.

I began to talk about his uncalled for comments about Bob Schwartz. "You mean the two Bob Schwartzes," he said. "You walked right into that. And don't tell me what's uncalled for."

I walked away. Let him stew in his lack of pain.

I am in a *lot* of pain, and there is no one to hear it.

⊗

A couple of days ago, one of the Ucross visual artists asked another resident, a novelist, "What's your new book about?"

The novelist wouldn't say. "Writers don't like to talk about what they're working on."

Which is certainly true for me. Talking about it feels like a jinx. It's not just superstition. Once I've told someone else the story, what's the point of writing it down?

And once the story is told, it's no longer malleable. For many years, whenever I talked with friends about childhood memories, I told the story of going to Niagara Falls. World War II was over; gas rationing had ended. My father took his old Buick out of storage and we took a family vacation, driving north through New York State. I was still an only child. On this trip, which happened in the fall of 1945 or perhaps the following spring, I was not yet one and a half.

All that, I know from the story my parents told. But I have a strong memory of that trip to Niagara Falls. I always describe it as my earliest memory. It is dark outside, and the surface of the water reflects the play of colored lights.

When I tell my father this story, he says it's impossible. He says I must have seen a picture in a magazine. He says just after the war, there were no colored lights.

I could do some research and see which of us is right. But I have told this story so many times, to so many people, that it's become the truth. I *remember* those dancing lights. I see them when I close my eyes. They're my earliest memory, and they're not about to change.

So, an axiom: telling a story often takes the place of writing it down. And a corollary: saying that something happened, even if it didn't, somehow makes it real. And something else: telling the story or writing it down moves the memory outside of one's self. Not just the memory: "what really happened" or "what I think went on." The emotions that surround the memory also move outside. And when they're shared, they dissipate. This is the power of testimony; why, for example, alcoholics tell their stories over and over at AA meetings; why war crimes tribunals help heal the wounds of genocide.

But every story can be told from many points of view. A black eye, a divorce, a family story: who can possibly own the truth?

⊕

Thursday evening, December 4, 1986

I developed breathing problems in the late afternoon, and the only thing I can figure out is that I have begun to think quite seriously again about leaving—even to the point of thinking that this would not be abandoning David and Eli. I don't know whether leaving Paul makes me aware that leaving is a possibility that I can survive or whether it's just Stu's dogged refusal to communicate with me. (Although the refusal itself is communicated all too well and in not a very pleasant manner.) But I feel ready, even eager, to start a new life on my own.

And unable (or reluctant?) to tell Stu.

⊛

It snowed last night as I walked a mile or so up a dirt road to the "end of the session" Ucross cocktail party at Sharon Dynak's dome house, thinking of Wisconsin. I headed into the wind; by the time I arrived, my purple parka and brown hair were frosted white. All the other residents went by car, and the ones from California, especially, thought I must be a little crazy to be out in "this weather." But after twenty winters in Madison, this weather, the snow and cold, define December for me. And it is, once again, December.

When I walked back, the night was very dark. The moon, curved and slight as a nail-paring, rises late, and clouds obscured all the stars. I could see the sweep of headlights from an occasional car on the highway; lights from a couple of ranches; a glow from the distant intersection where Highways 14 and 16 diverge. Sharon gave me a flashlight, but I didn't need it. The snow-covered road wound like a luminous ribbon between the dark hills, showing me the way.

⊛

Saturday night, December 6, 1986

Incredible, ugly twenty-four hours just past—and it's all over now, baby blue.

I spent yesterday at work. On the way home, I stopped to pick up a pizza. Bill and Linda came for dinner and dominoes and stayed until eleven. Stu was incredibly uptight, and Bill commented on how tense David was, watching Stu's every move. Before the Langes arrived, Stu told me that David's teacher had called again. She said David was very angry and suggested getting "help" for him. In school, he'd traced the veins on his arm in ink; this isn't the first time.

331

During the domino game, Stu said something very depressed and fatalistic about being tired of life, and David said, "That's what people say who are thinking about suicide."

After the Langes left, Stu seemed willing to talk and hadn't had much to drink (I thought). We didn't get very far.

"I can't live with the kind of hostile frigidity I've been getting from you," I said.

"You could warm me up if you'd only try," Stu said. "Just love me a little." He grabbed my hand and pulled it toward his crotch. "Come on," he wheedled, "you can do it."

I backed away from him. "I can't warm you up when you're encased in ice. I do love you, but you need to get some help." I said I thought his life was tragic. "You need to talk to me, to reach out to people, not close yourself off like this."

He got very upset. "I don't need any help but your love. I'll change my will and commit suicide before I see some shrink."

About twelve-thirty, I suggested that one way of combating depression was to keep busy. Stu's been out of work for almost four years. "You don't have to get a job. It could be volunteer work or getting involved in politics. But you need to find something productive to do."

He got sarcastic. "You want me to be like Oliver North?" he asked. "There's someone *really* productive." (He despises Oliver North.) Then after repeating innumerable times that I have to show that I love him by making love in midday, he said, "All you do during the day is occupy your time so that you can avoid me."

I said that I work during the day.

He sneered. "You're not working all the time. You take time out to write poetry." He compared writing poetry to the kind of "productive" work that Oliver North does.

I went up to the third floor to avoid further conversation.

He followed me upstairs, basically to say that he'd been thinking that we should rent an apartment for me to live in for two or three months or so. I said I didn't want to leave. "If I do leave, it won't be temporary. It will be for good, and I'll take the kids with me."

"Won't they have some say in where they go?"

"The courts will decide."

He punched me in the face, three times. I got away from him and cowered near the window in the dormer alcove on the lake side of the house. (Bad move! A dormer is an easy place to get trapped.) He became very contrite, almost immediately. He begged me to hit him; he wanted to hold me, to make me feel better. He called me "melodramatic" and told me to "stop acting" when I said I didn't want him to touch me or to bring me ice for my eye. I just wanted him to leave the room, but he wouldn't. And he wouldn't let me leave either.

Finally, he agreed to let me go downstairs to get ice. But as soon as I came back up, he was all over me again. He wanted me to let him hold me, to go to bed with him, to let him hold the ice pack—and again he trapped me in the dormer when I tried to get away.

After about twenty minutes of this (I'd guess), I said I had to pee. He laughed and said he did too. He went to the third-floor bathroom. I grabbed my purse from my desk chair and ran downstairs and out of the house, but I didn't get out of the driveway before he came out the kitchen door, in shirtsleeves, and blocked the driveway with his hands on the hood of the car. It was very cold, but we had a stand-off for about ten minutes—I in the locked car, prepared to sleep there if necessary.

At last he gave up and went inside, and I drove to a seedy motel on the strip near the interstate, checked in about two and slept until eight.

✦

I start back to Madison on Friday, December 5, a date of leavings, or new beginnings. I take with me the completed first draft of the memoir—a version that's twice as long as it should be and will need extensive rewriting. And with more than a wink to my father, to Stu, to my own hardheaded rationalist, I take Ulm, a plush antelope named for a nearby railroad crossing. In the past few weeks, herds of real antelope have come down from the hills to graze in the range-land near Ulm. I would take them home if I could, but real antelope require more open space than Wisconsin has to offer. Anyway, I know that Ulm, with his cuddly tan-and-white body and quizzical expression will serve my needs quite well. He sat with me on the plaid couch downstairs as I read the entire first draft. Keep going, he insisted. This is important. Don't worry if it seems like crap. You can improve it. Just keep writing. On Friday, he will take the place of honor in the front seat of my car. When we get to Madison Saturday night, I will give him free range of my house.

⊛

Saturday night, December 6, 1986

This morning, I drove to University Hospital and had my face checked. I was pretty sure nothing was wrong, other than the swelling and black and blue, but I wanted an official record of the battering. The resident encouraged me to call the police. The dispatcher wouldn't take a report on the phone. He said I should go to the police station and have a photo taken.

On the way, I stopped to see Helen. I told her that I was going to file for divorce. By this time my face really looked awful, and Helen was, of course, terribly upset. We cried.

And then Stu showed up, cool as a cucumber, with the kids. David was very remote, Eli very warm (but tentative). Stu apparently told them on the way out of the house that I wasn't around (in case they hadn't noticed!) and that he hit me "accidentally" because I said that they would have to live with me. Eli especially wanted me to know that they wanted to live with us both, even if we were in different houses. He looked so serious.

Stu apologized for hitting me, and they all asked when I was coming home and would I go to the Y with them this afternoon.

I decided that I triggered Stu's violence last night when I threatened to leave. I thought that I could probably appear neutral enough about my plans to make it through the weekend at home without provoking more violence. That would give me the time to talk with Carol Madsen and decide whether to take the kids and leave or to get an injunction against Stu, so he would have to move out. Stu and the kids left Helen's after I said I'd be back in an hour or two.

I got home about one-thirty. Stu was still very apologetic, wanting me to forgive him, to kiss and make up. I tried to remain noncommittal. He made a big show of planning the rest of the day for the family. First he said

334

we would all go to the Y to swim. Then he scratched that plan. Instead, we hung around the house all afternoon, spending some of the time in bed. Stu wanted us to nap together. I lay down with him, but I was much too tense to sleep. He had gotten TV dinners for the kids and wanted to take me out to eat. I made it clear I did not want to go to a fancy restaurant with my black eye, but I agreed to go to a movie, where it would be dark. We all went to the five o'clock show of *Star Trek IV* and came home to eat TV dinners and Chinese takeout.

During dinner, Stu said he wanted to talk after the kids were in bed. "I don't have anything to say," I warned him. But I agreed to listen. I wondered if he would say he'd decided to get help for his drinking—though he had a drink with dinner, and I could tell from his breath that last night he'd had a lot to drink.

After the kids went to bed, Stu put his arms around me. I tensed and said, "It will be a long time before I can relax when you touch me."

"Don't be ridiculous. Just shake it off," he told me. "You've done it before, you can do it again. Just make yourself get over it." Then he said he thought that I was right, last night, when I said he had to tell me what was bothering him. "I've eaten too much anger over the past six months. You have to listen to my complaints about things like the mess you leave in the kitchen, and accept them." Then he added, "A lot of good came out of our conversation last night. We made progress, even though the evening had its problems."

I almost threw up.

I will be driving east on Interstate 90 this weekend, the eleventh anniversary of the weekend I plotted my escape. The only police I will see are the highway patrol. I won't have to deal with them unless they catch me speeding or I have an accident or the car breaks down.

It's a long time, twenty years or more, since I thought of all cops as "pigs." But I'm still uneasy in their presence, even when they're trying to help. Eleven years ago, the Madison police didn't want to let me go home after I filed my domestic violence report. They thought I would get beat up again. They wanted to take me to the house and stand guard while I packed up some clothes and left to stay with a friend. They worried about my safety. But they also said that they would be legally responsible if they let me go back to a place they knew to be unsafe.

I managed to convince them that I knew what I was doing. Or maybe they weren't convinced. Anyway, they let me go. I spent the weekend acting, lying, keeping a secret. Pretending I was going to stay with Stu. Covering up, as best I could, my extreme anxiety.

This weekend I only feel anxious about the weather. Will it snow? Will the highway be slippery? On the way to Ucross, I almost lost control of the car on an icy bridge. Signs posted all through the Black Hills warn that the bridges freeze before the road surface, but I was coming down out of the hills, headed into Wyoming at eighty-five miles an hour, and just for an instant, I forgot. The car skidded—I felt the tires slip—and careened into the passing lane. I must have turned into the skid, or maybe I was just lucky. The tires recovered their grip, but for several minutes, it seemed, the car whipped from side to side, rocking wildly. Then it calmed down, and I had time to be grateful that Wyoming is so thinly populated. There were no other cars around.

Sometimes you get lucky. Sometimes you get a gift.

❧

Monday morning, December 8, 1986

I am sick with fear, anger, sadness—and in a tiny corner of my brain, where the long-term planning goes on—optimism and relief.

Yesterday morning, I talked with Carol Madsen, who said I have only two legal alternatives. I can leave with David and Eli, so long as Stu knows where they are. Or I can kick Stu out with a temporary injunction and restraining order.

I called Helen and told her I had decided not to sneak out with the kids. She agreed that, however awful this is for Stu, it is more "dignified" for me to stay in the house.

So we played happy family for another day. We went to the Y; Stu did laundry; Eli, David, and Stu cooked dinner for Helen and me. I became terrified when Stu started to insist that I act less cold to him. "Why can't you get over it?" he wanted to know. And I got teary when I talked to friends. David's teacher said, "How sad for you all," and Beth said she was crying to know this was happening.

And then in the evening, I began to imagine the process server coming to the door, and I began to feel very sorry for Stu and upset that I'm making his life hell. (*I'm* making *his* life hell!?) So I called Rachel, who I knew would help strengthen my resolve.

And finally I went to bed about twelve and was able to sleep, mostly, until about six-thirty or so, I'd guess, when Stu curled around me like a spoon and I became terrified again.

⊛

Monday, December 8, 1986. I pick David and Eli up after school. "Where would you like to go?" I ask them, once they're in the car. "We need to have a serious talk."

"What about?" David asks.

"I'll tell you—why don't we go to Ella's?" I suggest the place we always go for birthdays, an ice cream parlor and kosher deli decorated with mechanical toys: a robot "greeter" at the entrance, a tall tin Ferris wheel, a Superman who swoops across the ceiling, turns, and swoops back again. Outside, there's a real carousel, but I'm sure it's closed for the season.

"What are you going to tell us?" David asks again.

Driving across town, I say that we can't go home. "I'm afraid of Stu. I can't live with him anymore. I'm going to move out, but not right away. Sometime this afternoon, he's going to learn that he can't be there when I am. He's going to have to leave, until I find a new place to live. We'll stay away overnight and go back home after he's gone."

David is very teary. Eli is angry. "When will you let us see Stu again?"

"I don't know, but I promise, it will be soon."

Eli orders a sundae. David orders a chocolate milkshake. I ask for a cup of coffee. But they don't have much appetite, and of course, neither do I.

I ask, "Do you want to stay at the Thompsons' tonight, or should we go to a motel?"

They choose Howard Johnson's. They want to go to the pool. We register and cross the street to the mall for swim suits, toothbrushes, underwear. Suddenly, we're having an adventure. While they swim, I make phone calls: to Carol Madsen, to Helen, to Stu. He needs to know where we are.

We go to the coffee shop for supper. David and Eli seem to accept our situation. In fact, they seem almost relieved. They ask me a lot of questions: "Does Helen know what's happening? How poor will you be without Stu? Where's your new house going to be? Will you have a computer? Will we live with both of you?"

I answer as best I can.

They seem to understand that with a black eye, afraid, I have no choice but to leave.

⊛

Monday night, December 8, 1986
Howard Johnson's

It's been a very long, exhausting day, starting with a breakfast meeting about the *Marriage and the Family* course. I was so tense that I couldn't eat anything. I drank half a cup of decaf and took my tea scone with me. In fact that and a bowl of clam chowder are all I've eaten all day.

After the meeting, I drove out to Carol's office. I was there until twelve-thirty, filling out papers to file in court. I was able to go through with it all, but I would hardly say I was calm. To work for a couple of hours, and then picked the kids up at school.

I have not had breathing difficulties nor even eye tics since Stu hit me.

I am surprised at how good, if exhausted, I feel right now. I'm wearing a new blue velour nightshirt I picked up at Penney's, and it's positively smashing. I feel sexy and ready to take on the world. Including Stu. And although the shit has not yet hit the fan, because the papers were not served this afternoon—I'm ready. Not lulled into complacency by his crooning into the phone that he loves me and, "You can stay away as long as you need to." Confident that in the long run, things will be all right.

✺

I cannot help but take my black eye, my swollen lid, my bruised and puffy cheek, into the light of day. I have to drive the kids to school; I have to go to work; I have to shop for groceries; I have to rent a house; I have to appear in court. "What happened?" people ask.

I am in no mood to make up stories. "My husband slugged me," I say. I tell my friends. I tell my kids' teachers. I tell my colleagues. I tell total strangers who stop me on the street. The words shock a lot of people. Saying them seems important: they are my reason for leaving Stu, the justification for my escape. My husband slugged me. That's the fact. Subject, verb, direct object. Pulling no punches. No one—not even I—could insist that I should stay in such an abusive relationship.

Still, I wonder, did I somehow ask to be slugged? Am I responsible for the outrage that set me free? After all, I set the terms when I said I would no longer tolerate physical violence.

In the midst of my move, between court dates, with my black eye fading to yellows and greens, I pose these questions to Paul Bergeson.

He won't answer me directly. "You probably looked different," he says. "Stu probably got the message that you'd changed. That he couldn't control you anymore."

I was ready to leave.

It seems fair to say: Stu gave me a black eye.

✺

The Gift

Tuesday, December 16, 1986

This afternoon, I took the kids to Northwest Fabrics for fake fur David needs for a school project. The woman who was measuring the fabric took one look at me and said, "You must have been in an accident."

I said, "No, someone hit me."

She nodded, as if she'd known it all along. And she said, "My second husband did that to me." Then she described lying on an emergency room table, getting her face stitched up, while the doctor asked whether she was going to report the beating to the police.

"I didn't," she said. "I was scared that he'd come after me again." But later, she left her husband. "And here I am, ten years later, and everybody's fine." Her son is an Eagle Scout and her children make all A's. She told me, "You'll be all right."

I felt a tremendous sense of sisterhood. A camaraderie.

It sort of fit into a conversation I had with Bill Lange, who came by for lunch. He was encouraging me to write about the differences between the way men and women react to my black eye. Men always want to know what happened, and when I tell them that Stu slugged me, they're shocked. They get terribly upset. Some of them hug me. Some of them cry. Women are much less emotional, much more matter-of-fact. They don't have to ask what happened. They see the black eye, and they know.

I said to Bill, "I can't write about it."

"Just a short article," he said.

I objected. "Stu would have a fit."

Bill said, "You can write it. You're not with him any more, remember?" He paused. "You'll get used to that."

Afterword

"You can't end it *there!*" Just about every person who read a draft of this book insisted that they wanted more of my story. But they all had different ideas about what I should put in an epilogue. One person wanted to know, "What happened next?" Another reader wondered if I'd found a new man. Someone asked, "How did your kids turn out?" A close friend wanted more about my life as a writer. "Where does the drive to write come from? What need does it satisfy?" And a social worker who has worked with victims of domestic violence told me, "It's really important for women like you to know that it's *normal* to take such a long time to leave. You have to write more about that."

Let me take care of the easy things first. My kids are fine. David is an artist—I think of him as a "conceptual artist," but he calls himself a sculptor—whose work has been featured in the *New York Times* and *Spin* magazine. Eli just finished two years in the Peace Corps, teaching English in Africa. Although they lived with me after I left Stu, they maintain strong and loving ties to their father. Like most young adults, they are coming to terms with the difficult truth that mothers and fathers are human beings, and that both their parents are burdened with the usual load of human frailties.

I haven't "found a man." (Or a woman, either, for that matter.) I have built a full and satisfying life that is currently focused on writing and music. A few years ago, I started cello lessons, and I now play in an orchestra that doesn't require auditions and in small chamber groups. I sing in a Yiddish choir. I am far from the "cold

drafty barn of a life" I described in January 1986. But I don't have a
lover. I long ago gave up my childhood fantasy about a knight in
shining armor who would ride up on a great white steed and trans-
form my life. Still, in the years since my children left home, I have
often wished to be someone's most special person in the world. This
lonely desire became almost unbearable for several months after my
father died. And yet, I wonder: if someone desirable appeared on the
horizon, would I once again try to fit myself into the image he desired? If I did, then where would I be? It feels much easier to be
me—the real me, the happy me—unattached.

What happened after Stu punched me? I learned, firsthand, how
class and race intersect with domestic abuse. I returned to our house,
accompanied by a very big male friend, the morning after Stu was
served with a restraining order that required him to move out. A
locksmith met us, prepared to change the locks. But Stu's car was
still in the garage. The locksmith had his company call the police.
Two squad cars arrived with three patrolmen, one a rookie. This
very nervous young man told Stu to leave. Stu refused. He insisted
that his lawyer had told him he could stay. Eventually, one of the experienced cops told Stu that if he didn't start packing his things, he'd
be arrested. Stu said, almost taunting, "You mean you'd put hand-
cuffs on me?"

"You'd better pack a few things. Let's go," the officer repeated.
Then we all watched as Stu made trip after trip down the stairs and
out of the house, carrying hangars full of shirts and pants and box
after box of other clothes and financial papers. Finally, I protested.
The officer re-read the restraining order, which allowed Stu to take
only "a few personal effects." He told Stu to leave the papers behind.
Stu, very angry, got into his car and left.

Several weeks later, a citizen-relations officer called me from the
police department. When I described the scene, this person was incredulous. "You know he got away with that because he's white and
you live on the lake," he said. "If he was black or poor, those guys

wouldn't have put up with his arguments. They'd have hauled him right off to jail."

I didn't want Stu to go to jail. I just wanted him out of the house until I could find someplace else to live. Under the circumstances, it's just as well that the cops were impressed by Stu's money, his race, his evident education. He was lucky, and so was I. In fact, what strikes me most, looking back, is how fortunate I have been. My grandmother said, "It's just as easy to fall in love with someone rich as someone poor." That may or may not be true. But it's definitely easier to be divorced from someone with substantial assets. For a short time after I moved out of the house, I was unemployed. My ability to pay the rent each month rested on the assumption that Stu would come through with child support. (He always did.) Then a grant I had written was funded, and I was employed again. Eventually, a judge determined that most of our assets were "commingled" and that they had to be equally divided. I no longer live in a big house on a lake, but my life is solidly upper-middle class—as I knew it would be.

What if I had not had a good education, the prospect of a decent job, the money for therapists and lawyers? What if I knew that life as a single mother would mean long hours working for little pay, no health insurance, child care a constant worry? How long would I have stayed married? Would I ever have left?

After all, even in my privileged position, even after a year of therapy sessions that cost thousands of dollars, I was committed to staying with Stu, to making our marriage work. I entered therapy in December 1985 with the question, "Should I stay in my marriage or leave it?" By the time I terminated therapy, in November 1986, Paul Bergeson had opened me up to feeling. That meant I could write. It was when I began to *feel* that the poetry started to come. (And poetry remains most important to me as a link to emotion.) But when I began to feel, I felt enormous pain.

At the time I terminated therapy, I was very clear about my plans: I was going to stay married. (I've often wondered whether Paul thought that he had failed. I'm sure he wanted me to leave.) I was going to continue to work to improve the marriage through what Paul wryly called "'individual' family therapy." I knew this would be difficult; that Stu would likely continue to be verbally abusive; that I could not share myself, emotionally, with him. That was OK, I decided; I had women friends I could talk with, and I could try to share the pain through writing. I hoped that would be enough.

But in July I had told Stu, "No more physical violence." And I meant it. It's clear, reading my old journal, that I had an unhealthy tolerance for emotional abuse. But I didn't think of myself as a battered wife. I didn't want to see myself that way.

And then Stu gave me the black eye. I didn't need a mirror to know it was past time to leave.

⊛

Those are the particulars of my life. *Black Eye* is one woman's story—mine. But in many respects, it is also the story of a generation of women who came of age in the 1960s: raised to believe in Prince Charming, sexually freed by the pill, and caught, with our friends and partners, in a disorienting social and economic revolution that, whether or not we call ourselves "feminists," has inevitably affected our lives. All the women of my generation have experienced, in one way or another, the social and political violence that was Vietnam. We all know that the American economy requires two wage earners to support a middle-class family, and that this—as much as "women's liberation"—has shattered the assumptions about marriage and family with which we were raised.

Family history and individual psychology determine the trajectory of each of our lives in the context of social conditions, political events, and historical accident. I would like to think that most of the women of my generation have not suffered domestic abuse; that as children they were shielded from political and economic insecurity by loving parents and other caring adults; that they developed the emotional resources required to create healthy families despite the disorienting circumstance of radical social change. But domestic abuse is notorious for its invisibility. No one knew I suffered abuse until I told them; until I started walking around with a discolored, swollen eye.

It is essential that we pay attention to the way the political, social, and economic environments affect our families, especially in a world shadowed by the violence and uncertainty imposed by terror and war. Societies that breed economic, political, and social insecurity threaten the development of healthy individuals living in healthy families. We can escape our childhood homes, we can break up with our boyfriends, we can leave our spouses and even our children, but we cannot divorce ourselves from the times in which we live.

References

Intimate Strangers, p. 49

Rubin, Lillian B., *Intimate Strangers: Men and Women Together* (New York: Harper & Row, 1983).

True Colors, p. 87

Woititz, Janet Geringer, *Marriage on the Rocks: Learning to Live with Yourself and an Alcoholic* (Pompano Beach, Fla.: Health Communications, Inc., 1979).

J Jumped for It, p. 202

Russo, Francine, "The Faces of Hedda Nussbaum," *New York Times Magazine,* March 30, 1997, pp. 26–29.

Cause and Effect, p. 253

Kramer, Peter, *Should You Leave? A Psychiatrist Explains Intimacy and Autonomy—and the Nature of Advice* (New York: Simon & Schuster Trade, 1997).

Trouble on Its Way, p. 259

Fox, Faulkner, "Lucy," *Prairie Schooner,* Summer 1997, p. 165.

Enormous Rage, p. 301

Rothstein, Edward, "Rude Awakenings from 60's Dreams," *New York Times,* May 1, 1997.

Enormous Rage, p. 301

Belluck, Pam, "A Woman's Killer Is Likely to Be Her Partner, a Study Finds," *New York Times,* March 31, 1997.

References

Enormous Rage, p. 307

Sams, Jamie, and David Carson, *Medicine Cards: The Discovery of Power through the Ways of Animals* (Rochester, Vt.: Bear and Co., 1988), p. 186.

The Gift, p. 318

Damasio, Antonio, *Descartes' Error: Emotion, Reason, and the Human Brain* (New York: G. P. Putnam's Sons, 1994).

Acknowledgments

Authors need many kinds of help. I learned this when my first child was a week old and I had to make the hour-and-a-half-long drive from Davis to Berkeley to conduct an interview for a magazine article I'd been assigned. I loaded the van with my newborn, my visiting mother-in-law, the diaper bag, a stroller, a tape recorder, and a steno pad. Helen took David and all the baby gear to the University of California art library while I went off to be a journalist. I thought she should share the byline.

I am indebted to many people, without whom *Black Eye* would not exist. Some of the most important, including my sons, my mother-in-law, my sister Shelly, my therapists, my lawyer, and a number of friends, appear—with fictitious names—in the narrative, and I won't break their cover here. Others, who provided essential support in the early to mid-1980s when I struggled with cancer, small children, and a difficult marriage, include Karen Dummer, Betty MacDonald, Amy Nickles, Jeanne Vergeront, and other early members of the Board of Directors of the Madison Children's Museum, as well as Bert Adams, Pat Anderson, and my colleagues at the Wisconsin Educational Communications Board. Oncologists Saul Rosenberg and Henry Kaplan at Stanford Hospital and Tom Davis at the University of Wisconsin Hospital and Clinics literally saved my life. In 1987 and 1988 the University of Wisconsin offered me support as a "returning adult woman student," and my first writing teacher, Ron Wallace, convinced me that I really was a poet.

When I decided to try to shape my experience into a book, Joan Drury and Kelly Kager made my time at Norcroft: A Writing Retreat for Women truly astonishing. Sharon Dynak and the staffs of the Ucross Foundation and Vermont Studio Center gave me similar gifts in Wyoming and Vermont. And my colleagues at Wisconsin Public Radio—especially Molly Bentley, Deborah Bilder, Mary Lou Finnegan, Jim Fleming, Marv Nonn, Steve Paulson, and Anne Strainchamps of *To the*

349

Best of Our Knowledge—encouraged me to take time off to write, even when it made their own work more difficult.

I'm especially grateful to those who have read and commented on various drafts of *Black Eye*. Robin Chapman gently insisted that I take the story beyond its original journal form. Susan Elbe, Ann Hoyt, Jesse Lee Kercheval, Celeste Robins, Heather Sellers, Alison Townsend, Alan Venable, and Gail Venable offered valuable critical suggestions. Thanks also to the poet friends and critics extraordinaire who've encouraged me to write and to improve my poems through the years: Robin Chapman, Anne-Marie Cusac, Susan Elbe, Rasma Haidri, Catherine Jagoe, Jesse Lee Kercheval, Sara Parrell, Alison Townsend, and Susan Wicks. And to the Biking Babes, especially Diane Lauver, Liz McBride, Kathy Waack, and Janet Zimmerman, who keep me pedaling, whatever the weather, toward a better life.